2nd EDITION

RAILWAY ATLAS
THEN & NOW

Paul Smith and Keith Turner

The diminutive and non-timetabled Wimbledon Park Staff Halt viewed on 26 January 2014 with Class 450 EMU No.450071 approaching whilst Class 450 EMU No.450090 is parked alongside Wimbledon Park Depot. *Paul Smith*

Ian Allan
PUBLISHING

Site clearance being undertaken at Louth station on 6 October 1991; it was opened by the Great Northern Railway on 1 March 1848 and closed completely by BR on 31 December 1980. The listed station building, on the right, was converted into apartments whilst the remainder of the site was utilized mainly for housing.   *Paul Smith*

First published 2012
Reprinted 2012, 2013 (twice), 2014

This second edition first published 2015

ISBN 978 0 7110 3833 2

Published by Ian Allan Publishing, Addlestone, Surrey KT15 2SF

Printed in Bulgaria.

Visit the Ian Allan Publishing website at www.ianallanpublishing.com

INTRODUCTION

Class 318 EMU No.318253 approaching Hyndland station from the east on 8 June 2011. The station had been opened on 5 November 1960 in connection with the electrification of the line and replaced the original ex-LNER station which was on a short stub to the east. *Paul Smith*

This atlas is the first of its kind. Not only does it provide, in one volume, a direct comparison between the extensive railway system of Great Britain on the first day of the 1923 Grouping of virtually all the railway concerns into the 'Big Four' – the Great Western Railway (GWR), the Southern Railway (SR), the London Midland & Scottish Railway (LMS) and the London & North Eastern Railway (LNER) – and the stripped-down one of today, but also records the current use made of abandoned lines and closed stations.

The 'Then' maps are based on the relevant (amended and corrected) maps in the Ian Allan *British Railways Pre-Grouping Atlas and Gazetteer*; the 'Now' maps show all open lines and stations of the current national network (together with any other railways more than one mile in length) plus a record of all closed lines and stations now open to the general public in a different guise – be they preserved railways, tramways, roads, cycle trails, shops, museums or whatever.

Out of respect for privacy those stations converted into private residences or commercial premises have not – with a few exceptions – been noted. (2012)

INTRODUCTION TO THE SECOND EDITION

With this second, enlarged, edition of the Atlas, updated to 1 January 2015, a 20% increase in the scale of the maps has made possible an increase in the size of the lettering used which, together with a slight modification of the colour coding, has enhanced their readibility. At the same time the opportunity has been taken to extend the geographical coverage to include Lundy and the Channel Islands, whilst adding additional information such as the location of smaller railway museums, the reuse of industrial and tramroad trackbeds, and the names of all the stations opened and closed between the start of 1923 and 2015 (and those currently under construction).

Keith Turner, **Kidderminster** and Paul Smith, Kings Heath, **Birmingham** 2015

THE COMPILERS

KEITH TURNER

PAUL SMITH

"Last train's gone." Since their closure, many railway branches have been resurfaced as walks and cycleways, with the total mileage of such leisure trails increasing year on year. Here Keith consults the map at the former Merstone station on the Isle of Wight before deciding in which direction to explore. *M Donnison*

No such problems for Paul as he awaits the next train to Birmingham Moor Street from his local station, Yardley Wood. *S Salmon*

KEY TO MAP PAGES

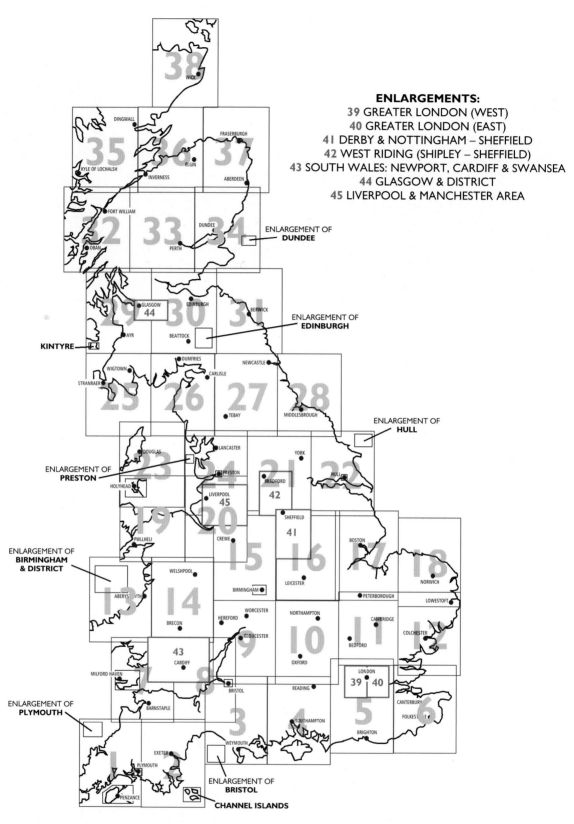

ENLARGEMENTS:
39 GREATER LONDON (WEST)
40 GREATER LONDON (EAST)
41 DERBY & NOTTINGHAM – SHEFFIELD
42 WEST RIDING (SHIPLEY – SHEFFIELD)
43 SOUTH WALES: NEWPORT, CARDIFF & SWANSEA
44 GLASGOW & DISTRICT
45 LIVERPOOL & MANCHESTER AREA

ENLARGEMENT OF **DUNDEE**

ENLARGEMENT OF **EDINBURGH**

ENLARGEMENT OF **HULL**

ENLARGEMENT OF **PRESTON**

KINTYRE

ENLARGEMENT OF **BIRMINGHAM & DISTRICT**

ENLARGEMENT OF **PLYMOUTH**

ENLARGEMENT OF **BRISTOL**

CHANNEL ISLANDS

'Then' maps are indicated by the numeral and the *'Now'* maps by the numeral followed by the letter A.
'Then' and *'Now'* maps are located opposite each other for easy reference

SCALE OF MAPS 1-38 IS **6.7 MILES : 1 INCH**

iv

KEY - 1 JANUARY 1923 MAPS

STANDARD GAUGE LINES

National network with all timetabled passenger stations open as of 1 January 1923 .... YARDLEY WOOD PLATFORM

Principal untimetabled (private/workmen's/restricted access) stations open as of 1 January 1923 AUCHLOCHAN HALT*

Freight-only branches (some with workmen's services) ....

Significant lines closed to all traffic pre-1923; stations not marked ....

Engine sheds open as of 1 January 1948 (plus steam depots opened by BR) ....

Railway works open as of 1 January 1948 ....

NARROW GAUGE & MINIATURE LINES

Passenger-carrying railways with principal stations open as of 1 January 1923 .... TAN-Y-BWLCH

Military, industrial and private estate railways, and independent public railways less than 1 mile in length are not marked.

KEY - 1 JANUARY 2015 MAPS

STANDARD GAUGE LINES

National network with all timetabled passenger stations open as of 1 January 2015 .... KIDDERMINSTER

Untimetabled (seasonal/workmen's/restricted access) stations open as of 1 January 2015 .... FALLS OF CRUACHAN*

Stations with no services as of 1 January 2015 .... WEDGWOOD†

Lines/stations under construction (with projected opening dates) .... NEWTONGRANGE [2015]

Freight-only branches ....

Lines/stations on 1923 maps closed to all traffic as of 1 January 2015 (including lines/stations
    opened post-1922) ....

Stations opened and closed between 1 January 1923 and 1 January 2015 .... EASTHOPE HALT

Motive power depots still standing as of 1 January 2015 ....

Railway works still extant/open as of 1 January 2015 ....

Diesel and electric depots operational in 2010* ....

Lines on 1923 maps now part of the London Underground network; only termini and
    converted/shared stations marked ....

Mothballed lines ....

Lines relaid as light rail/metro/tramway systems; only termini and converted/shared stations
    marked ....

    — off-trackbed sections ....

Preserved lines with principal stations open as of 1 January 2015 .... HIGHLEY

    — envisaged extensions ....

Lines (and industrial railways and tramroads of any gauge) relaid as narrow gauge/miniature
    railways with principal stations open as of 1 January 2015 .... LLANUWCHLLYN

    — envisaged extensions ....

Trackbeds (and those of industrial railways and tramroads of any gauge) officially designated
    bridle/cycle/walkways and permissive footpaths ....

Trackbeds now roadways A40

Trackbeds with other specific usage ....

* As listed in "*Ian Allan ABC Railway Depots*" (Paul Smith & Philip Stuart, 2010. ISBN 978 0 7110 3482 2) and subsequently updated.

BROAD GAUGE, NARROW GAUGE & MINIATURE LINES

Commercial passenger railways with principal stations open as of 1 January 2015 .... LLANBERIS

Preserved/heritage railways with principal stations open as of 1 January 2015 .... LLANBADARN

MUSEUMS/HERITAGE CENTRES

Railway-focused museums or heritage centres not confined to a particular heritage line ....

Military, industrial, private estate and amusement park railways, and independent public railways less than 1 mile in length or less than 10¼in gauge are not marked.

MAP 1

MAP 7

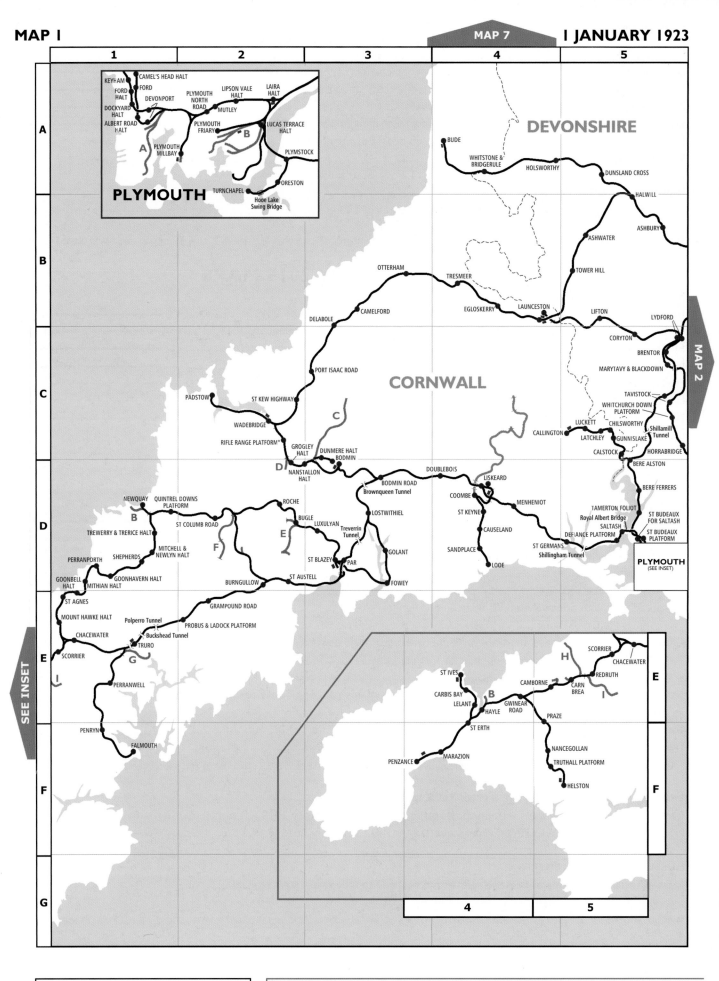

PLYMOUTH (inset)

KEYHAM
CAMEL'S HEAD HALT
FORD HALT
FORD
DEVONPORT
DOCKYARD HALT
PLYMOUTH NORTH ROAD
LIPSON VALE HALT
LAIRA HALT
ALBERT ROAD HALT
MUTLEY
PLYMOUTH FRIARY
LUCAS TERRACE HALT
A
PLYMOUTH MILLBAY
B
PLYMSTOCK
TURNCHAPEL
ORESTON
Hooe Lake Swing Bridge

PLYMOUTH

DEVONSHIRE

BUDE
WHITSTONE & BRIDGERULE
HOLSWORTHY
DUNSLAND CROSS
HALWILL
ASHBURY
ASHWATER
TOWER HILL
OTTERHAM
TRESMEER
EGLOSKERRY
LAUNCESTON
LIFTON
LYDFORD
CAMELFORD
DELABOLE
CORYTON
BRENTOR
MARYTAVY & BLACKDOWN
PORT ISAAC ROAD

CORNWALL

TAVISTOCK
WHITCHURCH DOWN PLATFORM
PADSTOW
ST KEW HIGHWAY
C
LUCKETT
CHILSWORTHY
Shillamill Tunnel
WADEBRIDGE
CALLINGTON
LATCHLEY
GUNNISLAKE
RIFLE RANGE PLATFORM*
GROGLEY HALT
DUNMERE HALT
BODMIN
CALSTOCK
HORRABRIDGE
D
NANSTALLON HALT
DOUBLEBOIS
BERE ALSTON
BODMIN ROAD
Brownqueen Tunnel
LISKEARD
BERE FERRERS
NEWQUAY
QUINTREL DOWNS PLATFORM
ROCHE
COOMBE
MENHENIOT
TAMERTON FOLIOT
ST BUDEAUX FOR SALTASH
B
LUXULYAN
BUGLE
LOSTWITHIEL
ST KEYNE
Royal Albert Bridge
SALTASH
ST BUDEAUX PLATFORM
TREWERRY & TRERICE HALT
ST COLUMB ROAD
Treverrin Tunnel
CAUSELAND
DEFIANCE PLATFORM
F
MITCHELL & NEWLYN HALT
E
GOLANT
ST GERMANS
Shillingham Tunnel
PERRANPORTH
SHEPHERDS
ST BLAZEY
PAR
SANDPLACE
PLYMOUTH (SEE INSET)
GOONBELL HALT
GOONHAVERN HALT
BURNGULLOW
ST AUSTELL
FOWEY
LOOE
MITHIAN HALT
ST AGNES
GRAMPOUND ROAD
MOUNT HAWKE HALT
Polperro Tunnel
PROBUS & LADOCK PLATFORM
CHACEWATER
Buckshead Tunnel
SCORRIER
TRURO
SCORRIER
G
CHACEWATER
H
SEE INSET
PERRANWELL
REDRUTH
ST IVES
CAMBORNE
CARN BREA
I
CARBIS BAY
B
LELANT
HAYLE
GWINEAR ROAD
PRAZE
PENRYN
FALMOUTH
ST ERTH
PENZANCE
MARAZION
NANCEGOLLAN
TRUTHALL PLATFORM
HELSTON

MAP 2

SEE INSET

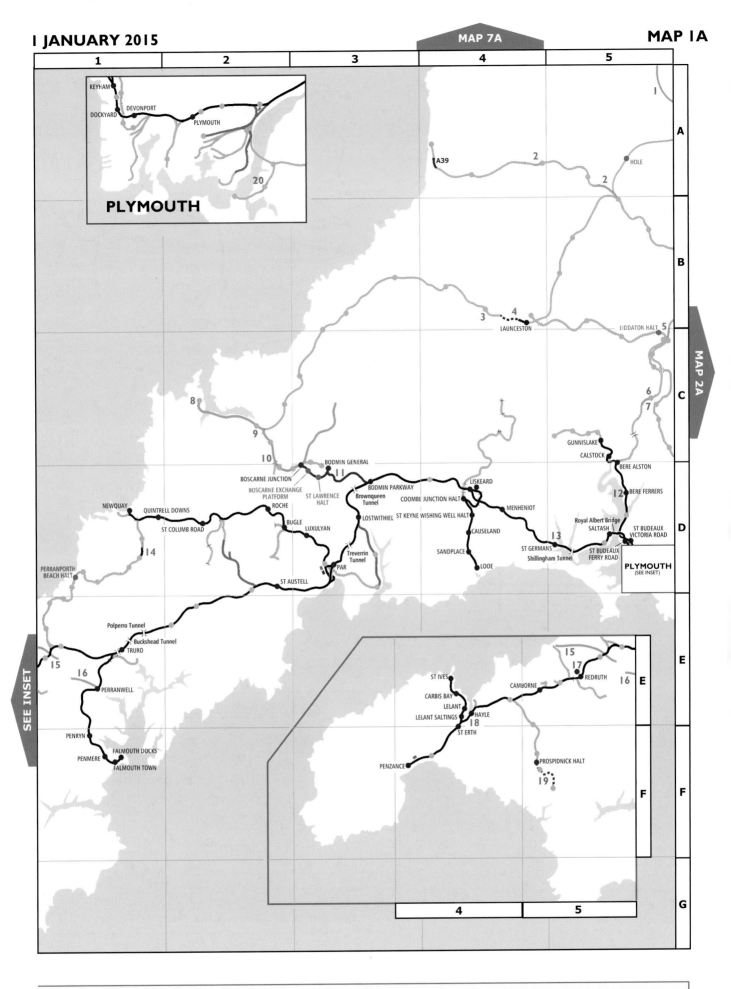

MAP 7A

PLYMOUTH

KEYHAM
DOCKYARD
DEVONPORT
PLYMOUTH
20

HOLE
A39
2
2
2
LIDDATON HALT 5
3 4
LAUNCESTON
6
7
GUNNISLAKE
CALSTOCK
BERE ALSTON
8
BERE FERRERS
9
12
10
BODMIN GENERAL
BOSCARNE JUNCTION
11
LISKEARD
BOSCARNE EXCHANGE
PLATFORM
BODMIN PARKWAY
ST LAWRENCE
HALT
Brownqueen
Tunnel
COOMBE JUNCTION HALT
NEWQUAY
QUINTRELL DOWNS
ROCHE
MENHENIOT
Royal Albert Bridge
ST COLUMB ROAD
BUGLE
LUXULYAN
LOSTWITHIEL
ST KEYNE WISHING WELL HALT
SALTASH
ST BUDEAUX
VICTORIA ROAD
14
CAUSELAND
13
PLYMOUTH
(SEE INSET)
PERRANPORTH
BEACH HALT
Treverrin
Tunnel
PAR
SANDPLACE
ST GERMANS
Shillingham Tunnel
ST BUDEAUX
FERRY ROAD
ST AUSTELL
LOOE
Polperro Tunnel
Buckshead Tunnel
TRURO
15
17
15
16
CAMBORNE
REDRUTH
16 E
PERRANWELL
ST IVES
CARBIS BAY
LELANT
LELANT SALTINGS
HAYLE
18
PENRYN
PENMERE
FALMOUTH DOCKS
FALMOUTH TOWN
ST ERTH
PROSPIDNICK HALT
PENZANCE
19

SEE INSET

4   5

LEGEND FOR **MAP 1A**
The former goods shed is now the BETTY FISHER CENTRE
for community projects
10 CAMEL TRAIL. www.sustrans.org.uk
11 BODMIN & WENFORD RAILWAY.
www.bodminrailway.co.uk
12 BERE FERRERS: Now a heritage centre with former dining car
restaurant and holiday accommodation available in two
converted sleeping cars. www.tamarbelle.co.uk

13 ST GERMANS: Holiday accommodation available in two
converted carriages. www.railholiday.co.uk
14 1ft 3in gauge [one section] and 10¼in gauge [one section]
LAPPA VALLEY STEAM RAILWAY. www.lappavalley.co.uk
15 & 16 Parts of the COAST TO COAST MINERAL TRAMWAYS
TRAIL on the trackbeds of the PORTREATH TRAMROAD (15)
and the REDRUTH & CHASEWATER RAILWAY (16).
www.westcountrywalks.com

17 MOSELEY INDUSTRIAL NARROW GAUGE TRAMWAY
& TOY MUSEUM, with a 2ft gauge operational line.
www.tumblydownfarm.co.uk
18 HAYLE: Holiday accommodation available in a converted
carriage. www.railholiday.co.uk
19 HELSTON RAILWAY. www.helstonrailway.co.uk
20 Part of the ERME-PLYM TRAIL. www.ldwa.org.uk

MAP 2   MAP 7   MAP 8   1 JANUARY 1923

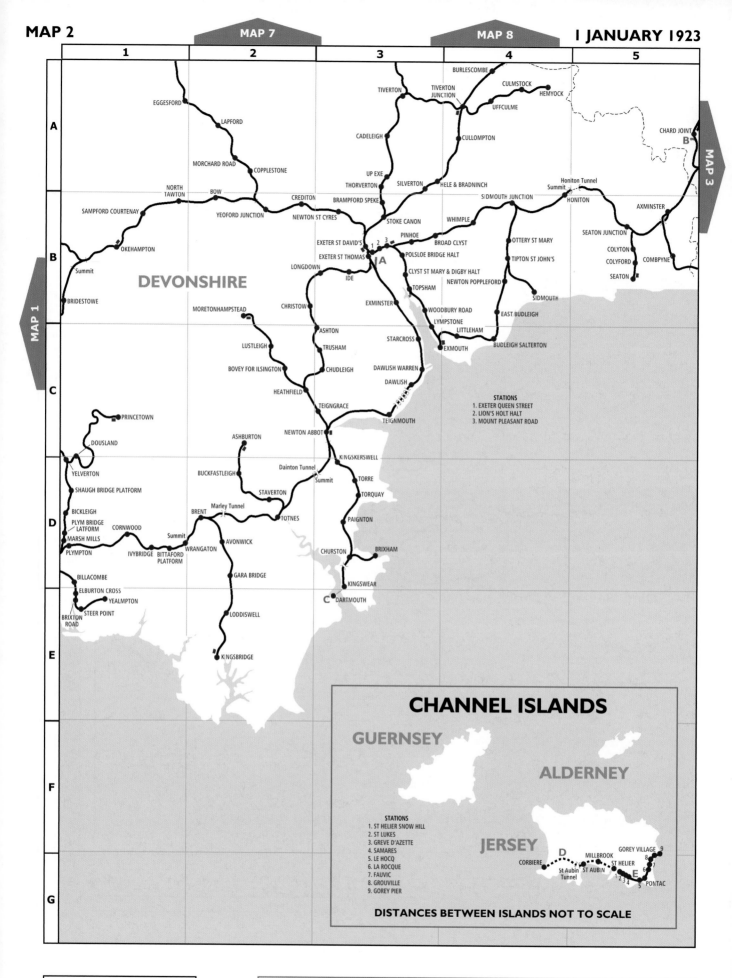

MAP 1
MAP 3
MAP 7
MAP 8

DEVONSHIRE

EGGESFORD
LAPFORD
MORCHARD ROAD
COPPLESTONE
NORTH TAWTON
BOW
SAMPFORD COURTENAY
YEOFORD JUNCTION
OKEHAMPTON
Summit
BRIDESTOWE
CREDITON
NEWTON ST CYRES
BRAMPFORD SPEKE
STOKE CANON
PINHOE
EXETER ST DAVID'S
EXETER ST THOMAS
LONGDOWN
IDE
A
CHRISTOW
EXMINSTER
ASHTON
TRUSHAM
STARCROSS
LUSTLEIGH
BOVEY FOR ILSINGTON
CHUDLEIGH
DAWLISH WARREN
HEATHFIELD
DAWLISH
TEIGNGRACE
TEIGNMOUTH
MORETONHAMPSTEAD
ASHBURTON
NEWTON ABBOT
KINGSKERSWELL
Dainton Tunnel
Summit
TORRE
TORQUAY
BUCKFASTLEIGH
STAVERTON
PAIGNTON
PRINCETOWN
DOUSLAND
YELVERTON
SHAUGH BRIDGE PLATFORM
BICKLEIGH
PLYM BRIDGE PLATFORM
MARSH MILLS
PLYMPTON
CORNWOOD
BRENT
Marley Tunnel
Summit
WRANGATON
AVONWICK
IVYBRIDGE
BITTAFORD PLATFORM
BILLACOMBE
ELBURTON CROSS
YEALMPTON
STEER POINT
BRIXTON ROAD
GARA BRIDGE
LODDISWELL
KINGSBRIDGE
CHURSTON
BRIXHAM
KINGSWEAR
C DARTMOUTH

TIVERTON
TIVERTON JUNCTION
BURLESCOMBE
CULMSTOCK
HEMYOCK
UFFCULME
CADELEIGH
CULLOMPTON
UP EXE
THORVERTON
SILVERTON
HELE & BRADNINCH
WHIMPLE
SIDMOUTH JUNCTION
Honiton Tunnel Summit
HONITON
AXMINSTER
CHARD JOINT
B
BROAD CLYST
POLSLOE BRIDGE HALT
CLYST ST MARY & DIGBY HALT
TOPSHAM
NEWTON POPPLEFORD
OTTERY ST MARY
TIPTON ST JOHN'S
SEATON JUNCTION
COLYTON
COLYFORD
COMBPYNE
SEATON
WOODBURY ROAD
LYMPSTONE
LITTLEHAM
SIDMOUTH
EAST BUDLEIGH
BUDLEIGH SALTERTON
EXMOUTH

STATIONS
1. EXETER QUEEN STREET
2. LION'S HOLT HALT
3. MOUNT PLEASANT ROAD

CHANNEL ISLANDS

GUERNSEY

ALDERNEY

JERSEY

STATIONS
1. ST HELIER SNOW HILL
2. ST LUKES
3. GREVE D'AZETTE
4. SAMARES
5. LE HOCQ
6. LA ROCQUE
7. FAUVIC
8. GROUVILLE
9. GOREY PIER

CORBIERE
St Aubin Tunnel
ST AUBIN
D
MILLBROOK
ST HELIER
E
GOREY VILLAGE
PONTAC

DISTANCES BETWEEN ISLANDS NOT TO SCALE

LEGEND FOR **MAP 2**
A Canal basin branch
B Town branch
C Ferry service from KINGSWEAR
D 3ft 6in gauge JERSEY RAILWAY
E Independent JERSEY EASTERN RAILWAY

1 CADELEIGH: DEVON RAILWAY CENTRE with 2ft gauge and 7¼in gauge operational lines. www.devonrailwaycentre.co.uk
2 CULLOMPTON: Site occupied by M5 Cullompton Services.
3 DARTMOOR RAILWAY. www.dartmoorrailway.com
4 Part of the GRANITE WAY. www.devoncyclehire.co.uk
5 OTTERY ST MARY: Now a youth club
6 2ft 9in gauge SEATON TRAMWAY. www.tram.co.uk
7 CHRISTOW: Home of the (private) EXETER & TEIGN VALLEY

RAILWAY with holiday accommodation available in a converted brake van. www.teignrail.co.uk
8 BOVEY: Now the Bovey Tracey Heritage Centre. www.visitsouthdevon.co.uk
9 Part of the TEMPLER WAY on the trackbed of the HAYTOR GRANITE RAILWAY. www.teignbridge.gov.uk
10 ASHBURTON: Now the Station Garage
11 SOUTH DEVON RAILWAY. www.southdevonrailway.co.uk

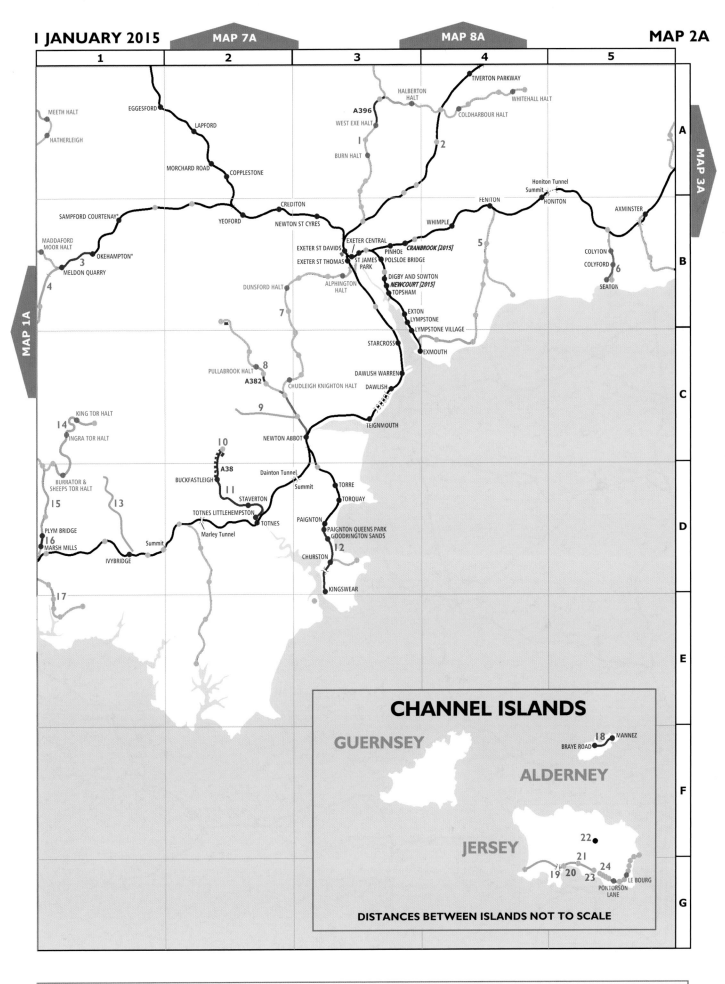

CHANNEL ISLANDS

GUERNSEY

ALDERNEY

JERSEY

DISTANCES BETWEEN ISLANDS NOT TO SCALE

MAP 1A

MAP 3A

LEGEND FOR **MAP 2A**

12 DARTMOUTH STEAM RAILWAY.
www.dartmouthrailriver.co.uk
13 Part of the TWO MOORS WAY on the trackbed of the
REDLAKE TRAMWAY. www.devon.gov.uk
14 DOUSLAND TO PRINCETOWN RAILWAY TRACK.
www.divinedartmoorwalks.co.uk
15 Part of the WEST DEVON WAY
16 PLYM VALLEY RAILWAY. www.plymrail.co.uk

17 Part of the ERME-PLYM TRAIL. www.ldwa.org.uk
18 ALDERNEY RAILWAY: Preserved quarry/military railway.
www.alderneyrailway.com
19 St Aubin Tunnel: Now used by a cycle-hire business
20 ST AUBIN: Station building and hotel now Saint Brelade
Parish Hall
21 MILLBROOK: Station building now the Old Station Café

22 PALLOT STEAM HERITAGE MUSEUM.
www.pallotmuseum.co.uk
23 ST HELIER: Former station building and site now the
Liberation Station for the island's buses
24 ST HELIER SNOW HILL: Site cleared as a car park

MAP 3　　MAP 9　　1 JANUARY 1923

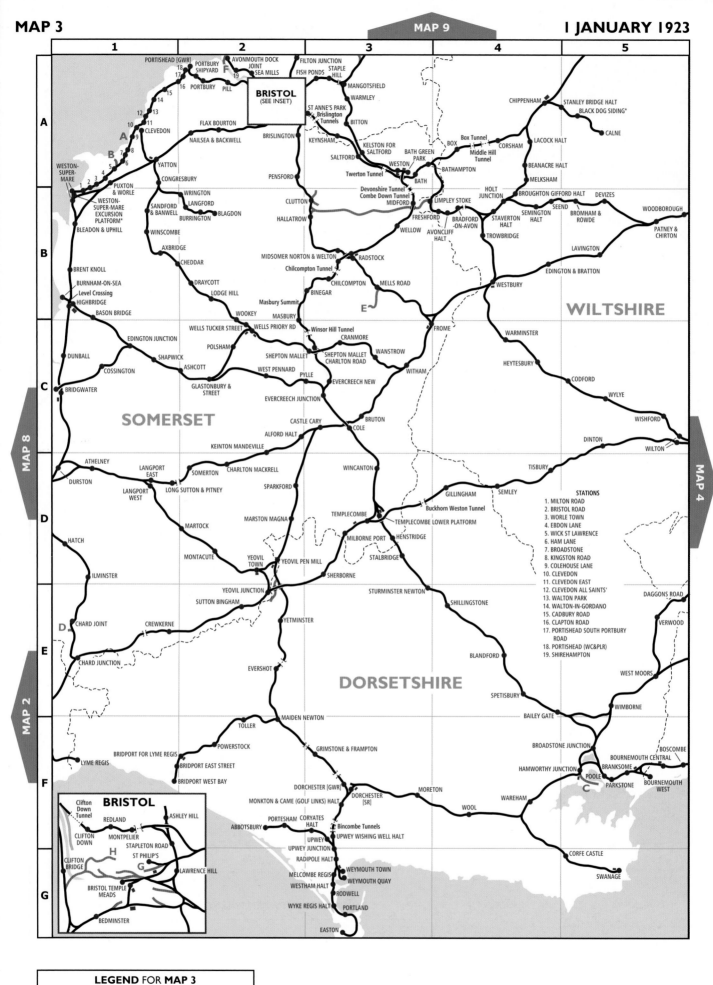

MAP 8
MAP 2
MAP 9
MAP 4

SOMERSET

WILTSHIRE

DORSETSHIRE

STATIONS
1. MILTON ROAD
2. BRISTOL ROAD
3. WORLE TOWN
4. EBDON LANE
5. WICK ST LAWRENCE
6. HAM LANE
7. BROADSTONE
8. KINGSTON ROAD
9. COLEHOUSE LANE
10. CLEVEDON
11. CLEVEDON EAST
12. CLEVEDON ALL SAINTS'
13. WALTON PARK
14. WALTON-IN-GORDANO
15. CADBURY ROAD
16. CLAPTON ROAD
17. PORTISHEAD SOUTH PORTBURY ROAD
18. PORTISHEAD (WC&PLR)
19. SHIREHAMPTON

BRISTOL
(SEE INSET)

BRISTOL
Clifton Down Tunnel
Clifton Down
REDLAND
ASHLEY HILL
MONTPELIER
STAPLETON ROAD
CLIFTON BRIDGE
ST PHILIP'S
H
G
LAWRENCE HILL
BRISTOL TEMPLE MEADS
BEDMINSTER

LEGEND FOR **MAP 3**
A WESTON, CLEVEDON & PORTISHEAD LIGHT RAILWAY
B Wick St Lawrence Wharf branch
C Hamworthy branch
D Town branch
E Vobster Colliery branch
F Avonmouth Dock branches
G Avonside Wharf branch
H Cannon's Marsh branch

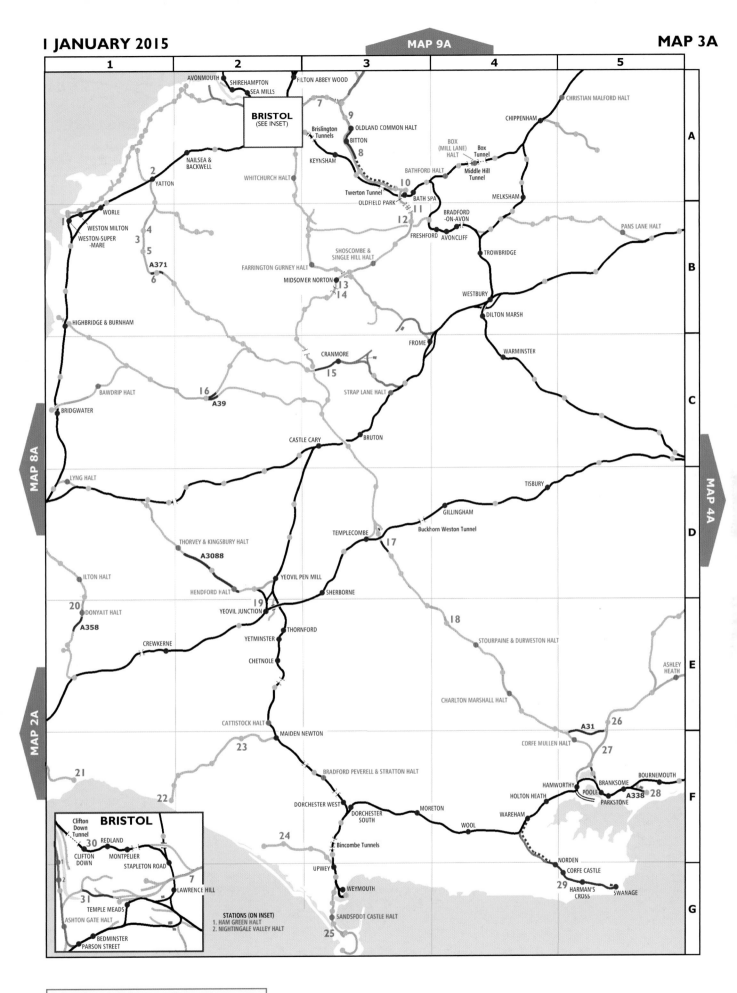

MAP 8A

MAP 4A

MAP 2A

AVONMOUTH
SHIREHAMPTON
SEA MILLS
FILTON ABBEY WOOD

BRISTOL
(SEE INSET)

7

9

OLDLAND COMMON HALT

Brislington
Tunnels

BITTON

CHRISTIAN MALFORD HALT

CHIPPENHAM

BOX
(MILL LANE)
HALT

Box
Tunnel

8

KEYNSHAM

BATHFORD HALT

Middle Hill
Tunnel

NAILSEA &
BACKWELL

2

YATTON

WHITCHURCH HALT

10

Twerton Tunnel

MELKSHAM

WORLE

OLDFIELD PARK

BATH SPA

WESTON MILTON

11

WESTON-SUPER
-MARE

4

12

BRADFORD
-ON-AVON

PANS LANE HALT

3

FRESHFORD

5

AVONCLIFF

A371

6

TROWBRIDGE

SHOSCOMBE &
SINGLE HILL HALT

FARRINGTON GURNEY HALT

WESTBURY

HIGHBRIDGE & BURNHAM

MIDSOMER NORTON

13

DILTON MARSH

14

FROME

WARMINSTER

BAWDRIP HALT

CRANMORE

15

BRIDGWATER

16

A39

STRAP LANE HALT

CASTLE CARY

BRUTON

LYNG HALT

TISBURY

THORVEY & KINGSBURY HALT

GILLINGHAM

A3088

Buckhorn Weston Tunnel

TEMPLECOMBE

17

ILTON HALT

YEOVIL PEN MILL

HENDFORD HALT

SHERBORNE

18

DONYATT HALT

19

20

YEOVIL JUNCTION

STOURPAINE & DURWESTON HALT

A358

THORNFORD

CREWKERNE

YETMINSTER

ASHLEY
HEATH

CHETNOLE

CHARLTON MARSHALL HALT

A31

26

CATTISTOCK HALT

CORFE MULLEN HALT

27

MAIDEN NEWTON

21

23

BOURNEMOUTH

BRADFORD PEVERELL & STRATTON HALT

HAMWORTHY

BRANKSOME

22

HOLTON HEATH

POOLE

A338

28

DORCHESTER WEST

MORETON

WAREHAM

PARKSTONE

DORCHESTER
SOUTH

WOOL

24

Bincombe Tunnels

NORDEN

UPWEY

CORFE CASTLE

29

HARMAN'S
CROSS

SWANAGE

WEYMOUTH

SANDSFOOT CASTLE HALT

25

BRISTOL

Clifton
Down
Tunnel

30

REDLAND

CLIFTON
DOWN

MONTPELIER

2

STAPLETON ROAD

7

31

LAWRENCE HILL

TEMPLE MEADS

ASHTON GATE HALT

BEDMINSTER
PARSON STREET

STATIONS (ON INSET)
1. HAM GREEN HALT
2. NIGHTINGALE VALLEY HALT

MAP 4
MAP 10

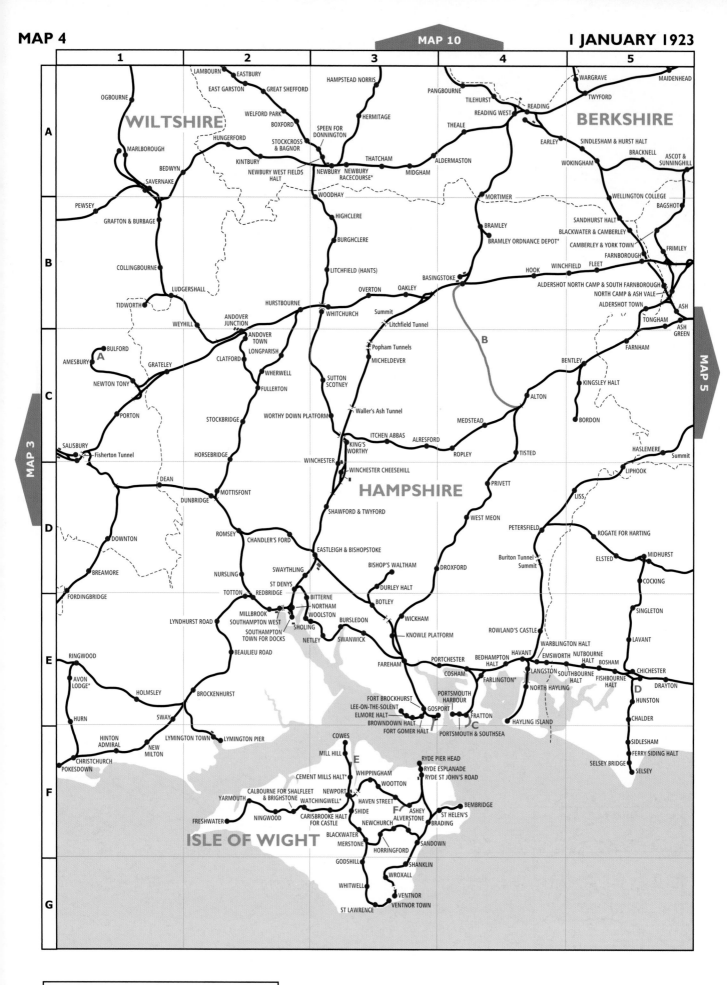

MAP 3

MAP 5

LEGEND FOR **MAP 4**

A Military network served at BULFORD and AMESBURY
B Former BASINGSTOKE & ALTON LIGHT RAILWAY
C EAST SOUTHSEA branch, services suspended
D CHICHESTER – SELSEY: Independent HUNDRED OF MANHOOD &
   SELSEY TRAMWAY
E Medina Wharf branch
F Quarry branch by racecourse: passenger specials used as
   grandstands on race days.

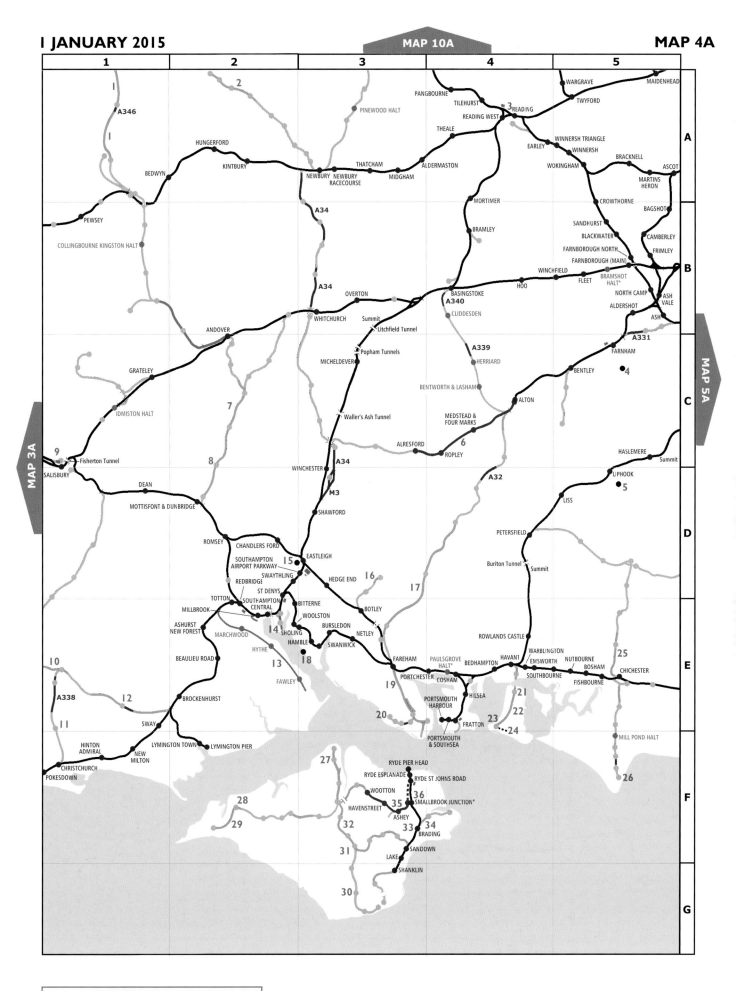

MAP 5A

MAP 3A

LEGEND FOR MAP 4A
FOR THE LEGEND TO THIS MAP,
PLEASE SEE PAGE vi

MAP 5   MAP 11   1 JANUARY 1923

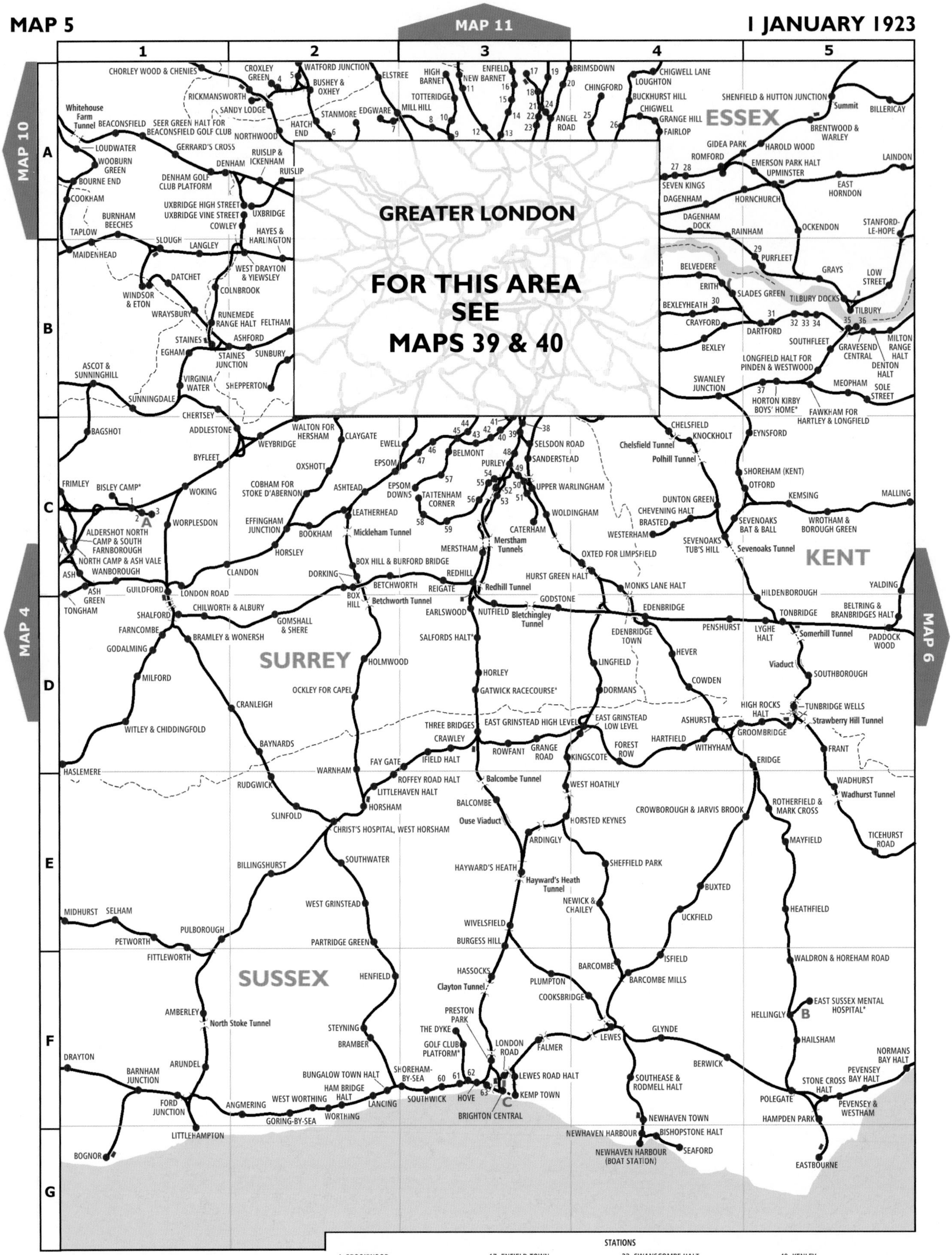

MAP 10

MAP 4

MAP 6

GREATER LONDON

FOR THIS AREA
SEE
MAPS 39 & 40

ESSEX

KENT

SURREY

SUSSEX

STATIONS

1. BROOKWOOD	33. SWANSCOMBE HALT
2. BROOKWOOD CEMETERY NORTH STATION	34. NORTHFLEET
3. BROOKWOOD CEMETERY SOUTH STATION	35. ROSHERVILLE
4. WATFORD WEST	36. GRAVESEND WEST STREET
5. WATFORD HIGH STREET	37. FARNINGHAM ROAD & SUTTON-AT-HONE
6. HEADSTONE LANE	38. EAST CROYDON
7. THE HALE FOR MILL HILL	39. SOUTH CROYDON
8. MILL HILL FOR MILL HILL BARRACKS	40. WADDON
9. FINCHLEY (CHURCH END)	41. WEST CROYDON
10. WOODSIDE PARK	42. WALLINGTON
11. OAKLEIGH PARK	43. BEECHES HALT
12. NEW SOUTHGATE FOR COLNEY HATCH	44. CARSHALTON
13. BOWES PARK	45. SUTTON
14. PALMER'S GREEN & SOUTHGATE	46. CHEAM
15. WINCHMORE HILL	47. EWELL FOR WORCESTER PARK
16. GRANGE PARK	48. PURLEY OAKS
17. ENFIELD TOWN	49. KENLEY
18. BUSH HILL PARK	50. WHYTELEAFE
19. CHURCHBURY	51. WARLINGHAM
20. PONDERS END	52. COULSDON & SMITHAM DOWNS
21. LOWER EDMONTON HIGH LEVEL	53. COULSDON & CANE HILL
22. SILVER STREET	54. REEDHAM HALT
23. WHITE HART LANE	55. SMITHAM
24. LOWER EDMONTON LOW LEVEL	56. CHIPSTEAD & BANSTEAD DOWNS
25. HIGHAMS PARK & HALE END	57. BANSTEAD & BURGH HEATH
26. WOODFORD	58. TADWORTH & WALTON-ON-THE-HILL
27. GOODMAYES	59. KINGSWOOD & BURGH HEATH
28. CHADWELL HEATH	60. FISHERGATE HALT
29. PURFLEET RIFLE RANGE HALT	61. PORTSLADE
30. BARNEHURST	62. DYKE JUNCTION HALT
31. STONE CROSSING HALT	63. HOLLAND ROAD HALT
32. GREENHITHE	

LEGEND FOR MAP 5
A Brookwood Cemetery branch
B Independent East Sussex Mental Hospital railway
C Brighton seafront: 2ft 8½in gauge BRIGHTON
ELECTRIC RAILWAY

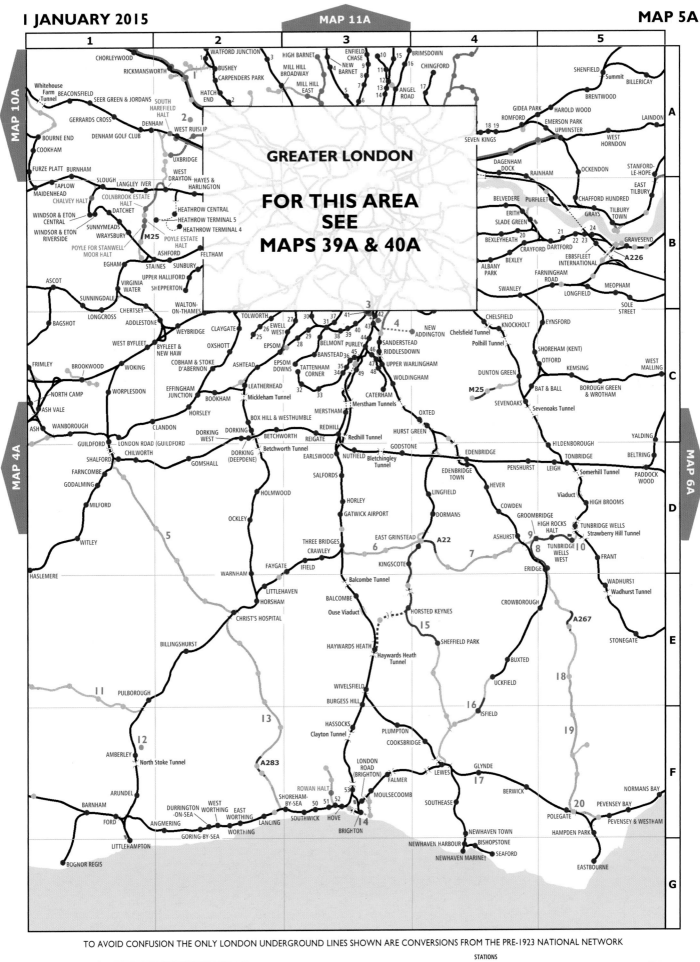

GREATER LONDON

FOR THIS AREA
SEE
MAPS 39A & 40A

MAP 10A

MAP 4A

MAP 6A

TO AVOID CONFUSION THE ONLY LONDON UNDERGROUND LINES SHOWN ARE CONVERSIONS FROM THE PRE-1923 NATIONAL NETWORK

STATIONS

1. WATFORD HIGH STREET	13. SILVER STREET	25. CHESSINGTON SOUTH	37. CARSHALTON	49. COULSDON SOUTH
2. HEADSTONE LANE	14. WHITE HART LANE	26. CHESSINGTON NORTH	38. CARSHALTON BEECHES	50. FISHERSGATE
3. ELSTREE & BOREHAMWOOD	15. SOUTHBURY	27. STONELEIGH	39. WALLINGTON	51. PORTSLADE
4. OAKLEIGH PARK	16. PONDERS END	28. EWELL EAST	40. WADDON	52. ALDRINGTON
5. NEW SOUTHGATE	17. HIGHAMS PARK	29. CHEAM	41. WEST CROYDON	53. PRESTON PARK
6. BOWES PARK	18. GOODMAYES	30. WEST SUTTON	42. EAST CROYDON	
7. PALMERS GREEN	19. CHADWELL HEATH	31. SUTTON	43. SOUTH CROYDON	
8. WINCHMORE HILL	20. BARNEHURST	32. TADWORTH	44. PURLEY OAKS	
9. GRANGE PARK	21. STONE CROSSING	33. KINGSWOOD	45. REEDHAM	
10. ENFIELD TOWN	22. GREENHITHE FOR BLUEWATER	34. CHIPSTEAD	46. KENLEY	
11. BUSH HILL PARK	23. SWANSCOMBE	35. WOODMANSTERNE	47. WHYTELEAFE	
12. EDMONTON GREEN	24. NORTHFLEET	36. COULSDON TOWN	48. WHYTELEAFE SOUTH	

ESSEX

KENT

WOODHAM FERRERS
BATTLESBRIDGE
FAMBRIDGE
ALTHORNE
BURNHAM-ON-CROUCH
HOCKLEY
WICKFORD
RAYLEIGH
ROCHFORD
PITSEA
PRITTLEWELL
BENFLEET
LEIGH-ON-SEA
SOUTHEND-ON-SEA FOR WESTCLIFF & THORPE BAY
WESTCLIFF-ON-SEA
SOUTHEND-ON-SEA
SHOEBURYNESS
CORRINGHAM*
Canvey Island
THORPE BAY
KYNOCHTOWN*
THAMESHAVEN

URALITE HALT
CLIFFE
HIGH HALSTOW HALT
MIDDLE STOKE HALT
GRAIN CROSSING HALT
SHARNAL STREET
PORT VICTORIA
SHEERNESS-ON-SEA
SHEERNESS EAST
HIGHAM
STROOD
BELUNCLE HALT
QUEENBOROUGH PIER
EAST MINSTER-ON-SEA
MINSTER-ON-SEA
EASTCHURCH
QUEENBOROUGH
GILLINGHAM
BRAMBLEDOWN HALT
HARTY ROAD HALT
LEYSDOWN
CUXTON
RAINHAM
KINGS FERRY BRIDGE NORTH HALT
CHATHAM
KINGS FERRY BRIDGE SOUTH HALT
ROCHESTER
NEWINGTON
WHITSTABLE HARBOUR
MARGATE SANDS
WESTGATE-ON-SEA
MARGATE EAST
BIRCHINGTON-ON-SEA
MARGATE WEST
BROADSTAIRS
SITTINGBOURNE
WHITSTABLE TOWN & TANKERTON
HERNE BAY
RAMSGATE TOWN
HALLING
TEYNHAM
TANKERTON HALT
MINSTER JUNCTION (THANET)
RAMSGATE HARBOUR
SNODLAND
SOUTH STREET HALT
GROVE FERRY
EBBSFLEET & CLIFFSEND HALT
AYLESFORD
FAVERSHAM
BLEAN & TYLER HILL HALT
STURRY
CHISLET COLLIERY HALT
WOODNESBOROUGH COLLIERY
SANDWICH ROAD
EAST MALLING HALT
SELLING
SELLING TUNNEL
CANTERBURY WEST
CANTERBURY EAST
ASH TOWN
MAIDSTONE EAST
BEARSTED & THURNHAM
STAPLE
SANDWICH
BARMING
HOLLINGBOURNE
CHILHAM
CHARTHAM
SOUTH CANTERBURY
BRIDGE
BEKESBOURNE
WINGHAM COLLIERY
EASTRY
ROMAN ROAD
EAST FARLEIGH
MAIDSTONE BARRACKS
HARRIETSHAM
ADISHAM
TOVIL
MAIDSTONE WEST
LENHAM
BISHOPSBOURNE
KNOWLTON
TILMANSTONE COLLIERY HALT
DEAL
TESTON CROSSING HALT
CHARING
BARHAM
SNOWDOWN & NONINGTON HALT
TILMANSTONE COLLIERY YARD*
WATERINGBURY
WALMER
HOTHFIELD
EYTHORNE
MARDEN
STAPLEHURST
WYE
ELHAM
SHEPHERD'S WELL
MARTIN MILL
HEADCORN
PLUCKLEY
LYDDEN TUNNEL
STONEHALL & LYDDEN HALT
KEARSNEY
HORSMONDEN
LYMINGE
GUSTON TUNNEL
FRITTENDEN ROAD
ASHFORD
DOVER PRIORY
DOVER HARBOUR
GOUDHURST
BIDDENDEN
SMEETH
SANDLING JUNCTION
DOVER MARINE
CRANBROOK
HIGH HALDEN ROAD
WESTENHANGER
FOLKESTONE WARREN HALT
TENTERDEN ST MICHAELS
HYTHE
FOLKESTONE HARBOUR
HAWKHURST
TENTERDEN TOWN
HAM STREET & ORLESTONE
SANDGATE
ROLVENDEN
ETCHINGHAM
WITTERSHAM ROAD
APPLEDORE
JUNCTION ROAD
BODIAM
NORTHIAM
BROOKLAND
NEW ROMNEY & LITTLESTONE-ON-SEA
SALEHURST HALT*
ROBERTSBRIDGE
RYE
LYDD
Mountfield Tunnel
WINCHELSEA
CAMBER SANDS
DOLEHAM HALT
SNAILHAM HALT
DUNGENESS
BATTLE
THREE OAKS & GUESTLING HALT
CROWHURST
WEST ST LEONARDS
ORE
SIDLEY
HASTINGS
BEXHILL-ON-SEA
ST LEONARDS WARRIOR SQUARE
BEXHILL
ST LEONARDS WEST MARINA

STATIONS
1. CHERITON HALT
2. SHORNCLIFFE CAMP
3. FOLKESTONE CENTRAL
4. FOLKESTONE JUNCTION

TUNNELS
1. Higham Tunnel
2. Strood Tunnel
3. Fort Pitt Tunnel
4. Chatham Tunnel
5. Gillingham Tunnel
6. Preston Hall Tunnels
7. Charlton Tunnel
8. Priory Tunnel
9. Harbour Tunnel
10. Abbotscliff Tunnel
11. Shakespeare Tunnel
12. Martello Tunnel
13. Saltwood Tunnel
14. Sandling Tunnel
15. Ore Tunnel
16. Mount Pleasant Tunnel
17. Hastings Tunnel
18. Bopeep Tunnel

LEGEND FOR MAP 6
A CORRINGHAM - KYNOCHTOWN: CORRINGHAM LIGHT RAILWAY
B Southend-on-Sea Pier: Home to 3ft 6in gauge SOUTHEND PIER RAILWAY
C Dockyard branch
D SHEPHERD'S WELL - WINGHAM COLLIERY and SANDWICH ROAD: EAST KENT LIGHT RAILWAY
E HEADCORN - ROBERTSBRIDGE: KENT & EAST SUSSEX LIGHT RAILWAY
F 3ft gauge RYE & CAMBER TRAMWAY
G Harbour branch

1 LEIGH-ON-SEA: Former up platform and building home to Leigh-on-Sea Sailing Club
2 Southend-on-Sea pier: Home to 3ft gauge SOUTHEND PIER RAILWAY. www.southend.gov.uk
3 Demonstration trains are operated in CHATHAM HISTORIC DOCKYARD by the North Kent Industrial Locomotive Society. www.dockyardrailway.co.uk
4 SNODLAND: Former station building now a restaurant

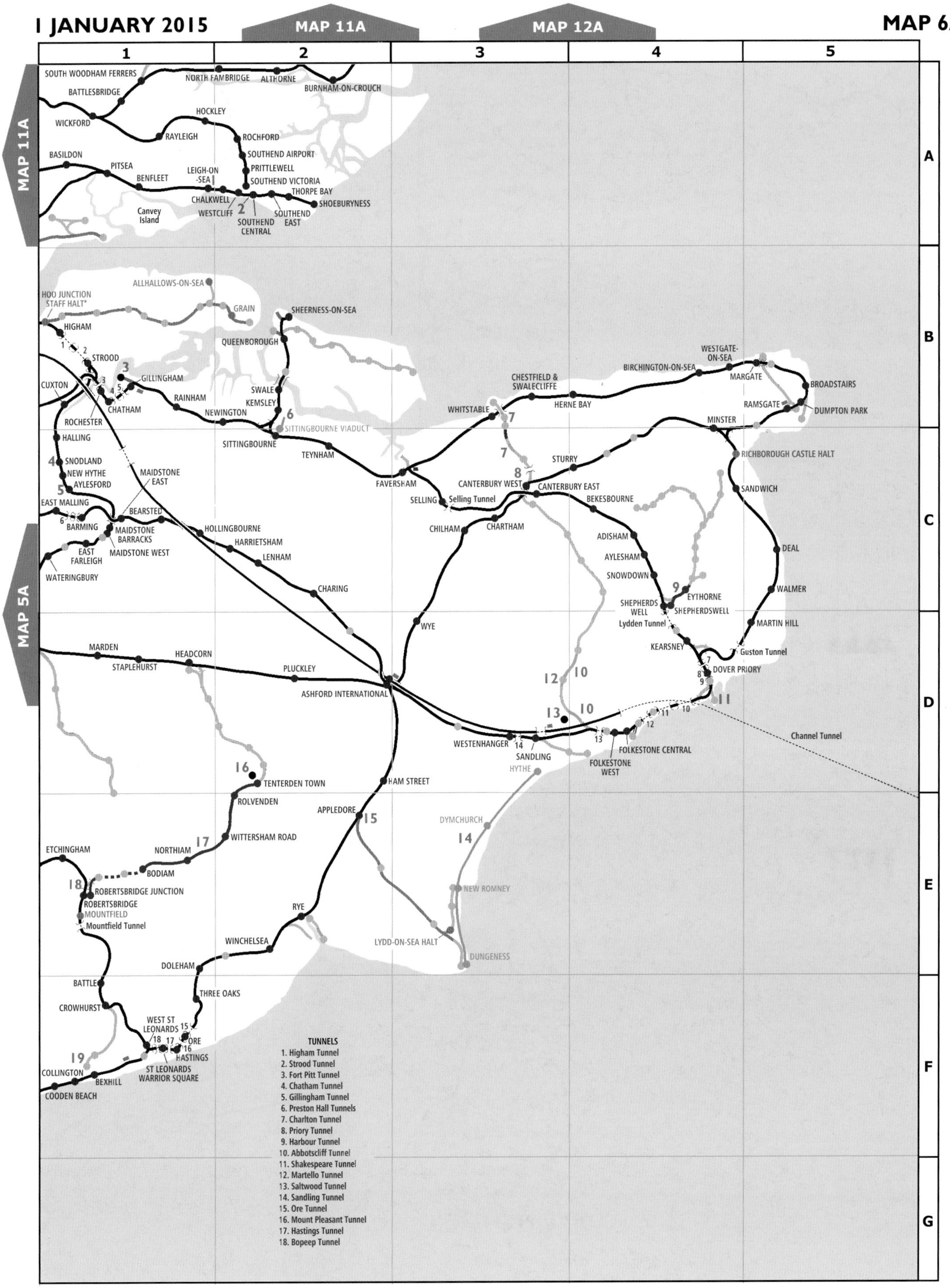

1   2   3   4   5

A   B   C   D   E   F   G

MAP 11A

MAP 5A

SOUTH WOODHAM FERRERS
NORTH FAMBRIDGE
ALTHORNE
BURNHAM-ON-CROUCH
BATTLESBRIDGE
HOCKLEY
WICKFORD
RAYLEIGH
ROCHFORD
BASILDON
SOUTHEND AIRPORT
PITSEA
PRITTLEWELL
BENFLEET
LEIGH-ON-SEA
SOUTHEND VICTORIA
THORPE BAY
CHALKWELL
WESTCLIFF
SOUTHEND EAST
SHOEBURYNESS
Canvey Island
2 SOUTHEND CENTRAL

HOO JUNCTION STAFF HALT*
ALLHALLOWS-ON-SEA
GRAIN
SHEERNESS-ON-SEA
HIGHAM
QUEENBOROUGH
1   2
STROOD
3
GILLINGHAM
WESTGATE-ON-SEA
BIRCHINGTON-ON-SEA
MARGATE
CUXTON
3
4 5
CHATHAM
RAINHAM
SWALE
KEMSLEY
CHESTFIELD & SWALECLIFFE
BROADSTAIRS
RAMSGATE
DUMPTON PARK
ROCHESTER
NEWINGTON
HERNE BAY
MINSTER
HALLING
SITTINGBOURNE VIADUCT
SITTINGBOURNE
6
WHITSTABLE
7
4 SNODLAND
NEW HYTHE
TEYNHAM
7
STURRY
RICHBOROUGH CASTLE HALT
5 AYLESFORD
MAIDSTONE EAST
FAVERSHAM
8
CANTERBURY WEST
CANTERBURY EAST
BEKESBOURNE
SANDWICH
EAST MALLING
BEARSTED
SELLING
SELLING TUNNEL
6 BARMING
MAIDSTONE BARRACKS
HOLLINGBOURNE
CHILHAM
CHARTHAM
ADISHAM
DEAL
EAST FARLEIGH
MAIDSTONE WEST
HARRIETSHAM
AYLESHAM
WATERINGBURY
LENHAM
SNOWDOWN
9
EYTHORNE
WALMER
CHARING
SHEPHERDS WELL
SHEPHERDSWELL
WYE
Lydden Tunnel
MARTIN HILL
MARDEN
HEADCORN
KEARSNEY
GUSTON TUNNEL
STAPLEHURST
PLUCKLEY
12
10
7
DOVER PRIORY
8
9
11
ASHFORD INTERNATIONAL
13
10
Channel Tunnel
WESTENHANGER
11   10
12
FOLKESTONE CENTRAL
14
13
16
TENTERDEN TOWN
HAM STREET
SANDLING
FOLKESTONE WEST
ROLVENDEN
APPLEDORE
DYMCHURCH
HYTHE
15
17
WITTERSHAM ROAD
14
ETCHINGHAM
NORTHIAM
NEW ROMNEY
BODIAM
18
ROBERTSBRIDGE JUNCTION
ROBERTSBRIDGE
RYE
MOUNTFIELD
Mountfield Tunnel
WINCHELSEA
LYDD-ON-SEA HALT
DOLEHAM
DUNGENESS
BATTLE
THREE OAKS
CROWHURST
WEST ST LEONARDS
15
ORE
18   17   16
HASTINGS
19
ST LEONARDS WARRIOR SQUARE
COLLINGTON
BEXHILL
COODEN BEACH

TUNNELS
1. Higham Tunnel
2. Strood Tunnel
3. Fort Pitt Tunnel
4. Chatham Tunnel
5. Gillingham Tunnel
6. Preston Hall Tunnels
7. Charlton Tunnel
8. Priory Tunnel
9. Harbour Tunnel
10. Abbotscliff Tunnel
11. Shakespeare Tunnel
12. Martello Tunnel
13. Saltwood Tunnel
14. Sandling Tunnel
15. Ore Tunnel
16. Mount Pleasant Tunnel
17. Hastings Tunnel
18. Bopeep Tunnel

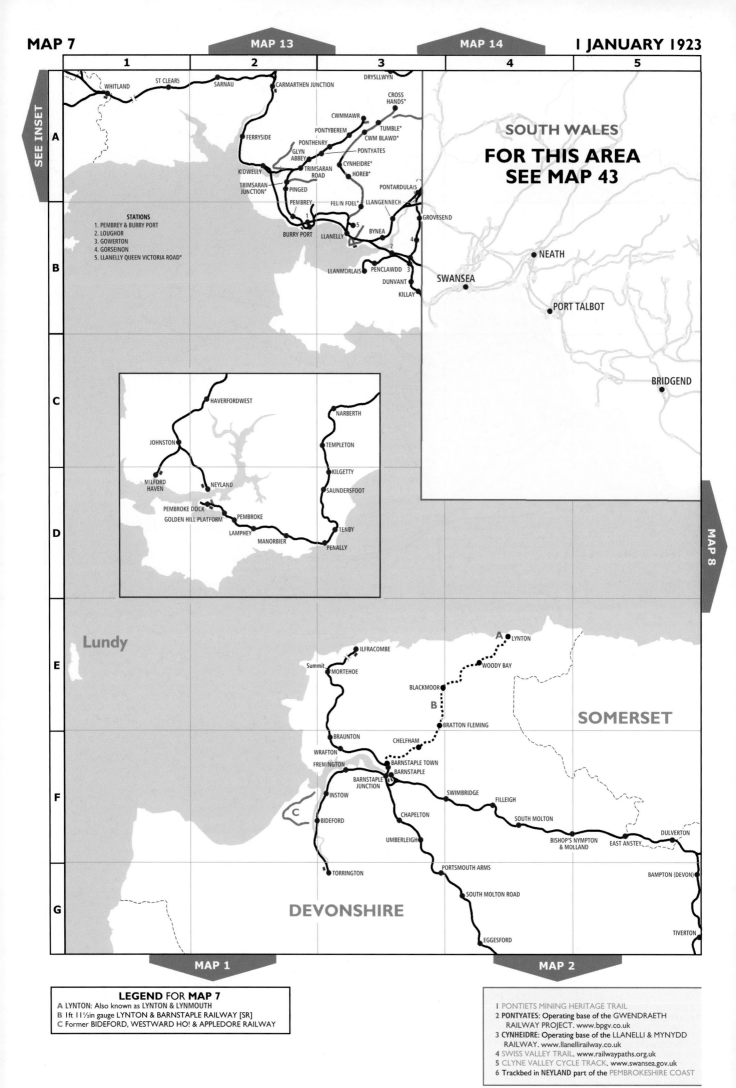

MAP 7

MAP 13

MAP 14

1 JANUARY 1923

1　　2　　3　　4　　5

SEE INSET

A

WHITLAND　ST CLEARS　SARNAU　CARMARTHEN JUNCTION　DRYSLLWYN

CROSS HANDS*

CWMMAWR

PONTYBEREM　TUMBLE*

FERRYSIDE　PONTHENRY　CWM BLAWD*

GLYN ABBEY　PONTYATES

KIDWELLY　TRIMSARAN ROAD　CYNHEIDRE*

TRIMSARAN JUNCTION*　HOREB*

PINGED　PONTARDULAIS

PEMBREY　FELIN FOEL*　LLANGENNECH

B

STATIONS
1. PEMBREY & BURRY PORT
2. LOUGHOR
3. GOWERTON
4. GORSEINON
5. LLANELLY QUEEN VICTORIA ROAD*

1

BURRY PORT　LLANELLY　BYNEA　GROVESEND

5

4

2

LLANMORLAIS　PENCLAWDD　3

DUNVANT　KILLAY

SOUTH WALES

**FOR THIS AREA
SEE MAP 43**

● NEATH

● SWANSEA

● PORT TALBOT

● BRIDGEND

C

HAVERFORDWEST　NARBERTH

JOHNSTON　TEMPLETON

MILFORD HAVEN　NEYLAND　KILGETTY

SAUNDERSFOOT

PEMBROKE DOCK　PEMBROKE

GOLDEN HILL PLATFORM　TENBY

LAMPHEY

MANORBIER

PENALLY

D

MAP 8

Lundy

E

A LYNTON

ILFRACOMBE

Summit　MORTEHOE　WOODY BAY

BLACKMOOR

B

BRATTON FLEMING

SOMERSET

CHELFHAM

BRAUNTON

WRAFTON　BARNSTAPLE TOWN

FREMINGTON　BARNSTAPLE

BARNSTAPLE JUNCTION

F

INSTOW　SWIMBRIDGE　FILLEIGH

BIDEFORD　CHAPELTON　SOUTH MOLTON

C　DULVERTON

UMBERLEIGH　BISHOP'S NYMPTON & MOLLAND　EAST ANSTEY

BAMPTON (DEVON)

G

TORRINGTON　PORTSMOUTH ARMS

SOUTH MOLTON ROAD

DEVONSHIRE

TIVERTON

EGGESFORD

MAP 1

MAP 2

LEGEND FOR MAP 7
A LYNTON: Also known as LYNTON & LYNMOUTH
B 1ft 11½in gauge LYNTON & BARNSTAPLE RAILWAY [SR]
C Former BIDEFORD, WESTWARD HO! & APPLEDORE RAILWAY

1 PONTIETS MINING HERITAGE TRAIL
2 PONTYATES: Operating base of the GWENDRAETH RAILWAY PROJECT. www.bpgv.co.uk
3 CYNHEIDRE: Operating base of the LLANELLI & MYNYDD RAILWAY. www.llanellirailway.co.uk
4 SWISS VALLEY TRAIL. www.railwaypaths.org.uk
5 CLYNE VALLEY CYCLE TRACK. www.swansea.gov.uk
6 Trackbed in NEYLAND part of the PEMBROKESHIRE COAST

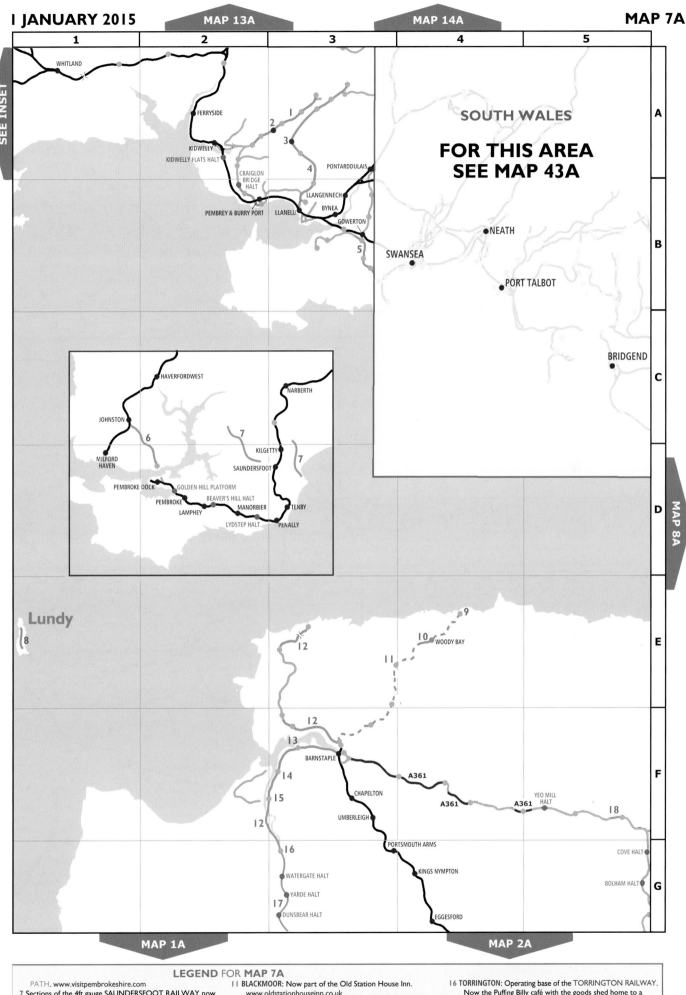

SEE INSET

MAP 13A

MAP 14A

1　2　3　4　5

A

WHITLAND

FERRYSIDE

1
2

KIDWELLY
3

KIDWELLY FLATS HALT
4

PONTARDDULAIS

CRAIGLON
BRIDGE
HALT

LLANGENNECH

PEMBREY & BURRY PORT
LLANELLI
BYNEA

GOWERTON

5

SOUTH WALES

FOR THIS AREA
SEE MAP 43A

NEATH

SWANSEA

PORT TALBOT

BRIDGEND

B

C

HAVERFORDWEST

NARBERTH

JOHNSTON
6

7

KILGETTY

MILFORD
HAVEN

SAUNDERSFOOT

7

PEMBROKE DOCK
GOLDEN HILL PLATFORM

BEAVER'S HILL HALT

PEMBROKE
LAMPHEY
MANORBIER

TENBY

LYDSTEP HALT
PENALLY

MAP 8A

D

Lundy

8

9

12

10
WOODY BAY

11

E

12

13

BARNSTAPLE

14

CHAPELTON

15

UMBERLEIGH

12

A361

A361

A361
YEO MILL
HALT

18

F

16

PORTSMOUTH ARMS

COVE HALT

WATERGATE HALT

KINGS NYMPTON

BOLHAM HALT

17
YARDE HALT

DUNSBEAR HALT

EGGESFORD

G

LEGEND FOR **MAP 7A**

PATH. www.visitpembrokeshire.com
7 Sections of the 4ft gauge SAUNDERSFOOT RAILWAY now
　walks, including part of the PEMBROKESHIRE COAST PATH
8 Former quarry tramroad. www.lundyisland.co.uk
9 LYNTON: Now partly holiday accommodation.
　e-mail:billthemovie@hotmail.com
10 1ft 11½in gauge LYNTON & BARNSTAPLE RAILWAY.
　www.lynton-rail.co.uk

11 BLACKMOOR: Now part of the Old Station House Inn.
　www.oldstationhouseinn.co.uk
12 Parts of the TARKA TRAIL. www.devon.gov.uk
13 FREMINGTON: Now the Quay Café. www.fremingtonquay.co.uk
14 INSTOW: Signal box preserved by BIDEFORD RAILWAY
　HERITAGE CENTRE (CIC). www.bidefordrailway.co.uk
15 BIDEFORD: Now the BIDEFORD RAILWAY HERITAGE
　CENTRE. www.bidefordrailway.co.uk

16 TORRINGTON: Operating base of the TORRINGTON RAILWAY.
　Now the Puffing Billy café with the goods shed home to a
　cycle-hire business. www.tarkavalleyrailway.co.uk
17 TARKA TRAIL south of TORRINGTON formerly the
　NORTH DEVON & CORNWALL LIGHT RAILWAY [SR]
18 Part of the EXE VALLEY WAY. www.devon.gov.uk

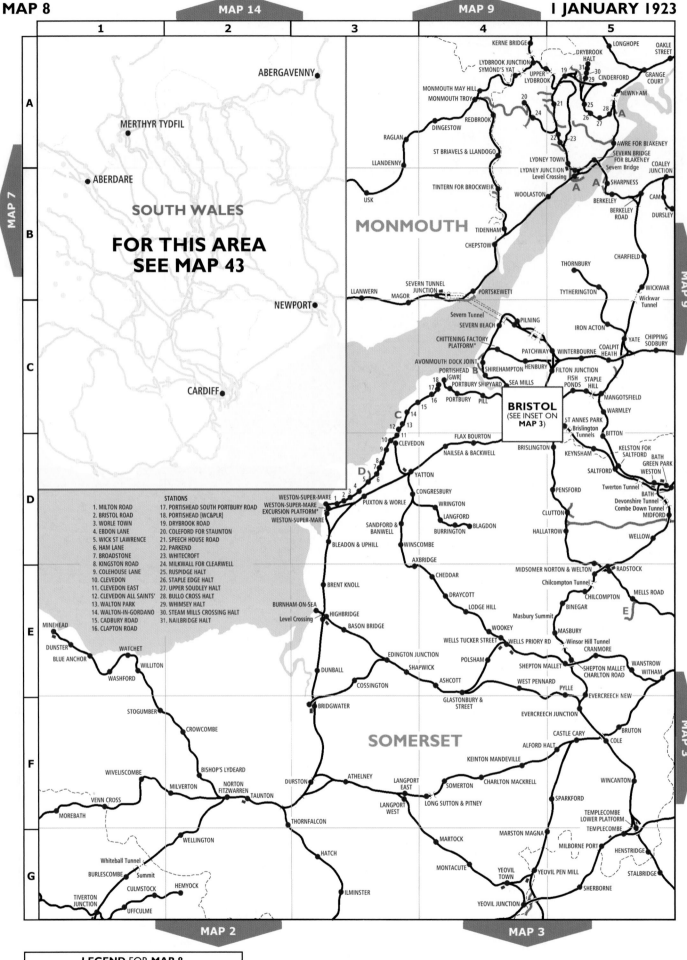

ABERGAVENNY

MERTHYR TYDFIL

ABERDARE

SOUTH WALES

FOR THIS AREA
SEE MAP 43

NEWPORT

CARDIFF

MONMOUTH

KERNE BRIDGE
LONGHOPE
OAKLE STREET
DRYBROOK HALT
LYDBROOK JUNCTION
SYMOND'S YAT
UPPER LYDBROOK
19
31
30
CINDERFORD
29
GRANGE COURT
MONMOUTH MAY HILL
MONMOUTH TROY
20
21
25
28
NEWNHAM
24
26
27
REDBROOK
22 23
RAGLAN
DINGESTOW
ST BRIAVELS & LLANDOGO
AWRE FOR BLAKENEY
SEVERN BRIDGE FOR BLAKENEY
LLANDENNY
LYDNEY TOWN
Severn Bridge
COALEY JUNCTION
USK
LYDNEY JUNCTION
Level Crossing
SHARPNESS
TINTERN FOR BROCKWEIR
WOOLASTON
BERKELEY
CAM
BERKELEY ROAD
DURSLEY
TIDENHAM
CHEPSTOW
THORNBURY
CHARFIELD
LLANWERN
SEVERN TUNNEL JUNCTION
MAGOR
PORTSKEWETT
TYTHERINGTON
WICKWAR
Wickwar Tunnel
Severn Tunnel
PILNING
SEVERN BEACH
IRON ACTON
YATE
CHIPPING SODBURY
CHITTENING FACTORY PLATFORM*
PATCHWAY
WINTERBOURNE
COALPIT HEATH
AVONMOUTH DOCK JOINT
PORTISHEAD [GWR]
SHIREHAMPTON
HENBURY
FILTON JUNCTION
PORTBURY SHIPYARD
SEA MILLS
FISH PONDS
STAPLE HILL
18
17
PORTBURY
PILL
MANGOTSFIELD
16
15
BRISTOL
(SEE INSET ON **MAP 3**)
ST ANNES PARK
WARMLEY
14
FLAX BOURTON
Brislington Tunnels
BITTON
12 13
NAILSEA & BACKWELL
BRISLINGTON
KELSTON FOR SALTFORD
11
CLEVEDON
KEYNSHAM
BATH GREEN PARK
10
9
YATTON
SALTFORD
WESTON
8
CONGRESBURY
Twerton Tunnel
BATH
7
WRINGTON
Devonshire Tunnel
5
PUXTON & WORLE
LANGFORD
PENSFORD
Combe Down Tunnel
4 6
WESTON-SUPER-MARE
1 2 3
SANDFORD & BANWELL
BLAGDON
MIDFORD
WESTON-SUPER-MARE EXCURSION PLATFORM*
BURRINGTON
CLUTTON
WELLOW
WESTON-SUPER-MARE
BLEADON & UPHILL
WINSCOMBE
HALLATROW
AXBRIDGE
MIDSOMER NORTON & WELTON
RADSTOCK
CHEDDAR
Chilcompton Tunnel
MELLS ROAD
BRENT KNOLL
DRAYCOTT
CHILCOMPTON
LODGE HILL
BINEGAR
BURNHAM-ON-SEA
Masbury Summit
Level Crossing
HIGHBRIDGE
WOOKEY
MASBURY
BASON BRIDGE
WELLS TUCKER STREET
WELLS PRIORY RD
Winsor Hill Tunnel
CRANMORE
MINEHEAD
EDINGTON JUNCTION
WANSTROW
DUNSTER
WATCHET
POLSHAM
SHEPTON MALLET
WITHAM
BLUE ANCHOR
SHAPWICK
SHEPTON MALLET CHARLTON ROAD
WILLITON
DUNBALL
ASHCOTT
WEST PENNARD
WASHFORD
COSSINGTON
PYLLE
EVERCREECH NEW
GLASTONBURY & STREET
BRIDGWATER
STOGUMBER
EVERCREECH JUNCTION
SOMERSET
CROWCOMBE
CASTLE CARY
BRUTON
ALFORD HALT
COLE
WIVELISCOMBE
BISHOP'S LYDEARD
KEINTON MANDEVILLE
MILVERTON
DURSTON
ATHELNEY
LANGPORT EAST
CHARLTON MACKRELL
WINCANTON
NORTON FITZWARREN
SOMERTON
VENN CROSS
TAUNTON
LONG SUTTON & PITNEY
SPARKFORD
MOREBATH
LANGPORT WEST
TEMPLECOMBE LOWER PLATFORM
THORNFALCON
TEMPLECOMBE
WELLINGTON
MARTOCK
MARSTON MAGNA
Whiteball Tunnel
HATCH
MILBORNE PORT
HENSTRIDGE
BURLESCOMBE
Summit
MONTACUTE
YEOVIL TOWN
YEOVIL PEN MILL
STALBRIDGE
TIVERTON JUNCTION
CULMSTOCK
HEMYOCK
ILMINSTER
SHERBORNE
UFFCULME
YEOVIL JUNCTION

STATIONS

1. MILTON ROAD	17. PORTISHEAD SOUTH PORTBURY ROAD
2. BRISTOL ROAD	18. PORTISHEAD [WC&PLR]
3. WORLE TOWN	19. DRYBROOK ROAD
4. EBDON LANE	20. COLEFORD FOR STAUNTON
5. WICK ST LAWRENCE	21. SPEECH HOUSE ROAD
6. HAM LANE	22. PARKEND
7. BROADSTONE	23. WHITECROFT
8. KINGSTON ROAD	24. MILKWALL FOR CLEARWELL
9. COLEHOUSE LANE	25. RUSPIDGE HALT
10. CLEVEDON	26. STAPLE EDGE HALT
11. CLEVEDON EAST	27. UPPER SOUDLEY HALT
12. CLEVEDON ALL SAINTS'	28. BULLO CROSS HALT
13. WALTON PARK	29. WHIMSEY HALT
14. WALTON-IN-GORDANO	30. STEAM MILLS CROSSING HALT
15. CADBURY ROAD	31. NAILBRIDGE HALT
16. CLAPTON ROAD	

LEGEND FOR **MAP 8**
A Dock branches
B Avonmouth Dock branches
C WESTON, CLEVEDON & PORTISHEAD LIGHT RAILWAY
D Wick St Lawrence Wharf branch
E Vobster Colliery branch

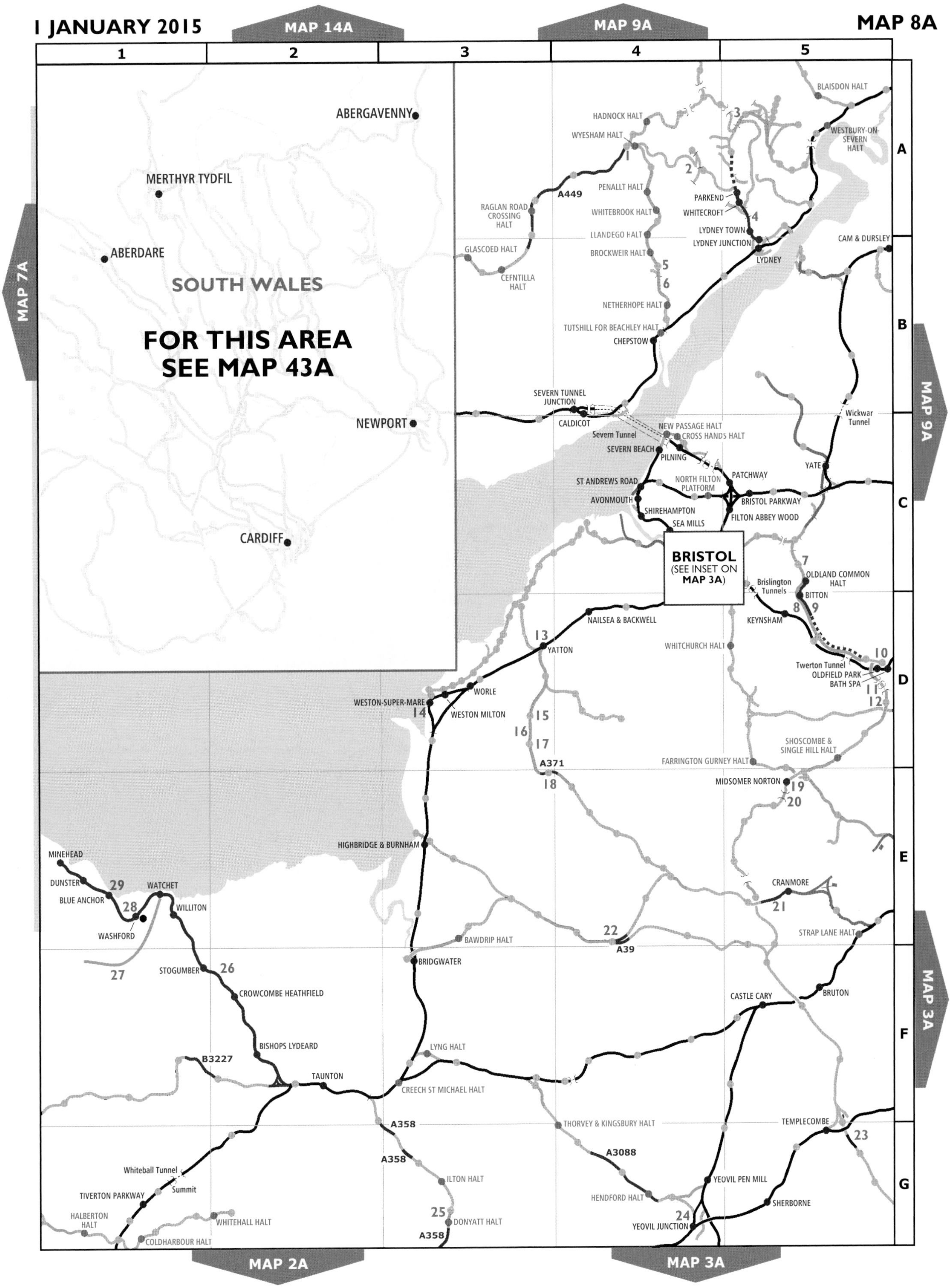

1   2   3   4   5

MAP 7A

MAP 9A

MAP 3A

A
B
C
D
E
F
G

ABERGAVENNY

MERTHYR TYDFIL

ABERDARE

SOUTH WALES

**FOR THIS AREA
SEE MAP 43A**

NEWPORT

CARDIFF

BLAISDON HALT

HADNOCK HALT
WYESHAM HALT

WESTBURY-ON-SEVERN HALT

PENALLT HALT

A449

RAGLAN ROAD
CROSSING
HALT

WHITEBROOK HALT

PARKEND
WHITECROFT

LLANDEGO HALT

LYDNEY TOWN
LYDNEY JUNCTION

CAM & DURSLEY

GLASCOED HALT

BROCKWEIR HALT

LYDNEY

CEFNTILLA
HALT

NETHERHOPE HALT

TUTSHILL FOR BEACHLEY HALT

CHEPSTOW

SEVERN TUNNEL
JUNCTION

Wickwar
Tunnel

CALDICOT

NEW PASSAGE HALT
CROSS HANDS HALT

Severn Tunnel

SEVERN BEACH

PILNING

YATE

ST ANDREWS ROAD

NORTH FILTON
PLATFORM

PATCHWAY

AVONMOUTH

BRISTOL PARKWAY

SHIREHAMPTON

FILTON ABBEY WOOD

SEA MILLS

BRISTOL
(SEE INSET ON
MAP 3A)

OLDLAND COMMON
HALT

Brislington
Tunnels

BITTON

NAILSEA & BACKWELL

KEYNSHAM

YATTON

WHITCHURCH HALT

Twerton Tunnel
OLDFIELD PARK
BATH SPA

WORLE

WESTON-SUPER-MARE

WESTON MILTON

SHOSCOMBE &
SINGLE HILL HALT

FARRINGTON GURNEY HALT

A371

MIDSOMER NORTON

MINEHEAD

DUNSTER
BLUE ANCHOR

WATCHET

WILLITON

CRANMORE

STRAP LANE HALT

WASHFORD

STOGUMBER

BAWDRIP HALT

A39

HIGHBRIDGE & BURNHAM

BRIDGWATER

CROWCOMBE HEATHFIELD

CASTLE CARY

BRUTON

BISHOPS LYDEARD

LYNG HALT

B3227

TAUNTON

CREECH ST MICHAEL HALT

A358

THORVEY & KINGSBURY HALT

TEMPLECOMBE

A358

A3088

ILTON HALT

YEOVIL PEN MILL

Whiteball Tunnel

TIVERTON PARKWAY
Summit

HENDFORD HALT

SHERBORNE

HALBERTON
HALT

WHITEHALL HALT

DONYATT HALT

YEOVIL JUNCTION

COLDHARBOUR HALT

A358

LEGEND FOR MAP 8A
FOR THE LEGEND TO THIS MAP,
PLEASE SEE PAGE vi

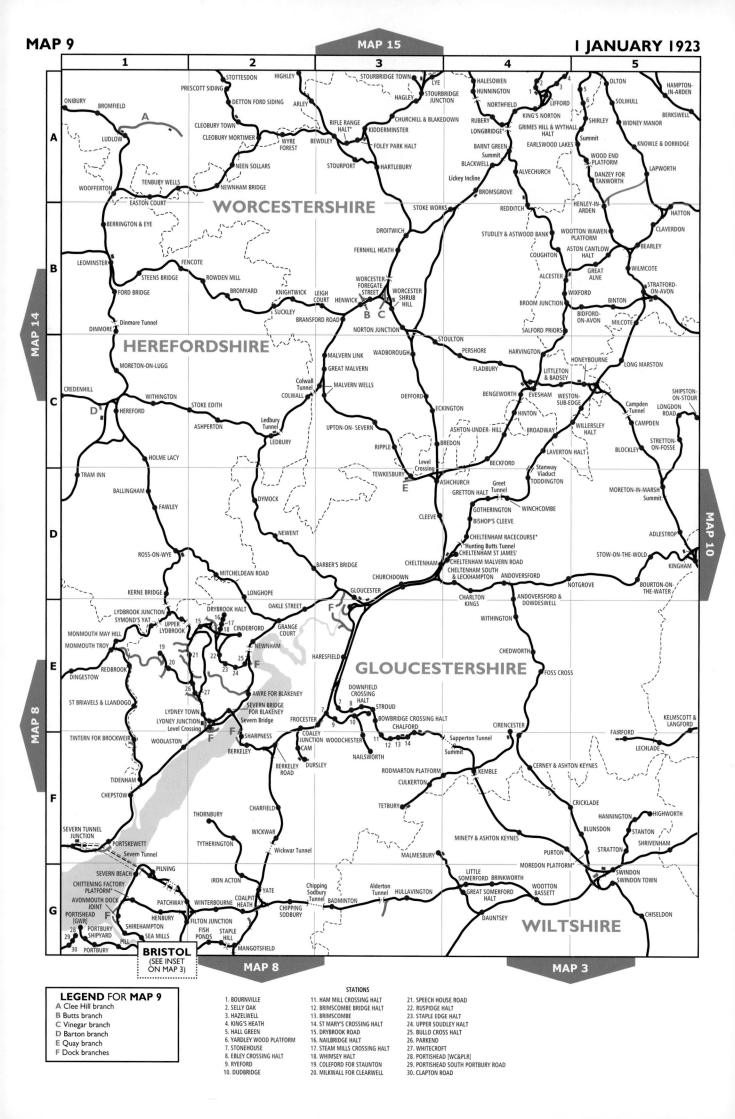

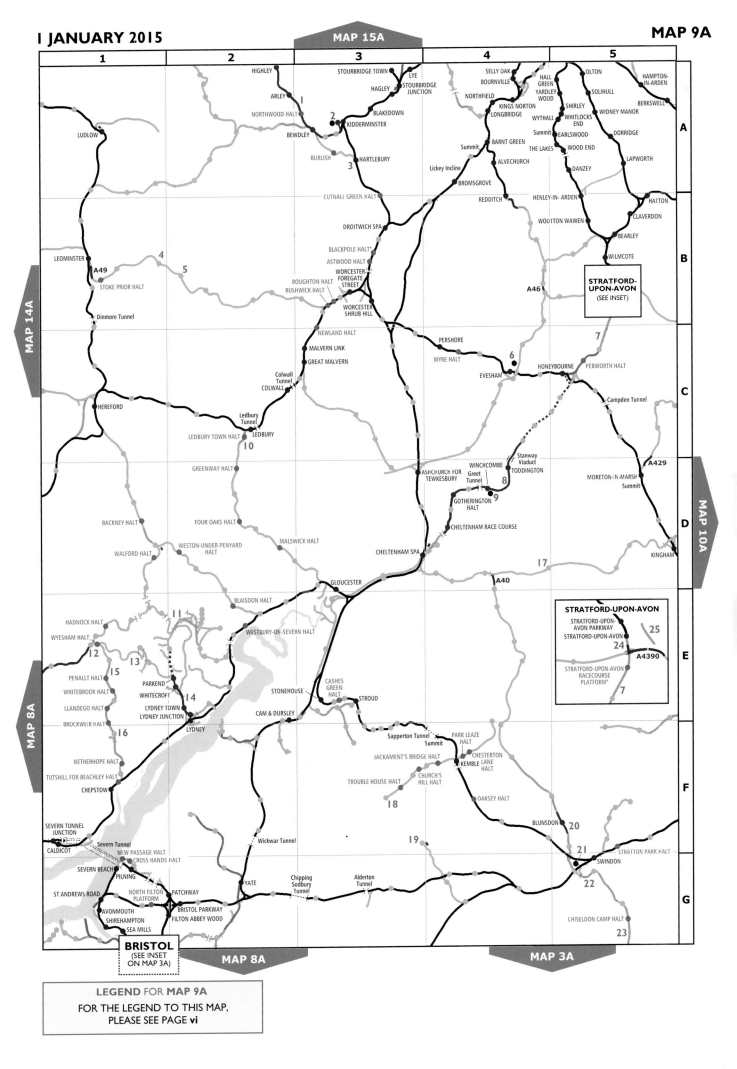

MAP 10   MAP 16   1 JANUARY 1923

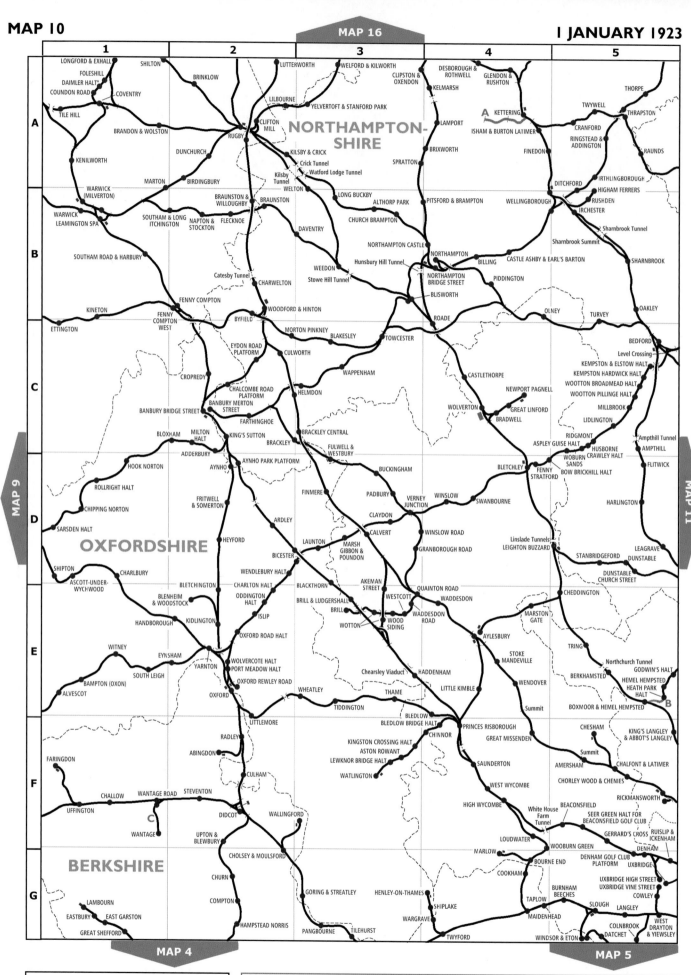

MAP 9
MAP 11
MAP 4
MAP 5

LEGEND FOR MAP 10

A Loddington branch
B Gasworks branch
C WANTAGE ROAD – WANTAGE: Independent WANTAGE TRAMWAY

1 Part of the COVENTRY WAY. www.acoventryway.org.uk
2 ELECTRIC RAILWAY MUSEUM. www.electricrailwaymuseum.co.uk
3 WELFORD & KILWORTH: Down platform shelter now preserved at the ELECTRIC RAILWAY MUSEUM
4 BRAMPTON VALLEY WAY. www.gps-routes.co.uk
5 GLENDON & RUSHTON: Currently subject to long-term restoration. www.glendonrushtonstation.org.uk

6 NORTHAMPTON & LAMPORT RAILWAY. www.nlr.org.uk
7 NORTHAMPTONSHIRE IRONSTONE RAILWAY. www.nirt.co.uk
8 IRCHESTER NARROW GAUGE RAILWAY MUSEUM. www.northamptonshire.gov.uk
9 RUSHDEN: Now the RUSHDEN TRANSPORT MUSEUM. www.rhts.co.uk
10 Part of the REDWAY cycleway network.

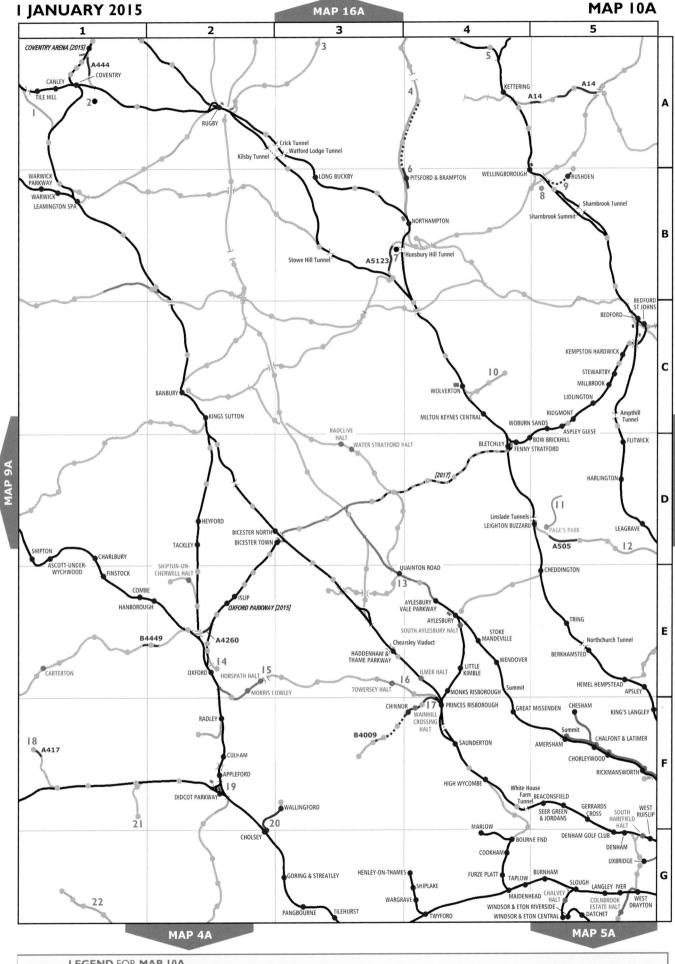

LEGEND FOR **MAP 10A**

www.milton-keynes.gov.uk
11 2ft gauge LEIGHTON BUZZARD RAILWAY.
  www.buzzrail.co.uk
12 DUNSTABLE – LUTON now a busway. www.busway.net
13 QUAINTON ROAD: Now part of the BUCKINGHAMSHIRE
  RAILWAY CENTRE. www.bucksrailcentre.org
14 OXFORD REWLEY ROAD: Station building rebuilt at
  BUCKINGHAMSHIRE RAILWAY CENTRE

15 Horspath Tunnel: Now a bat hibernaculum
16 PHOENIX TRAIL. www.gps-routes.co.uk
17 CHINNOR & PRINCES RISBOROUGH RAILWAY.
  www.chinnorrailway.co.uk
18 FARINGDON: Now a children's nursery
19 DIDCOT RAILWAY CENTRE. www.didcotrailwaycentre.org.uk
20 CHOLSEY & WALLINGFORD RAILWAY.
  www.cholsey-wallingford-railway.com

21 WANTAGE: Station office building occupied by an estate agent
22 LAMBOURN VALLEY WAY. www.ldwa.org.uk

MAP 11

MAP 17

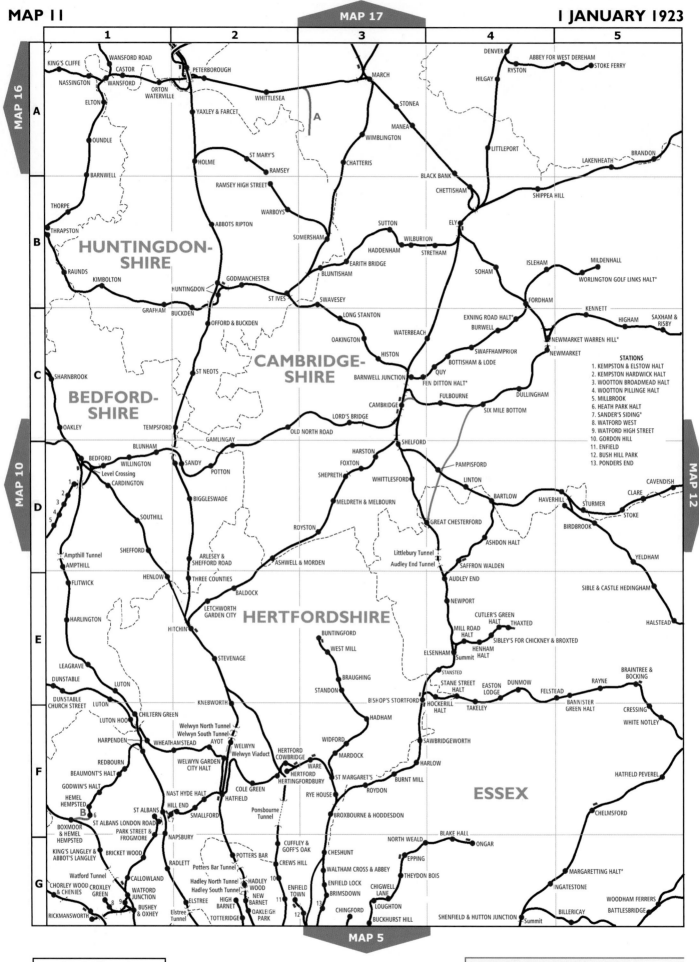

MAP 16

MAP 10

MAP 12

MAP 5

STATIONS
1. KEMPSTON & ELSTOW HALT
2. KEMPSTON HARDWICK HALT
3. WOOTTON BROADMEAD HALT
4. WOOTTON PILLINGE HALT
5. MILLBROOK
6. HEATH PARK HALT
7. SANDER'S SIDING*
8. WATFORD WEST
9. WATFORD HIGH STREET
10. GORDON HILL
11. ENFIELD
12. BUSH HILL PARK
13. PONDERS END

LEGEND FOR MAP 11
A Benwick branch
B Gasworks branch

1 RAILWORLD MUSEUM. www.railworld.net
2 NENE VALLEY RAILWAY. www.nvr.org.uk
3 BARNWELL: Station building re-erected at WANSFORD on the
  NENE VALLEY RAILWAY
4 SOMERSHAM: Station building re-erected at the private
  FAWLEY RAILWAY MUSEUM in Oxfordshire
5 EARITH BRIDGE: Site cleared as part of the Hermitage Marina
6 Parts of a busway and cycle track. www.the busway.info

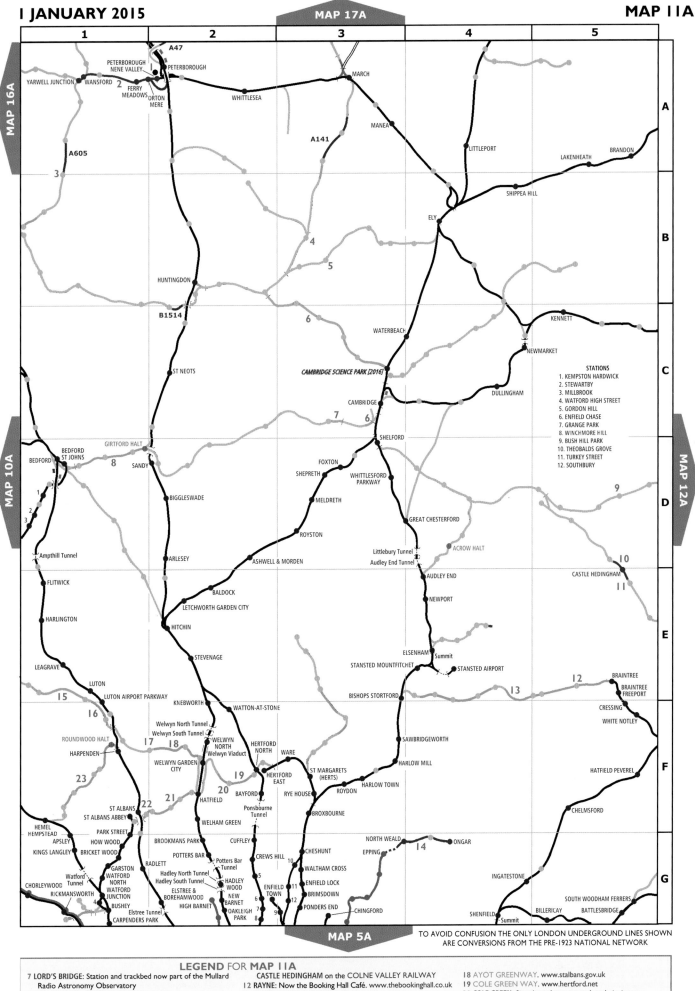

MAP 16A

MAP 10A

MAP 12A

MAP 5A

STATIONS
1. KEMPSTON HARDWICK
2. STEWARTBY
3. MILLBROOK
4. WATFORD HIGH STREET
5. GORDON HILL
6. ENFIELD CHASE
7. GRANGE PARK
8. WINCHMORE HILL
9. BUSH HILL PARK
10. THEOBALDS GROVE
11. TURKEY STREET
12. SOUTHBURY

TO AVOID CONFUSION THE ONLY LONDON UNDERGROUND LINES SHOWN
ARE CONVERSIONS FROM THE PRE-1923 NATIONAL NETWORK

LEGEND FOR MAP 11A

7 LORD'S BRIDGE: Station and trackbed now part of the Mullard
Radio Astronomy Observatory
8 BEDFORD TO SANDY COUNTRY WAY.
www.grps-routes.co.uk
9 CLARE: Buildings preserved as part of the Clare Country Park.
www.clare-uk.com
10 COLNE VALLEY RAILWAY. www.colnevalleyrailway.co.uk
11 SIBLE & CASTLE HEDINGHAM: Station building rebuilt at

CASTLE HEDINGHAM on the COLNE VALLEY RAILWAY
12 RAYNE: Now the Booking Hall Café. www.thebookinghall.co.uk
13 FLITCH WAY. www.visitessex.com
14 EPPING ONGAR RAILWAY. eorailway.co.uk
15 DUNSTABLE – LUTON: Now a busway. www.busway.net
16 Part of the LEA VALLEY WALK. www.leavalleywalk.org.uk
17 WHEATHAMPSTEAD: Site cleared and partly restored as a
leisure area

18 AYOT GREENWAY. www.stalbans.gov.uk
19 COLE GREEN WAY. www.hertford.net
20 COLE GREEN: Site cleared as a car park and picnic area
21 ALBAN WAY. www.stalbans.gov.uk
22 ST ALBANS: South signal box restored and open to the public.
www.sigbox.co.uk
23 NICKEY LINE. www.nickeyline.org

MAP 12   MAP 18   1 JANUARY 1923

MAP 11

MAP 6

NORFOLK

SUFFOLK

ESSEX

STOW BEDON
SPOONER ROW
ASHWELLTHORPE
FLORDON
HADDISCOE LOW LEVEL
HADDISCOE HIGH LEVEL
SOMERLEYTON
CORTON
ATTLEBOROUGH
FORNCETT
ALDEBY
Beccles Swing Bridge
LOWESTOFT NORTH
WRETHAM & HOCKHAM
ECCLES ROAD
GELDESTON
Oulton Broad Swing Bridge
OULTON BROAD
LOWESTOFT CENTRAL
ELLINGHAM
ROUDHAM JUNCTION
HARLING ROAD
TIVETSHALL
DITCHINGHAM
BUNGAY
BECCLES
CARLTON COLVILLE
EARSHAM
HOMERSFIELD
PULHAM MARKET
BRAMPTON
THETFORD
PULHAM ST MARY
HARLESTON
THETFORD BRIDGE
BURSTON
BARNHAM
DISS
HALESWORTH
B
BLYTHBURGH
SOUTHWOLD
WENHASTON
SEVEN HILLS HALT
MELLIS
STRADBROKE
WILBY
WALBERSWICK
EYE
HORHAM
INGHAM
WORLINGWORTH
LAXFIELD
C
DARSHAM
FINNINGHAM
THURSTON
BROCKFORD & WETHERINGSETT
KENTON
BURY ST EDMUNDS
ELMSWELL
MENDLESHAM
ASPALL & THORNDON
FRAMLINGHAM
SAXMUNDHAM
LEISTON
HAUGHLEY
PARHAM
THORPENESS HALT
WELNETHAM
STOWMARKET
MARLESFORD
D
COCKFIELD
NEEDHAM
WICKHAM MARKET
ALDEBURGH
LAVENHAM
CLAYDON
MELTON
GLEMSFORD
BRAMFORD
WESTERFIELD
WOODBRIDGE
BEALINGS
LONG MELFORD
E
DERBY ROAD
HADLEIGH
IPSWICH
F
SUDBURY
RAYDON WOOD
CAPEL
ORWELL
BENTLEY
TRIMLEY
FELIXSTOWE TOWN
BURES
HARWICH TOWN
FELIXSTOWE BEACH
MANNINGTREE
PARKESTON QUAY
FELIXSTOWE PIER
MISTLEY
DOVERCOURT BAY
EARLS COLNE
BRADFIELD
WRABNESS
WHITE COLNE
ARDLEIGH
CHAPPEL & WAKES COLNE
COLCHESTER
ST BOTOLPH'S
HYTHE
ALRESFORD
GREAT BENTLEY
WEELEY
KIRBY CROSS
WALTON-ON-THE-NAZE
MARKS TEY
WIVENHOE
THORINGTON
THORPE LE-SOKEN
FRINTON-ON-SEA
KELVEDON
KELVEDON LOW LEVEL
INWORTH
BRIGHTLINGSEA
TIPTREE
WITHAM
TOLLESHUNT D'ARCY
WICKHAM BISHOPS
TOLLESHUNT KNIGHTS
LANGFORD
TOLLESBURY
G
CLACTON-ON-SEA & SOUTHCLIFF
MALDON EAST & HEYBRIDGE
MALDON WEST HALT
BARON'S LANE HALT
COLD NORTON
FAMBRIDGE
ALTHORNE
SOUTHMINSTER
BURNHAM-ON-CROUCH

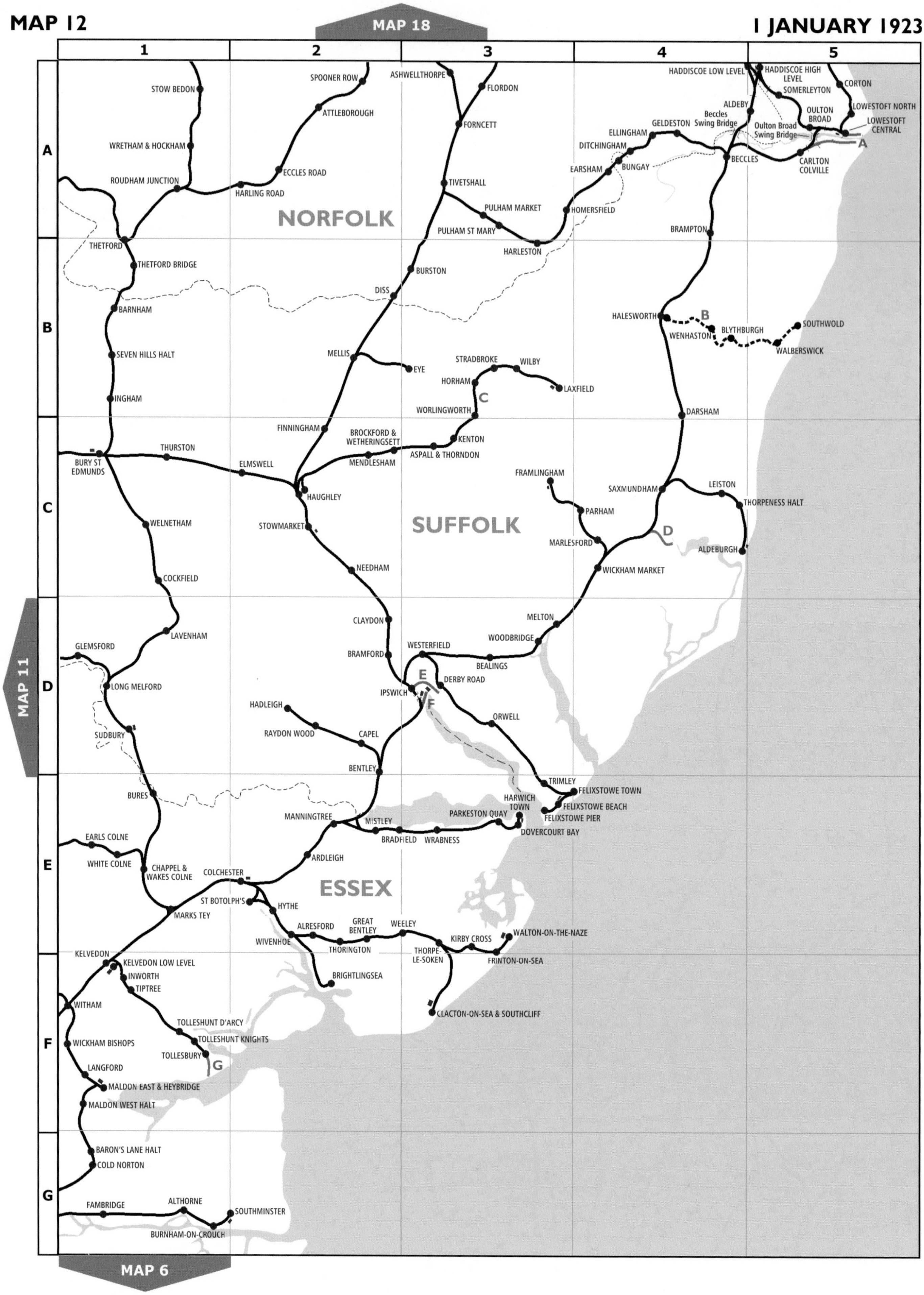

LEGEND FOR MAP 12

A Harbour branches
B 3ft gauge SOUTHWOLD RAILWAY
C HAUGHLEY - LAXFIELD: Independent MID-SUFFOLK LIGHT RAILWAY
D Snape branch
E Docks branch
F Griffin's Wharf branch
G Former TOLLESBURY PIER extension of the KELVEDON, TIPTREE & TOLLESBURY LIGHT RAILWAY

1 EAST ANGLIAN TRANSPORT MUSEUM with a 2ft gauge operational line. www.eatm.org.uk
2 BRAMPTON: Station building now at MANGAPPS RAILWAY MUSEUM
3 Parts of the SOUTHWOLD RAILWAY & BLYTH VALLEY WALK. www.southwoldrailway.co.uk
4 WENHASTON: Section of trackbed near station owned by the SOUTHWOLD RAILWAY TRUST as possible heritage

railway base. www.southwoldrailway.co.uk
5 BRESSINGHAM STEAM MUSEUM & GARDENS with operational lines of different gauges. bressingham.co.uk
6 LAXFIELD: Station building now at MANGAPPS RAILWAY MUSEUM
7 HORHAM: Station building now at MANGAPPS RAILWAY MUSEUM

MAP 18A

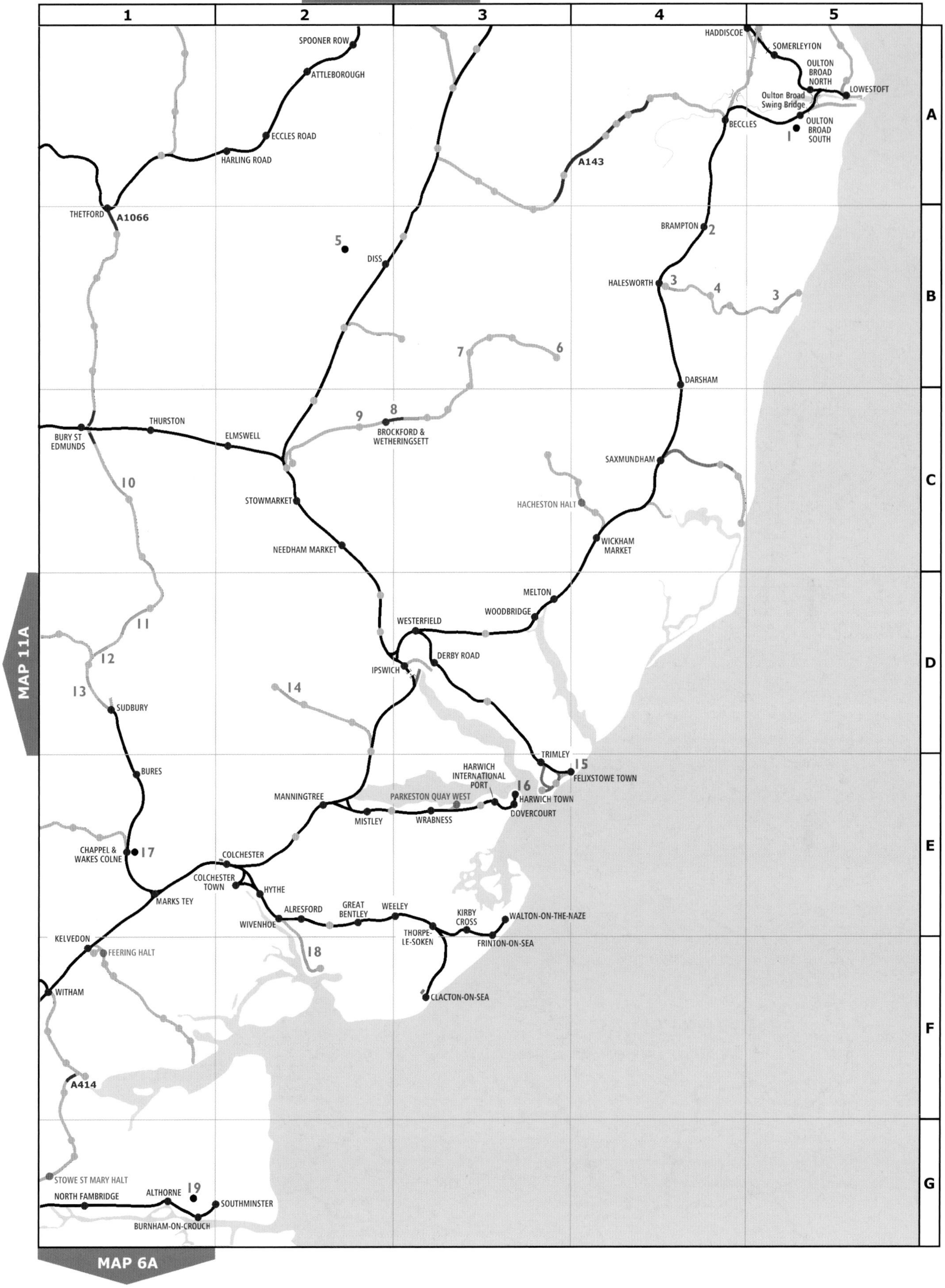
1
2
3
4
5
A
B
C
D
E
F
G
MAP 11A
MAP 6A
SPOONER ROW
ATTLEBOROUGH
ECCLES ROAD
HARLING ROAD
THETFORD
A1066
5
DISS
HADDISCOE
SOMERLEYTON
OULTON BROAD NORTH
LOWESTOFT
Oulton Broad Swing Bridge
BECCLES
OULTON BROAD SOUTH
1
A143
BRAMPTON
2
HALESWORTH
3
4
3
7
6
DARSHAM
9
8
BROCKFORD & WETHERINGSETT
THURSTON
ELMSWELL
BURY ST EDMUNDS
10
STOWMARKET
SAXMUNDHAM
HACHESTON HALT
WICKHAM MARKET
NEEDHAM MARKET
MELTON
WOODBRIDGE
WESTERFIELD
DERBY ROAD
IPSWICH
11
12
13
14
SUDBURY
TRIMLEY
15
FELIXSTOWE TOWN
BURES
HARWICH INTERNATIONAL PORT
16
HARWICH TOWN
DOVERCOURT
PARKESTON QUAY WEST
MANNINGTREE
MISTLEY
WRABNESS
CHAPPEL & WAKES COLNE
17
COLCHESTER
COLCHESTER TOWN
HYTHE
MARKS TEY
ALRESFORD
GREAT BENTLEY
WEELEY
KIRBY CROSS
WALTON-ON-THE-NAZE
WIVENHOE
THORPE-LE-SOKEN
FRINTON-ON-SEA
KELVEDON
FEERING HALT
18
WITHAM
CLACTON-ON-SEA
A414
STOWE ST MARY HALT
NORTH FAMBRIDGE
ALTHORNE
19
SOUTHMINSTER
BURNHAM-ON-CROUCH

LEGEND FOR MAP 12A

8 MID-SUFFOLK LIGHT RAILWAY. www.mslr.org.uk Holiday accommodation available in rebuilt original station building and converted carriage and guards vans. www.hoseasons.co.uk

9 **MENDLESHAM:** Station building re-erected at **BROCKFORD & WETHERINGSETT** on the **MID-SUFFOLK LIGHT RAILWAY**

10 Part of the ST EDMUND WAY. www.ldwa.org.uk

11 LAVENHAM WALK. www.nationaltrust.org.uk

12 LONGMELFORD OLD RAILWAY WALK. www.nationaltrust.org.uk

13 Parts of the THE VALLEY WALK. www.sudbury.org.uk

14 HADLEIGH RAILWAY WALK. www.badbergh.gov.uk

15 **FELIXSTOWE TOWN:** Former station buildings now part of a shopping centre

16 **HARWICH:** Quayside ticket office for railway steamers now a visitor centre

17 EAST ANGLIAN RAILWAY MUSEUM. www.earm.co.uk

18 CRAB & WINKLE PATH

19 MANGAPPS RAILWAY MUSEUM with a standard gauge operational line. www.mangapps.co.uk

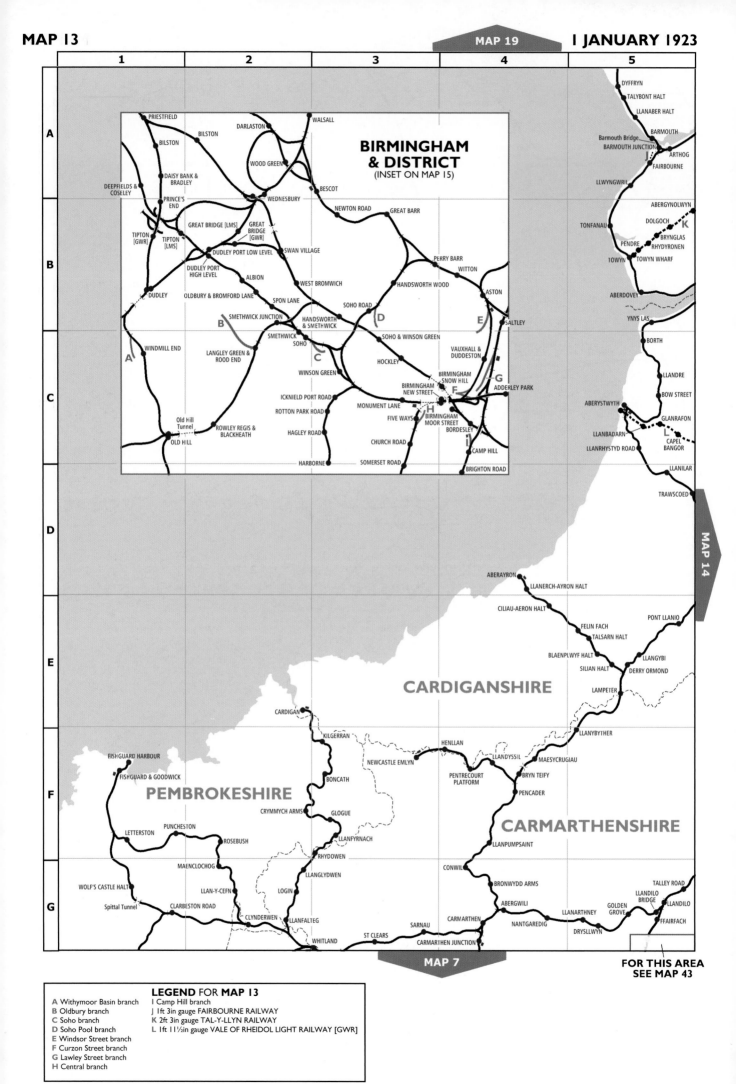

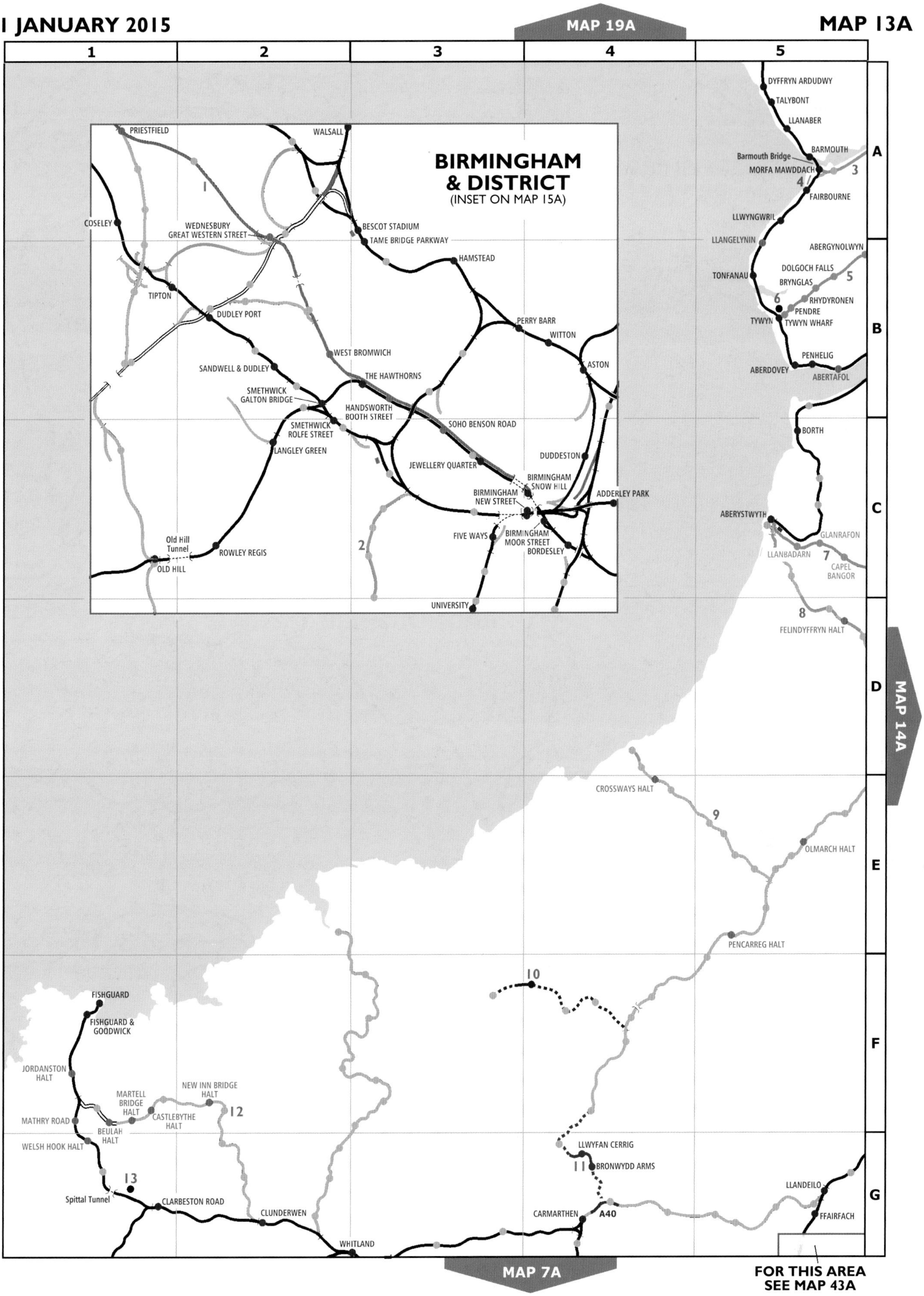

	1	2	3	4	5

DYFFRYN ARDUDWY
TALYBONT
LLANABER
BARMOUTH
Barmouth Bridge
MORFA MAWDDACH
FAIRBOURNE — **3**
4
LLWYNGWRIL
LLANGELYNIN
ABERGYNOLWYN
DOLGOCH FALLS
TONFANAU — **5**
BRYNGLAS
RHYDYRONEN
PENDRE
TYWYN WHARF
TYWYN — **6**
PENHELIG
ABERDOVEY
ABERTAFOL
BORTH
A
B

BIRMINGHAM & DISTRICT
(INSET ON MAP 15A)

PRIESTFIELD
WALSALL
COSELEY
WEDNESBURY GREAT WESTERN STREET — **1**
BESCOT STADIUM
TAME BRIDGE PARKWAY
HAMSTEAD
TIPTON
DUDLEY PORT
PERRY BARR
WITTON
ASTON
WEST BROMWICH
SANDWELL & DUDLEY
THE HAWTHORNS
SMETHWICK GALTON BRIDGE
HANDSWORTH BOOTH STREET
SMETHWICK ROLFE STREET
LANGLEY GREEN
SOHO BENSON ROAD
JEWELLERY QUARTER
DUDDESTON
BIRMINGHAM SNOW HILL
ADDERLEY PARK
Old Hill Tunnel
ROWLEY REGIS
OLD HILL
BIRMINGHAM NEW STREET
FIVE WAYS
BIRMINGHAM MOOR STREET
BORDESLEY
2
UNIVERSITY

ABERYSTWYTH — **7**
GLANRAFON
LLANBADARN
CAPEL BANGOR
8
FELINDYFFRYN HALT
C
MAP 14A
D

CROSSWAYS HALT
9
OLMARCH HALT
E

PENCARREG HALT

FISHGUARD
10
FISHGUARD & GOODWICK
JORDANSTON HALT
NEW INN BRIDGE HALT
MARTELL BRIDGE HALT
CASTLEBYTHE HALT
12
MATHRY ROAD
BEULAH HALT
WELSH HOOK HALT
13
Spittal Tunnel
CLARBESTON ROAD
CLUNDERWEN
LLWYFAN CERRIG
BRONWYDD ARMS
11
LLANDEILO
FFAIRFACH
CARMARTHEN
A40
WHITLAND
F
G

MAP 7A

FOR THIS AREA SEE MAP 43A

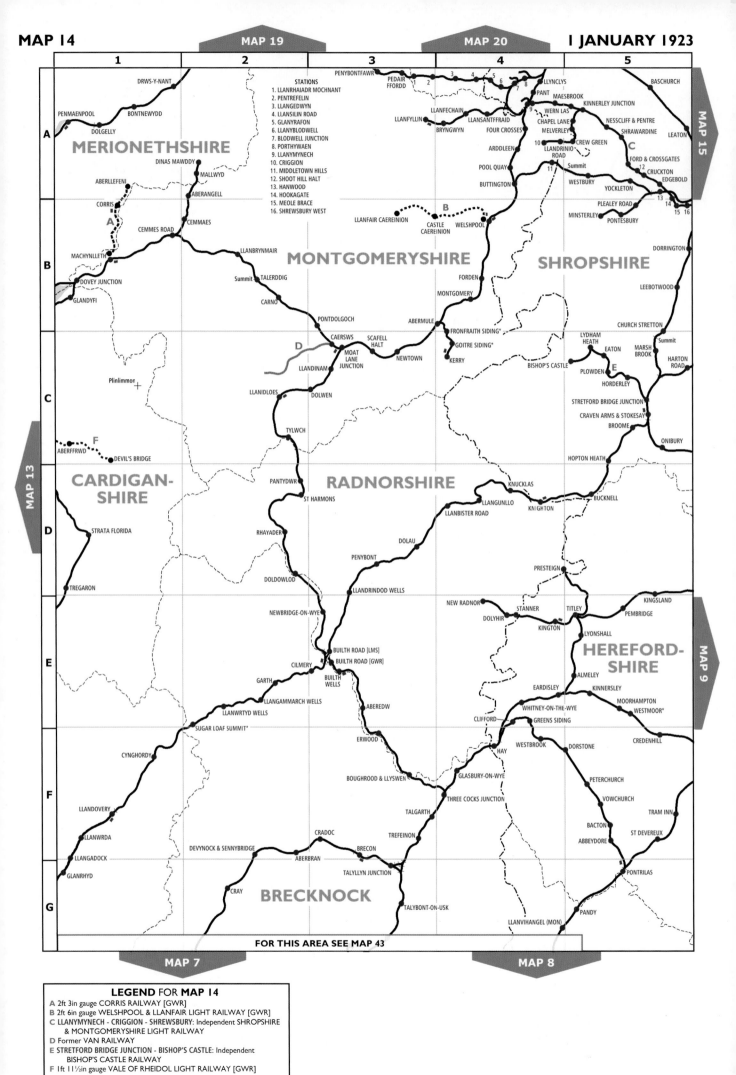

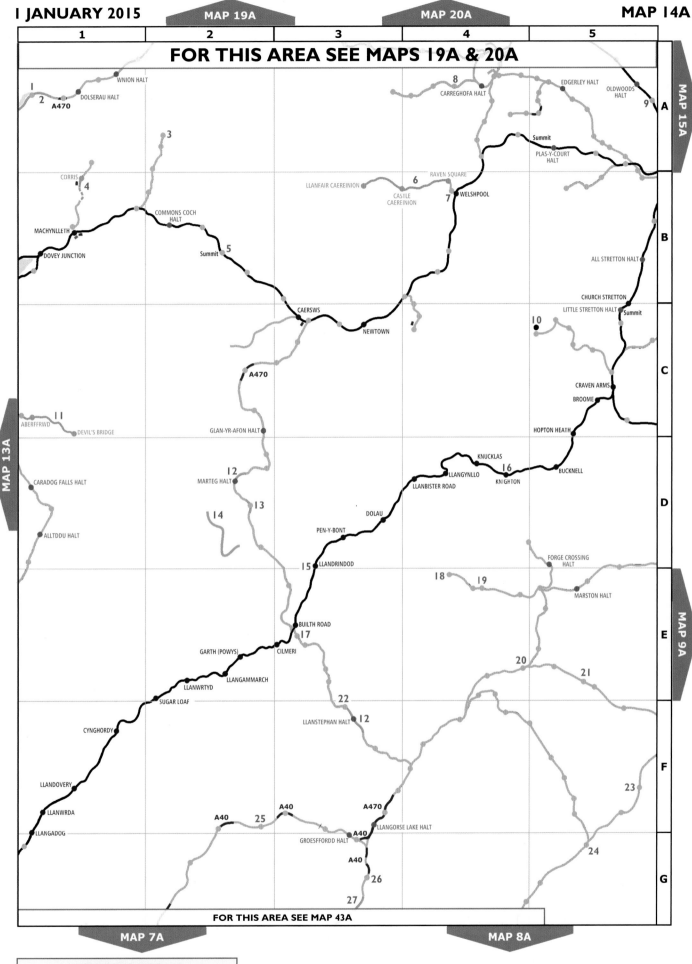

FOR THIS AREA SEE MAPS 19A & 20A

WNION HALT
DOLSERAU HALT
A470
CORRIS
MACHYNLLETH
DOVEY JUNCTION
COMMONS COCH HALT
Summit
CAERSWS
NEWTOWN
A470
ABERFFRWD
DEVIL'S BRIDGE
GLAN-YR-AFON HALT
CARADOG FALLS HALT
MARTEG HALT
ALLTDDU HALT
PEN-Y-BONT
DOLAU
LLANBISTER ROAD
LLANGYNLLO
LLANDRINDOD
BUILTH ROAD
GARTH (POWYS)
CILMERI
LLANGAMMARCH
LLANWRTYD
SUGAR LOAF
LLANSTEPHAN HALT
CYNGHORDY
LLANDOVERY
LLANWRDA
LLANGADOG
A40
A40
A470
GROESFFORDD HALT
LLANGORSE LAKE HALT
A40
A40

CARREGHOFA HALT
EDGERLEY HALT
OLDWOODS HALT
Summit
PLAS-Y-COURT HALT
LLANFAIR CAEREINION
RAVEN SQUARE
CASTLE CAEREINION
WELSHPOOL
ALL STRETTON HALT
CHURCH STRETTON
LITTLE STRETTON HALT
Summit
CRAVEN ARMS
BROOME
HOPTON HEATH
KNUCKLAS
KNIGHTON
BUCKNELL
FORGE CROSSING HALT
MARSTON HALT

MAP 15A
MAP 13A
MAP 9A

1 2 3 4 5
A
B
C
D
E
F
G

FOR THIS AREA SEE MAP 43A

LEGEND FOR MAP 14A
FOR THE LEGEND TO THIS MAP,
PLEASE SEE PAGE vii

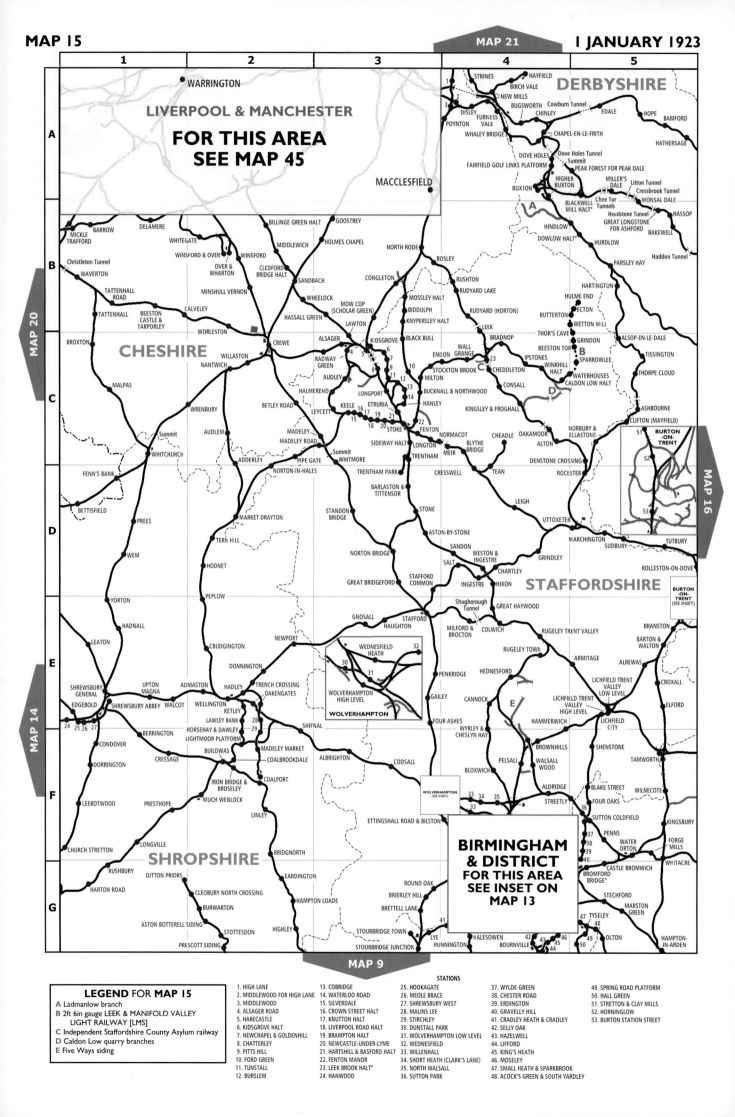

MAP 20

MAP 14

MAP 16

MAP 21

MAP 9

WARRINGTON

LIVERPOOL & MANCHESTER

FOR THIS AREA
SEE MAP 45

MACCLESFIELD

DERBYSHIRE

STRINES
HAYFIELD
BIRCH VALE
NEW MILLS
BUGSWORTH
Cowburn Tunnel
EDALE
HOPE
DISLEY
FURNESS VALE
CHINLEY
BAMFORD
POYNTON
WHALEY BRIDGE
CHAPEL-EN-LE-FRITH
HATHERSAGE
DOVE HOLES
FAIRFIELD GOLF LINKS PLATFORM
Dove Holes Tunnel Summit
PEAK FOREST FOR PEAK DALE
HIGHER BUXTON
MILLER'S DALE
Litton Tunnel
Cressbrook Tunnel
BUXTON
BLACKWELL MILL HALT*
Chee Tor Tunnels
MONSAL DALE
Headstone Tunnel
HASSOP
HINDLOW
GREAT LONGSTONE FOR ASHFORD
BAKEWELL
DOWLOW HALT*
HURDLOW
PARSLEY HAY
Haddon Tunnel

BILLINGE GREEN HALT
GOOSTREY
BARROW
DELAMERE
MICKLE TRAFFORD
WHITEGATE
HOLMES CHAPEL
NORTH RODE
BOSLEY
Christleton Tunnel
WAVERTON
WINSFORD & OVER
WINSFORD
MIDDLEWICH
CONGLETON
RUSHTON
HARTINGTON
TATTENHALL ROAD
OVER & WHARTON
CLEDFORD BRIDGE HALT
SANDBACH
RUDYARD LAKE
HULME END
ECTON
TATTENHALL
MINSHULL VERNON
MOSSLEY HALT
RUDYARD (HORTON)
BUTTERTON
BEESTON CASTLE & TARPORLEY
CALVELEY
WHEELOCK
MOW COP (SCHOLAR GREEN)
BIDDULPH
LEEK
BRADNOP
THOR'S CAVE
WETTON MILL
WORLESTON
HASSALL GREEN
KNYPERSLEY HALT
GRINDON
ALSOP-EN-LE-DALE
BROXTON
CHESHIRE
WILLASTON
CREWE
LAWTON
ALSAGER
KIDSGROVE
BLACK BULL
ENDON
WALL GRANGE
BEESTON TOR
IPSTONES
WINKHILL HALT
SPARROWLEE
TISSINGTON
NANTWICH
RADWAY GREEN
STOCKTON BROOK
CHEDDLETON
WATERHOUSES
CALDON LOW HALT
THORPE CLOUD
MALPAS
WRENBURY
AUDLEY
MILTON
CONSALL
WHITCHURCH
WRENBURY
BETLEY ROAD
HALMEREND
LONGPORT
BUCKNALL & NORTHWOOD
HANLEY
KINGSLEY & FROGHALL
ASHBOURNE
Summit
AUDLEM
KEELE
ETRURIA
NORMACOT
CLIFTON (MAYFIELD)
LEYCETT
STOKE
FENTON
CHEADLE
OAKAMOOR
NORBURY & ELLASTONE
MADELEY
SIDEWAY HALT
LONGTON
BLYTHE BRIDGE
ALTON
MADELEY ROAD
TRENTHAM
MEIR
DENSTONE CROSSING
PIPE GATE
Summit
WHITMORE
CRESSWELL
TEAN
ROCESTER
FENN'S BANK
NORTON-IN-HALES
TRENTHAM PARK
BARLASTON & TITTENSOR
BETTISFIELD
MARKET DRAYTON
STANDON BRIDGE
STONE
LEIGH
UTTOXETER
PREES
ASTON-BY-STONE
MARCHINGTON
SUDBURY
TUTBURY
WEM
TERN HILL
NORTON BRIDGE
SANDON
WESTON & INGESTRE
GRINDLEY
HODNET
SALT
ROLLESTON-ON-DOVE
YORTON
PEPLOW
GREAT BRIDGEFORD
STAFFORD COMMON
INGESTRE
CHARTLEY
HIXON
STAFFORDSHIRE
HADNALL
GNOSALL
STAFFORD
HAUGHTON
Shugborough Tunnel
GREAT HAYWOOD
BURTON-ON-TRENT (SEE INSET)
LEATON
CRUDGINGTON
NEWPORT
MILFORD & BROCTON
COLWICH
RUGELEY TRENT VALLEY
BRANSTON
SHREWSBURY GENERAL
UPTON MAGNA
ADMASTON
DONNINGTON
WEDNESFIELD HEATH
RUGELEY TOWN
ARMITAGE
BARTON & WALTON
EDGEBOLD
HADLEY
TRENCH CROSSING
OAKENGATES
PENKRIDGE
HEDNESFORD
ALREWAS
CROXALL
SHREWSBURY ABBEY
WALCOT
WELLINGTON
KETLEY
WOLVERHAMPTON HIGH LEVEL
GAILEY
LICHFIELD TRENT VALLEY LOW LEVEL
LAWLEY BANK
WOLVERHAMPTON
CANNOCK
LICHFIELD TRENT VALLEY HIGH LEVEL
ELFORD
HORSEHAY & DAWLEY
LIGHTMOOR PLATFORM
SHIFNAL
FOUR ASHES
HAMMERWICH
LICHFIELD CITY
CONDOVER
BERRINGTON
BUILDWAS
MADELEY MARKET
WYRLEY & CHESLYN HAY
BROWNHILLS
SHENSTONE
DORRINGTON
CRESSAGE
COALBROOKDALE
ALBRIGHTON
CODSALL
PELSALL
WALSALL WOOD
TAMWORTH
IRON BRIDGE & BROSELEY
COALPORT
BLOXWICH
ALDRIDGE
STREETLY
BLAKE STREET
FOUR OAKS
WILNECOTE
LEEBOTWOOD
PRESTHOPE
MUCH WENLOCK
LINLEY
ETTINGSHALL ROAD & BILSTON
WOLVERHAMPTON (SEE INSET)
SUTTON COLDFIELD
KINGSBURY
CHURCH STRETTON
LONGVILLE
BRIDGNORTH
PENNS
WATER ORTON
FORGE MILLS
RUSHBURY
DITTON PRIORS
EARDINGTON
ROUND OAK
BROMFORD BRIDGE*
CASTLE BROMWICH
WHITACRE
HARTON ROAD
SHROPSHIRE
CLEOBURY NORTH CROSSING
HAMPTON LOADE
BRIERLEY HILL
BRETTELL LANE
STECHFORD
MARSTON GREEN
BURWARTON
HIGHLEY
BIRMINGHAM & DISTRICT
FOR THIS AREA
SEE INSET ON
MAP 13
TYSELEY
BOLTON
HAMPTON-IN-ARDEN
ASTON BOTTERELL SIDING
STOTTESDON
STOURBRIDGE TOWN
HALESOWEN
BOURNVILLE
PRESCOT SIDING
STOURBRIDGE JUNCTION
LYE
HUNNINGTON

STATIONS

1. HIGH LANE	13. COBRIDGE	25. HOOKAGATE	37. WYLDE GREEN	49. SPRING ROAD PLATFORM
2. MIDDLEWOOD FOR HIGH LANE	14. WATERLOO ROAD	26. MEOLE BRACE	38. CHESTER ROAD	50. HALL GREEN
3. MIDDLEWOOD	15. SILVERDALE	27. SHREWSBURY WEST	39. ERDINGTON	51. STRETTON & CLAY MILLS
4. ALSAGER ROAD	16. CROWN STREET HALT	28. MALINS LEE	40. GRAVELLY HILL	52. HORNINGLOW
5. HARECASTLE	17. KNUTTON HALT	29. STIRCHLEY	41. CRADLEY HEATH & CRADLEY	53. BURTON STATION STREET
6. KIDSGROVE HALT	18. LIVERPOOL ROAD HALT	30. DUNSTALL PARK	42. SELLY OAK	
7. NEWCHAPEL & GOLDENHILL	19. BRAMPTON HALT	31. WOLVERHAMPTON LOW LEVEL	43. HAZELWELL	
8. CHATTERLEY	20. NEWCASTLE-UNDER-LYME	32. WEDNESFIELD	44. LIFFORD	
9. PITTS HILL	21. HARTSHILL & BASFORD HALT	33. WILLENHALL	45. KING'S HEATH	
10. FORD GREEN	22. FENTON MANOR	34. SHORT HEATH (CLARK'S LANE)	46. MOSELEY	
11. TUNSTALL	23. LEEK BROOK HALT*	35. NORTH WALSALL	47. SMALL HEATH & SPARKBROOK	
12. BURSLEM	24. HANWOOD	36. SUTTON PARK	48. ACOCK'S GREEN & SOUTH YARDLEY	

LEGEND FOR MAP 15

A Ladmanlow branch
B 2ft 6in gauge LEEK & MANIFOLD VALLEY LIGHT RAILWAY [LMS]
C Independent Staffordshire County Asylum railway
D Caldon Low quarry branches
E Five Ways siding

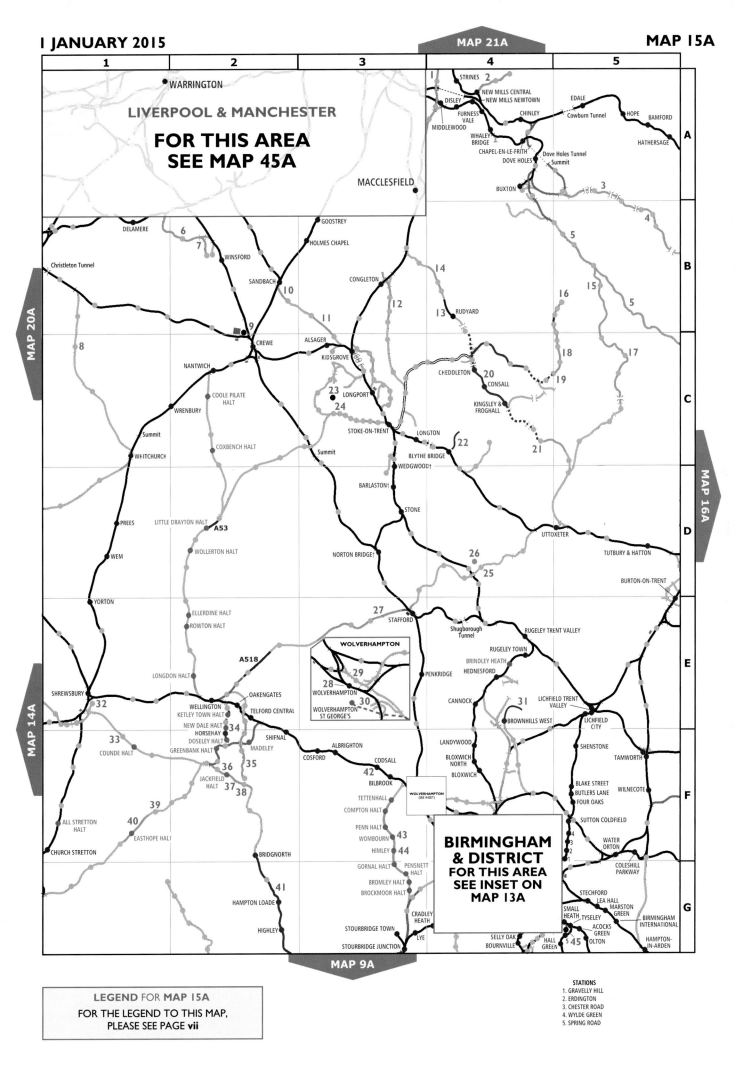

LEGEND FOR MAP 15A
FOR THE LEGEND TO THIS MAP,
PLEASE SEE PAGE vii

STATIONS
1. GRAVELLY HILL
2. ERDINGTON
3. CHESTER ROAD
4. WYLDE GREEN
5. SPRING ROAD

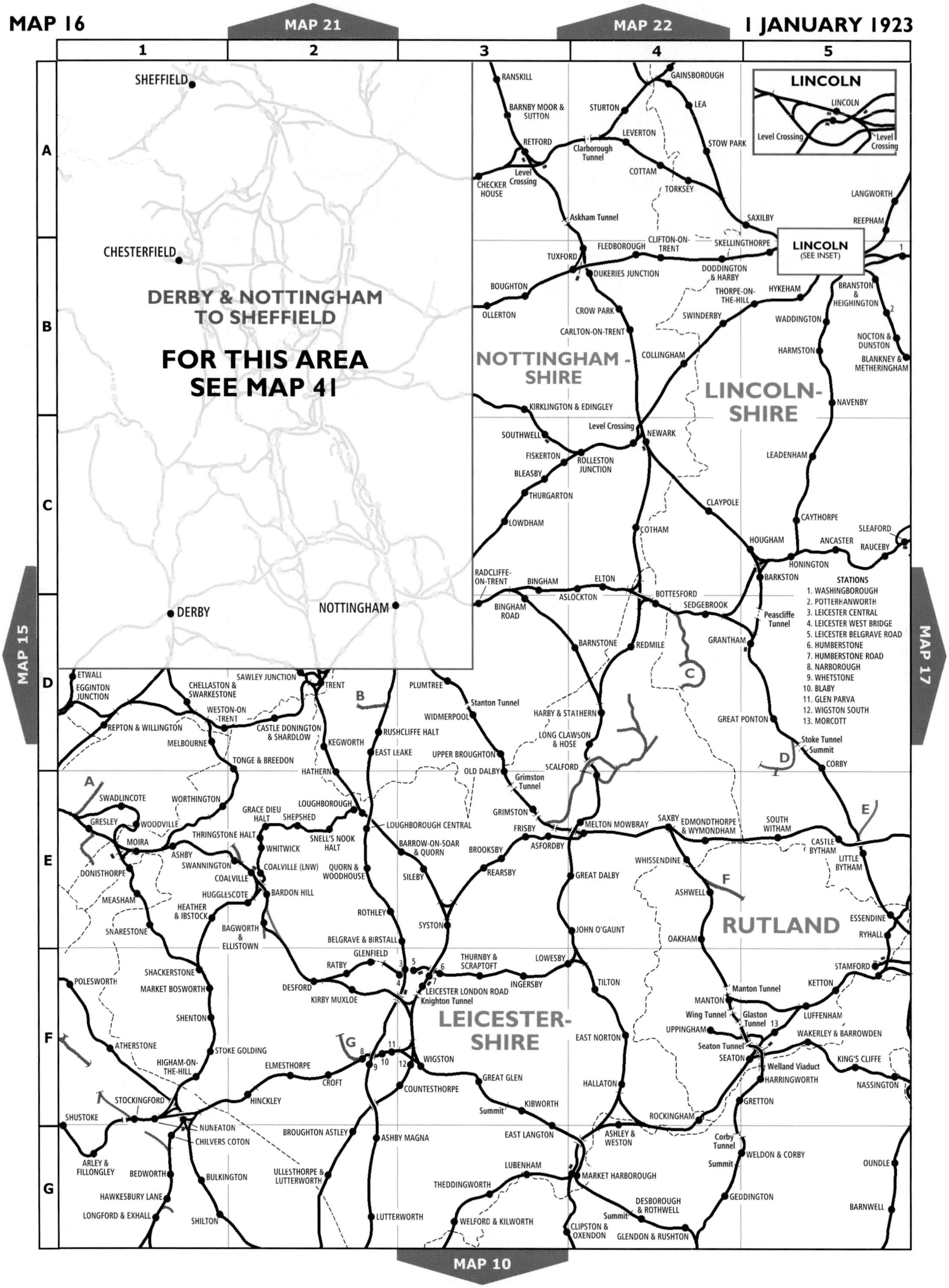

MAP 16 **MAP 21** **MAP 22** **1 JANUARY 1923**

1 2 3 4 5

LINCOLN

LINCOLN

Level Crossing LINCOLN Level Crossing

A

SHEFFIELD

RANSKILL
GAINSBOROUGH
BARNBY MOOR & SUTTON
STURTON
LEA
RETFORD
LEVERTON
STOW PARK
Clarborough Tunnel
COTTAM
Level Crossing
TORKSEY
CHECKER HOUSE
SAXILBY
LANGWORTH
Askham Tunnel
REEPHAM
CLIFTON-ON-TRENT
SKELLINGTHORPE

CHESTERFIELD

B

FLEDBOROUGH
LINCOLN (SEE INSET)
TUXFORD
DUKERIES JUNCTION
DODDINGTON & HARBY
HYKEHAM
BRANSTON & HEIGHINGTON

DERBY & NOTTINGHAM TO SHEFFIELD

FOR THIS AREA SEE MAP 41

BOUGHTON
THORPE-ON-THE-HILL
WADDINGTON
OLLERTON
CROW PARK
SWINDERBY
NOCTON & DUNSTON
CARLTON-ON-TRENT
HARMSTON
BLANKNEY & METHERINGHAM
COLLINGHAM
NOTTINGHAM-SHIRE
LINCOLN-SHIRE
NAVENBY
KIRKLINGTON & EDINGLEY

C

SOUTHWELL
Level Crossing
NEWARK
LEADENHAM
FISKERTON
ROLLESTON JUNCTION
BLEASBY
THURGARTON
CLAYPOLE
CAYTHORPE
LOWDHAM
SLEAFORD
COTHAM
HOUGHAM
ANCASTER
RAUCEBY
RADCLIFFE-ON-TRENT
BINGHAM
ELTON
HONINGTON
BARKSTON

DERBY
NOTTINGHAM
BINGHAM ROAD
ASLOCKTON
BOTTESFORD
SEDGEBROOK
Peascliffe Tunnel
BARNSTONE
REDMILE
GRANTHAM

STATIONS
1. WASHINGBOROUGH
2. POTTERHANWORTH
3. LEICESTER CENTRAL
4. LEICESTER WEST BRIDGE
5. LEICESTER BELGRAVE ROAD
6. HUMBERSTONE
7. HUMBERSTONE ROAD
8. NARBOROUGH
9. WHETSTONE
10. BLABY
11. GLEN PARVA
12. WIGSTON SOUTH
13. MORCOTT

D

ETWALL
EGGINTON JUNCTION
SAWLEY JUNCTION
TRENT
PLUMTREE
Stanton Tunnel
GREAT PONTON
CHELLASTON & SWARKESTONE
WESTON-ON-TRENT
WIDMERPOOL
HARBY & STATHERN
Stoke Tunnel Summit
REPTON & WILLINGTON
CASTLE DONINGTON & SHARDLOW
RUSHCLIFFE HALT
LONG CLAWSON & HOSE
CORBY
MELBOURNE
KEGWORTH
EAST LEAKE
UPPER BROUGHTON
SCALFORD
TONGE & BREEDON
HATHERN
OLD DALBY
Grimston Tunnel

E

SWADLINCOTE
WORTHINGTON
GRACE DIEU HALT
LOUGHBOROUGH
GRIMSTON
MELTON MOWBRAY
SAXBY
EDMONDTHORPE & WYMONDHAM
SOUTH WITHAM
GRESLEY
WOODVILLE
SHEPSHED
FRISBY
MOIRA
THRINGSTONE HALT
SNELL'S NOOK HALT
LOUGHBOROUGH CENTRAL
ASFORDBY
CASTLE BYTHAM
LITTLE BYTHAM
ASHBY
WHITWICK
BARROW-ON-SOAR & QUORN
BROOKSBY
GREAT DALBY
WHISSENDINE
DONISTHORPE
SWANNINGTON
COALVILLE (LNW)
QUORN & WOODHOUSE
REARSBY
ASHWELL
MEASHAM
COALVILLE
SILEBY
RUTLAND
ESSENDINE
HUGGLESCOTE
BARDON HILL
HEATHER & IBSTOCK
ROTHLEY
JOHN O'GAUNT
OAKHAM
RYHALL
SNARESTONE
SYSTON
BAGWORTH & ELLISTOWN
BELGRAVE & BIRSTALL
LOWESBY
STAMFORD

F

POLESWORTH
GLENFIELD
THURNBY & SCRAPTOFT
TILTON
KETTON
SHACKERSTONE
RATBY
INGERSBY
Manton Tunnel
MARKET BOSWORTH
DESFORD
LEICESTER LONDON ROAD
MANTON
LUFFENHAM
SHENTON
KIRBY MUXLOE
Knighton Tunnel
Wing Tunnel
Glaston Tunnel
WAKERLEY & BARROWDEN
LEICESTER-SHIRE
UPPINGHAM
KING'S CLIFFE
ATHERSTONE
STOKE GOLDING
WIGSTON
EAST NORTON
Seaton Tunnel
SEATON
HIGHAM-ON-THE-HILL
ELMESTHORPE
GREAT GLEN
Welland Viaduct
HARRINGWORTH
NASSINGTON
STOCKINGFORD
CROFT
COUNTESTHORPE
HALLATON
GRETTON

G

SHUSTOKE
HINCKLEY
KIBWORTH
Summit
ROCKINGHAM
NUNEATON
CHILVERS COTON
ASHLEY & WESTON
Corby Tunnel
WELDON & CORBY
OUNDLE
ARLEY & FILLONGLEY
BEDWORTH
BULKINGTON
BROUGHTON ASTLEY
ASHBY MAGNA
EAST LANGTON
MARKET HARBOROUGH
Summit
HAWKESBURY LANE
LUBENHAM
DESBOROUGH & ROTHWELL
GEDDINGTON
BARNWELL
LONGFORD & EXHALL
SHILTON
THEDDINGWORTH
Summit
LUTTERWORTH
WELFORD & KILWORTH
CLIPSTON & OXENDON
GLENDON & RUSHTON
ULLESTHORPE & LUTTERWORTH

MAP 15 **MAP 17** **MAP 10**

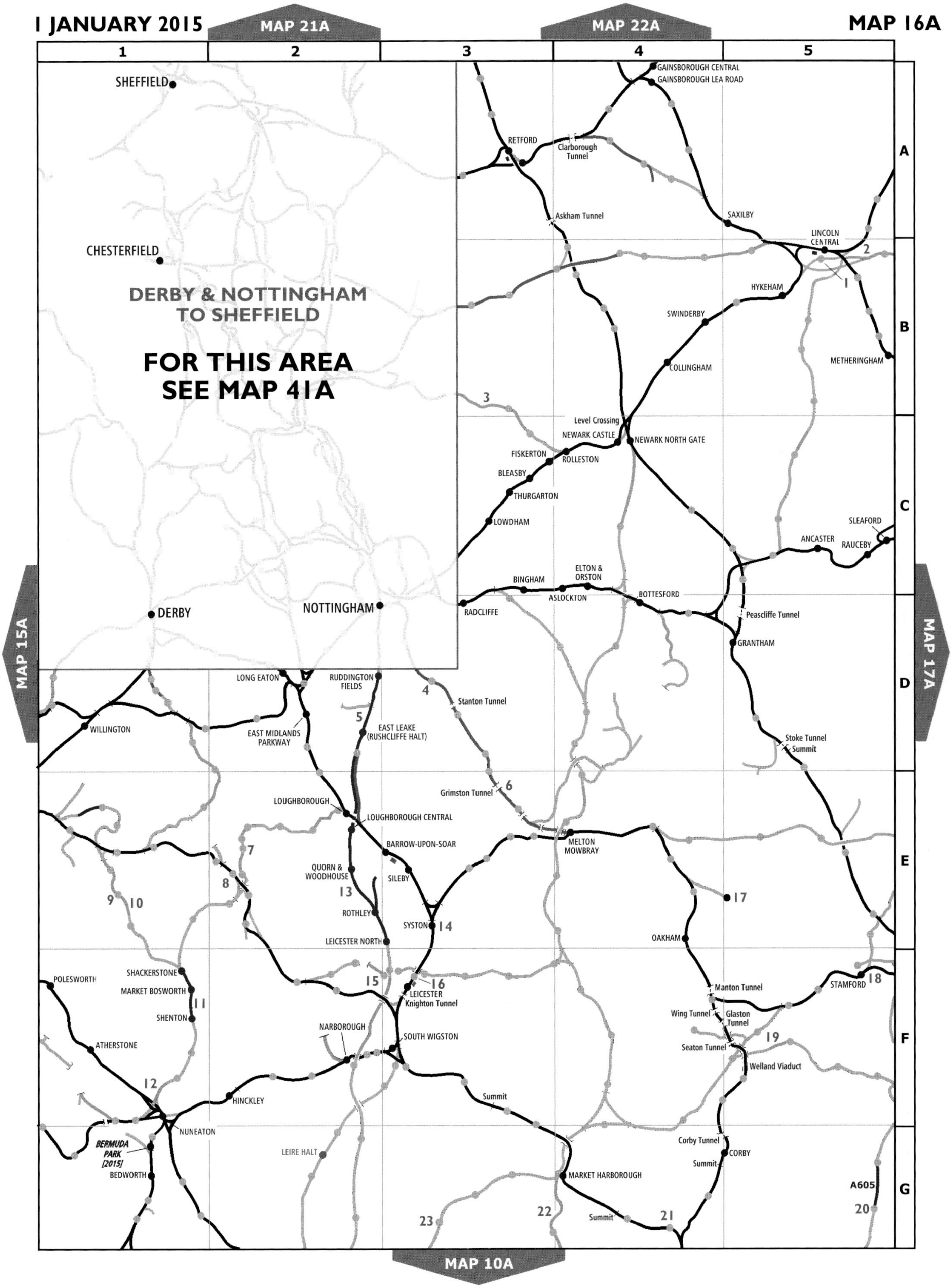

	1	2	3	4	5	

SHEFFIELD

GAINSBOROUGH CENTRAL
GAINSBOROUGH LEA ROAD

RETFORD

Clarborough
Tunnel

A

CHESTERFIELD

Askham Tunnel

SAXILBY

LINCOLN
CENTRAL

2

**DERBY & NOTTINGHAM
TO SHEFFIELD**

HYKEHAM

1

FOR THIS AREA
SEE MAP 41A

SWINDERBY

B

METHERINGHAM

COLLINGHAM

3

MAP 15A

Level Crossing
NEWARK CASTLE   NEWARK NORTH GATE

FISKERTON
BLEASBY   ROLLESTON
THURGARTON
LOWDHAM

SLEAFORD

ANCASTER
RAUCEBY

C

BINGHAM

ELTON &
ORSTON
ASLOCKTON

BOTTESFORD

RADCLIFFE

Peascliffe Tunnel

GRANTHAM

DERBY

NOTTINGHAM

MAP 17A

LONG EATON   RUDDINGTON
FIELDS

4
Stanton Tunnel

D

WILLINGTON

EAST MIDLANDS
PARKWAY

5
EAST LEAKE
(RUSHCLIFFE HALT)

Stoke Tunnel
Summit

Grimston Tunnel   6

LOUGHBOROUGH

LOUGHBOROUGH CENTRAL

MELTON
MOWBRAY

BARROW-UPON-SOAR

7

QUORN &
WOODHOUSE

SILEBY

E

8

13

17

9   10

ROTHLEY

SYSTON   14

LEICESTER NORTH

OAKHAM

POLESWORTH

SHACKERSTONE

MARKET BOSWORTH

11

15   16
LEICESTER
Knighton Tunnel

Manton Tunnel

STAMFORD   18

SHENTON

NARBOROUGH

Wing Tunnel   Glaston
Tunnel

19

ATHERSTONE

SOUTH WIGSTON

Seaton Tunnel

F

12

Welland Viaduct

HINCKLEY

Summit

BERMUDA
PARK
[2015]

NUNEATON

Corby Tunnel

BEDWORTH

LEIRE HALT

MARKET HARBOROUGH

Summit   CORBY

A605

G

23

22

Summit   21

20

LEGEND FOR MAP 16A

11 BATTLEFIELD STEAM RAILWAY. www.battlefieldline.co.uk
12 WEDDINGTON COUNTRY WALK
13 GREAT CENTRAL RAILWAY. www.gcrailway.co.uk
14 SYSTON: Former station building rebuilt at BUTTERLEY at the
    MIDLAND RAILWAY CENTRE.
    www.midlandrailway-butterley.co.uk
15 LEICESTER WEST BRIDGE: Site cleared as The Rally park
16 HUMBERSTONE ROAD: Station building rebuilt at SHENTON on

the BATTLEFIELD STEAM RAILWAY
17 ROCKS BY RAIL – THE LIVING IRONSTONE MUSEUM.
    www.rocks-by-rail.org
18 STAMFORD: Also home to a specialist railway bookshop.
    www.roberthumm.co.uk
19 Part of the JURASSIC WAY. www.ldwa.org.uk
20 BARNWELL: Station building re-erected at WANSFORD on the
    NENE VALLEY RAILWAY. www.nvr.org.uk

21 GLENDON & RUSHTON: Currently subject of a long-term
    restoration project. www.glendonrushtonstation.org.uk
22 BRAMPTON VALLEY WAY. www.gps-routes.co.uk
23 WELFORD & KILWORTH: Down platform shelter preserved at
    the ELECTRIC RAILWAY MUSEUM, Coventry.
    electricrailwaymuseum.co.uk

MAP 17   MAP 22   1 JANUARY 1923

1   2   3   4   5

A

B

C

D

E

F

G

LINCOLNSHIRE

MARKET RASEN
WICKENBY
SNELLAND
WRAGBY
LANGWORTH
KINGTHORPE
REEPHAM
WASHINGBOROUGH
FIVE MILE HOUSE
F
BRANSTON & HEIGHINGTON
POTTERHANWORTH
WADDINGTON
SOUTHREY
BARDNEY
NOCTON & DUNSTON
BLANKNEY & METHERINGHAM
NAVENBY
SCOPWICK & TIMBERLAND
DIGBY
RUSKINGTON
SLEAFORD
ANCASTER
RAUCEBY

SOUTH WILLINGHAM & HAINTON
EAST BARKWITH
WITHCALL
HALLINGTON
DONINGTON-ON-BAIN
HORNCASTLE
STIXWOULD
WOODHALL SPA
WOODHALL JUNCTION
CONINGSBY
TATTERSHALL
DOGDYKE
TUMBY WOODSIDE
NEW BOLINGBROKE
LANGRICK
HECKINGTON
HUBBERT'S BRIDGE
SWINESHEAD
BOSTON — B

FOTHERBY HALT
LOUTH
GRIMOLDBY
SALTFLEETBY
THEDDLETHORPE
LEGBOURNE ROAD
AUTHORPE
ABY
ALFORD
WILLOUGHBY
BURGH
SPILSBY
FIRSBY
HALTON HOLGATE
LITTLE STEEPING
THORPE CULVERT
STICKNEY
MIDVILLE
EAST VILLE
OLD LEAKE
SIBSEY
WAINFLEET

MABLETHORPE
SUTTON-ON-SEA
MUMBY ROAD
SEACROFT
SKEGNESS
HAVENHOUSE

ASWARBY & SCREDINGTON
HELPRINGHAM
KIRTON
BILLINGBOROUGH & HORBLING
DONINGTON ROAD
ALGARKIRK & SUTTERTON
GOSBERTON
SURFLEET
RIPPINGALE

HUNSTANTON
DOCKING
HEACHAM
SEDGEFORD
SNETTISHAM
DERSINGHAM
WOLFERTON

CORBY
MORTON ROAD
PINCHBECK
WHAPLODE
HOLBEACH
FLEET
LONG SUTTON
NORTH WOOTTON
HILLINGTON
GRIMSTON ROAD
NORTH DROVE
SPALDING
WESTON
MOULTON
GEDNEY
SUTTON BRIDGE
KING'S LYNN — B
BOURNE
COUNTER DRAIN
TWENTY
TERRINGTON
C
GAYTON ROAD
CASTLE BYTHAM
LITTLE BYTHAM
THURLBY
COWBIT
WALPOLE
CLENCHWARTON
SOUTH LYNN
MIDDLETON
EAST WINCH
TYDD
LITTLEWORTH
BRACEBOROUGH SPA
FERRY
NARBOROUGH
POSTLAND
ESSENDINE
FRENCH DROVE
WISBECH ST MARY
WISBECH
EMNETH
MIDDLE DROVE
MAGDALEN ROAD
RYHALL
SMEETH ROAD
TALLINGTON
DEEPING ST JAMES
PEAKIRK
MURROW
STOW
STAMFORD
UFFINGTON & BARNACK
ELMBRIDGE
BOYCE'S BRIDGE
KETTON
BARNACK
HELPSTON
THORNEY
Level Crossing
OUTWELL BASIN
OUTWELL VILLAGE
DOWNHAM
UFFORD BRIDGE
WRYDE
COLDHAM
D
UPWELL
WALTON
EYE GREEN FOR CROWLAND
GUYHIRNE
DENVER
RYSTON
ABBEY FOR WEST DEREHAM
WANSFORD ROAD
KING'S CLIFFE
CASTOR
PETERBOROUGH
MARCH
STOKE FERRY
NASSINGTON
WANSFORD
HILGAY
ORTON WATERVILLE
WHITTLESEA
STONEA
ELTON
E
YAXLEY & FARCET
WIMBLINGTON
MANEA
BRANDON
OUNDLE
LITTLEPORT
ST MARY'S
CHATTERIS
BARNWELL
HOLME
RAMSEY
BLACK BANK
LAKENHEATH

NORFOLK

CAMBRIDGE-SHIRE

MAP 16
MAP 18
MAP 11

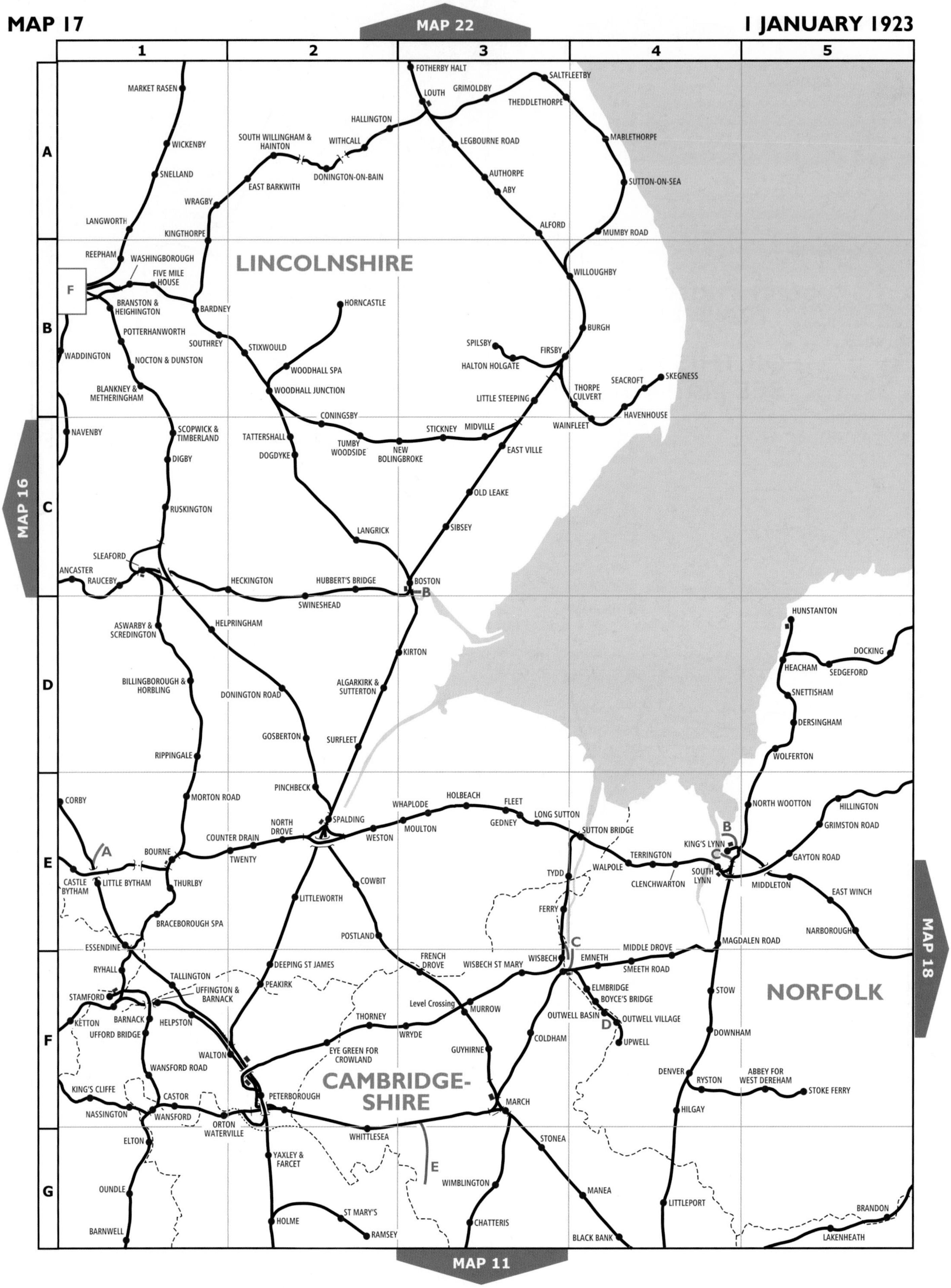

LEGEND FOR MAP 17
A Former EDENHAM & LITTLE BYTHAM RAILWAY
B Dock branches
C Harbour branches
D WISBECH & UPWELL TRAMWAY [LNER]
E Benwick branch
F Part of Lincoln. (See Inset in Map 16)

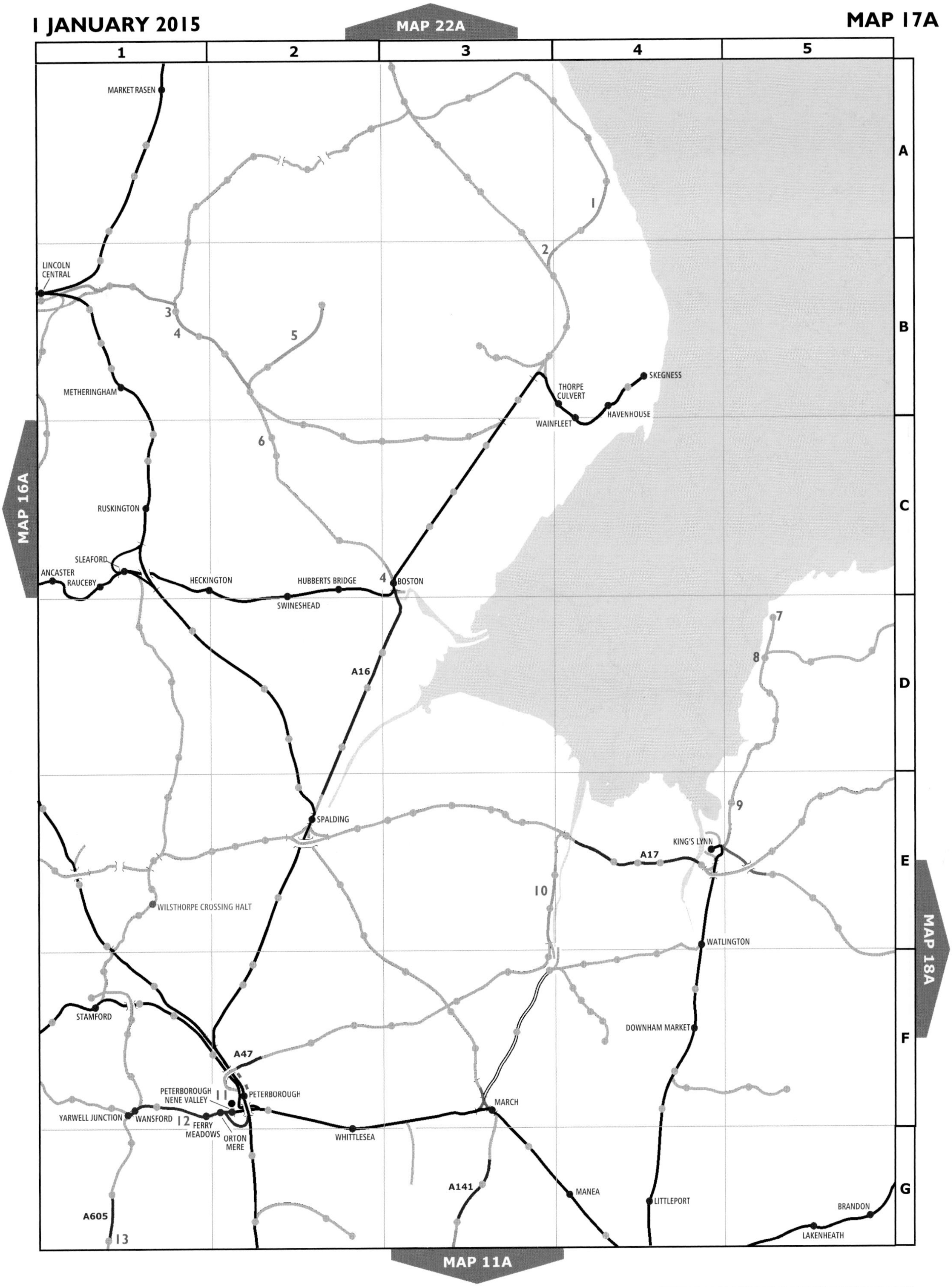

1   2   3   4   5

A

B

MAP 16A

C

MAP 18A

MARKET RASEN

LINCOLN CENTRAL

1

2

SKEGNESS
THORPE CULVERT
HAVENHOUSE
WAINFLEET

3
4
5

METHERINGHAM

6

RUSKINGTON

SLEAFORD
ANCASTER
RAUCEBY

HECKINGTON
SWINESHEAD
HUBBERTS BRIDGE
4 BOSTON

A16

7
8

9

SPALDING

WILSTHORPE CROSSING HALT

KING'S LYNN
A17

10

WATLINGTON

D

E

F

G

STAMFORD

A47

DOWNHAM MARKET

PETERBOROUGH NENE VALLEY
11 PETERBOROUGH
YARWELL JUNCTION
WANSFORD 12 FERRY MEADOWS
ORTON MERE
WHITTLESEA

MARCH

A141

A605

13

MANEA

LITTLEPORT

BRANDON

LAKENHEATH

LEGEND FOR MAP 17A

1 SUTTON BRANCH LINE WALKWAY
2 WILLOUGHBY BRANCH LINE NATURE RESERVE.
   www.linestrust.org.uk
3 BARDNEY: Replica station building houses the BARDNEY
   HERITAGE CENTRE with B&B accommodation in two
   converted goods vans. www.bardneyheritagecentre.com
4 WATER RAIL WAY. www.gps-routes.co.uk
5 SPA TRAIL (part of the VIKING WAY). www.woodhallspa.org.uk

6 TATTERSHALL: Home to the Tattershall Station Gallery &
   Pottery. www.paintmarks.co.uk
7 HUNSTANTON: Site cleared as a coach and car park; former
   coal shed now an art gallery
8 HEACHAM: Holiday accommodation available in former
   waiting room and a converted railway carriage.
   www.oldstationheacham.co.uk

9 NORTH WOOTTON: Former goods shed now local scouts
   and guides HQ
10 Part of the NENE WAY. www.ldwa.org.uk
11 RAILWORLD MUSEUM. www.railworld.net
12 NENE VALLEY RAILWAY. www.nvr.org.uk
13 BARNWELL: Former station building re-erected at
   WANSFORD on the NENE VALLEY RAILWAY.
   www.nvr.org.uk

MAP 18

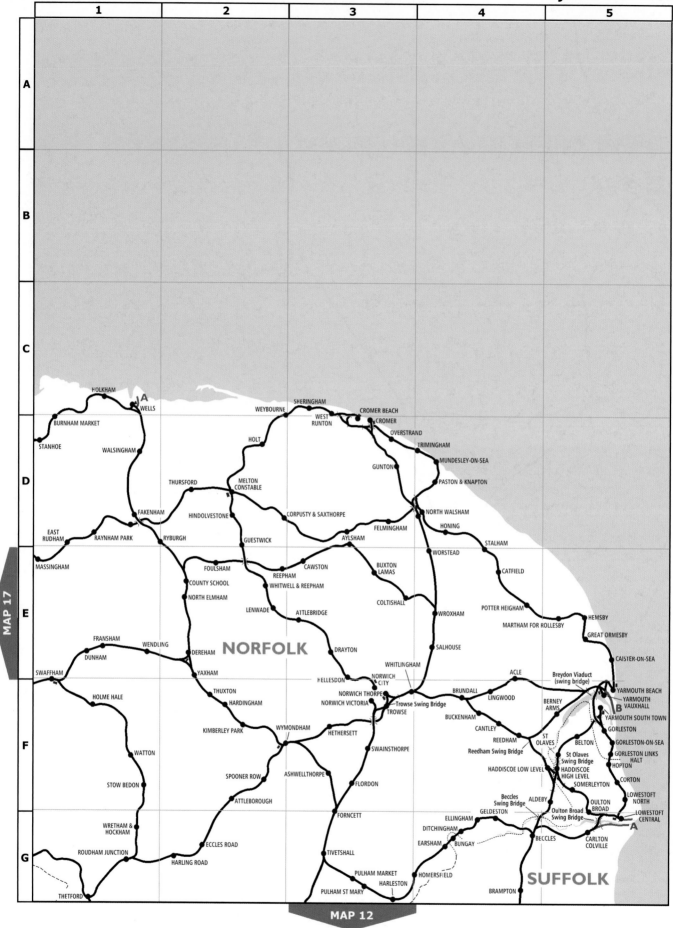

	1	2	3	4	5
A					
B					
C					
D					
E					
F					
G					

MAP 17

MAP 12

HOLKHAM
WELLS
BURNHAM MARKET
STANHOE
WALSINGHAM
SHERINGHAM
WEYBOURNE
WEST RUNTON
CROMER BEACH
CROMER
OVERSTRAND
TRIMINGHAM
HOLT
MUNDESLEY-ON-SEA
GUNTON
PASTON & KNAPTON
THURSFORD
MELTON CONSTABLE
FAKENHAM
HINDOLVESTONE
CORPUSTY & SAXTHORPE
NORTH WALSHAM
HONING
EAST RUDHAM
RAYNHAM PARK
RYBURGH
GUESTWICK
AYLSHAM
FELMINGHAM
WORSTEAD
STALHAM
MASSINGHAM
FOULSHAM
REEPHAM
CAWSTON
BUXTON LAMAS
CATFIELD
COUNTY SCHOOL
WHITWELL & REEPHAM
NORTH ELMHAM
LENWADE
ATTLEBRIDGE
COLTISHALL
POTTER HEIGHAM
HEMSBY
FRANSHAM
WENDLING
DEREHAM
WROXHAM
MARTHAM FOR ROLLESBY
GREAT ORMESBY
DUNHAM
YAXHAM
DRAYTON
SALHOUSE
CAISTER-ON-SEA
SWAFFHAM
WHITLINGHAM
ACLE
Breydon Viaduct (swing bridge)
NORFOLK
KELLESDON
NORWICH CITY
YARMOUTH BEACH
HOLME HALE
THUXTON
NORWICH THORPE
BRUNDALL
YARMOUTH VAUXHALL
HARDINGHAM
NORWICH VICTORIA
Trowse Swing Bridge
LINGWOOD
YARMOUTH SOUTH TOWN
TROWSE
BERNEY ARMS
GORLESTON
KIMBERLEY PARK
WYMONDHAM
HETHERSETT
BUCKENHAM
GORLESTON-ON-SEA
WATTON
SWAINSTHORPE
CANTLEY
REEDHAM
ST OLAVES
BELTON
GORLESTON LINKS HALT
HOPTON
SPOONER ROW
ASHWELLTHORPE
Reedham Swing Bridge
St Olaves Swing Bridge
HADDISCOE LOW LEVEL
HADDISCOE HIGH LEVEL
SOMERLEYTON
CORTON
STOW BEDON
FLORDON
Beccles Swing Bridge
ALDEBY
OULTON BROAD
LOWESTOFT NORTH
ATTLEBOROUGH
FORNCETT
GELDESTON
Oulton Broad Swing Bridge
LOWESTOFT CENTRAL
WRETHAM & HOCKHAM
ELLINGHAM
CARLTON COLVILLE
ROUDHAM JUNCTION
ECCLES ROAD
DITCHINGHAM
EARSHAM
BUNGAY
BECCLES
HARLING ROAD
TIVETSHALL
SUFFOLK
PULHAM MARKET
HOMERSFIELD
THETFORD
PULHAM ST MARY
HARLESTON
BRAMPTON

LEGEND FOR MAP 18
A Harbour branches
B Quay tramway

1 BURNHAM MARKET: Now the Railway Inn Hotel. www.hoste.com
2 10¼in gauge WELLS HARBOUR RAILWAY
3 WELLS (later WELLS-NEXT-THE-SEA): Station building now a bookshop and pottery. www.oldstationbookspots.co.uk
4 10¼in gauge WELLS & WALSINGHAM LIGHT RAILWAY. www.wellswalsinghamrailway.co.uk
5 NORTH NORFOLK RAILWAY. www.nnrailway.co.uk
6 Part of the WEAVERS' WAY. www.countrysideaccess.norfolk.gov.uk
7 STALHAM: Building re-erected at HOLT station on the NORTH NORFOLK RAILWAY
8 AYLSHAM [Ex-MGNJR]: Site cleared as a car park for the WEAVERS' WAY
9 15in gauge BURE VALLEY RAILWAY. www.bvrw.co.uk
10 BURE VALLEY WALK. www.bvrw.co.uk

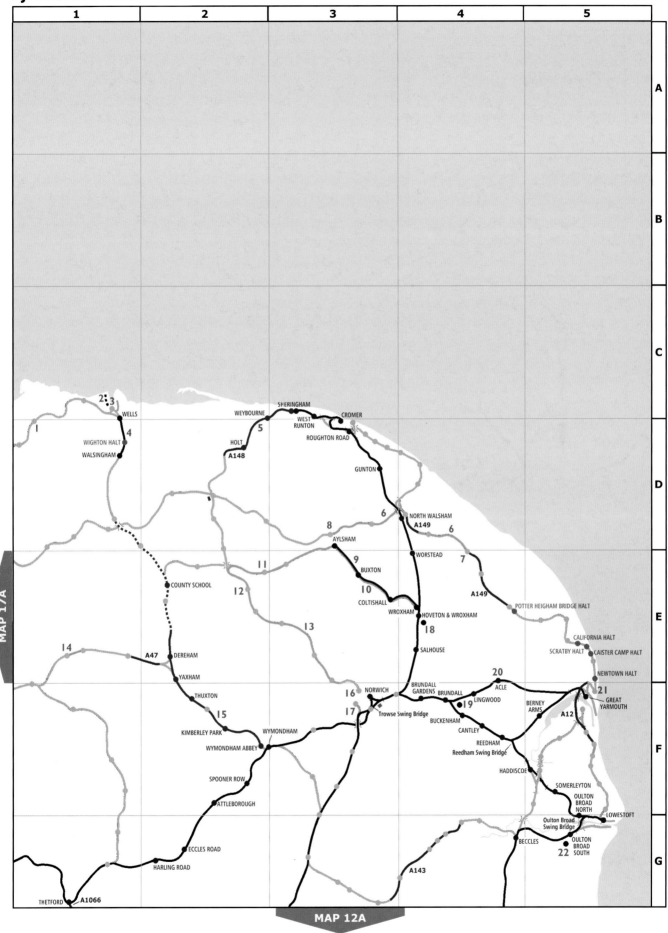

MAP 19

1 JANUARY 1923

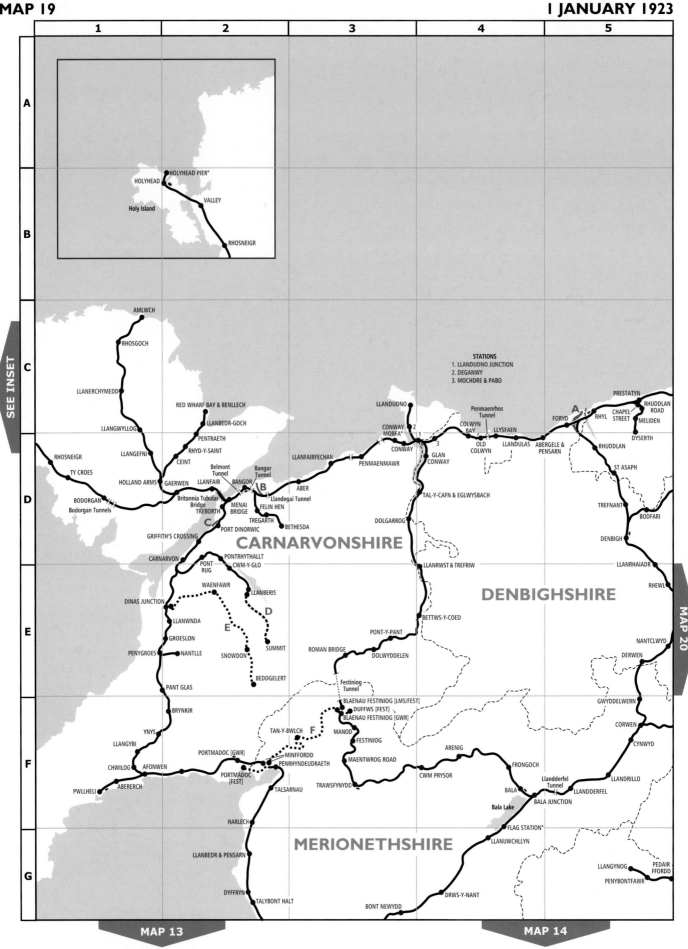

LEGEND FOR MAP 19
A Foryd Pier branch
B Port Penrhyn branch
C Port siding
D 800mm gauge SNOWDON MOUNTAIN TRAMROAD
E 1ft 11½in gauge WELSH HIGHLAND RAILWAY
F 1ft 11½in gauge FESTINIOG RAILWAY

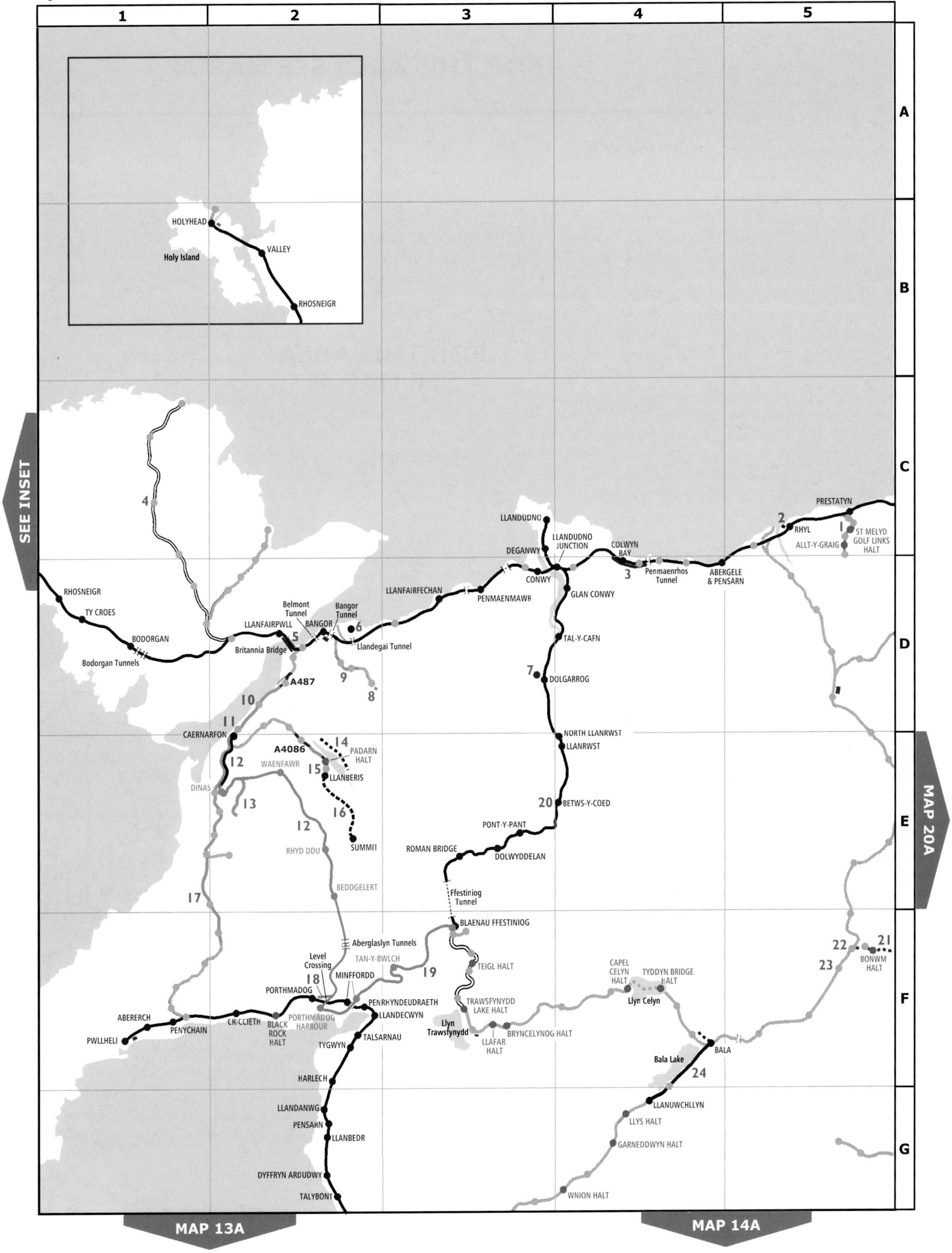

1 2 3 4 5

A

B

C

D

E

F

G

SEE INSET

MAP 20A

MAP 13A

MAP 14A

HOLYHEAD
VALLEY
Holy Island
RHOSNEIGR

4

PRESTATYN
RHYL
ST MELYD
GOLF LINKS
HALT
ALLT-Y-GRAIG
2
1

LLANDUDNO
LLANDUDNO
JUNCTION
DEGANWY
COLWYN
BAY
CONWY
Penmaenrhos
Tunnel
ABERGELE
& PENSARN
3
GLAN CONWY

RHOSNEIGR
TY CROES
BODORGAN
Bodorgan Tunnels

LLANFAIRFECHAN
PENMAENMAWR

TAL-Y-CAFN

Belmont
Tunnel
Bangor
Tunnel
LLANFAIRPWLL
BANGOR
6
Llandegai Tunnel
Britannia Bridge
5
A487
9
8

7 DOLGARROG

10

11
CAERNARFON
A4086
WAENFAWR
14
PADARN
HALT
15 LLANBERIS
16

NORTH LLANRWST
LLANRWST

12
DINAS
13
12
RHYD DDU
SUMMIT
BEDDGELERT
17

20 BETWS-Y-COED

PONT-Y-PANT
ROMAN BRIDGE
DOLWYDDELAN

Ffestiniog
Tunnel

Aberglaslyn Tunnels
TAN-Y-BWLCH
Level
Crossing
MINFFORDD
19
PORTHMADOG
18
BLAENAU FFESTINIOG
TEIGL HALT

CAPEL
CELYN
HALT
TYDDYN BRIDGE
HALT
Llyn Celyn

22
23
21
BONWM
HALT

ABERERCH
PENYCHAIN
CRICCIETH
BLACK
ROCK
HALT
PORTHMADOG
HARBOUR
PENRHYNDEUDRAETH
LLANDECWYN
TALSARNAU
TYGWYN
PWLLHELI

TRAWSFYNYDD
LAKE HALT
Llyn
Trawsfynydd
LLAFAR
HALT
BRYNCELYNOG HALT

BALA
Bala Lake
24

HARLECH

LLANDANWG
PENSARN
LLANBEDR

LLANUWCHLLYN
LLYS HALT
GARNEDDWYN HALT

DYFFRYN ARDUDWY
TALYBONT

WNION HALT

LEGEND FOR MAP 19A
FOR THE LEGEND TO THIS MAP,
PLEASE SEE PAGE vii

MAP 20

1 JANUARY 1923

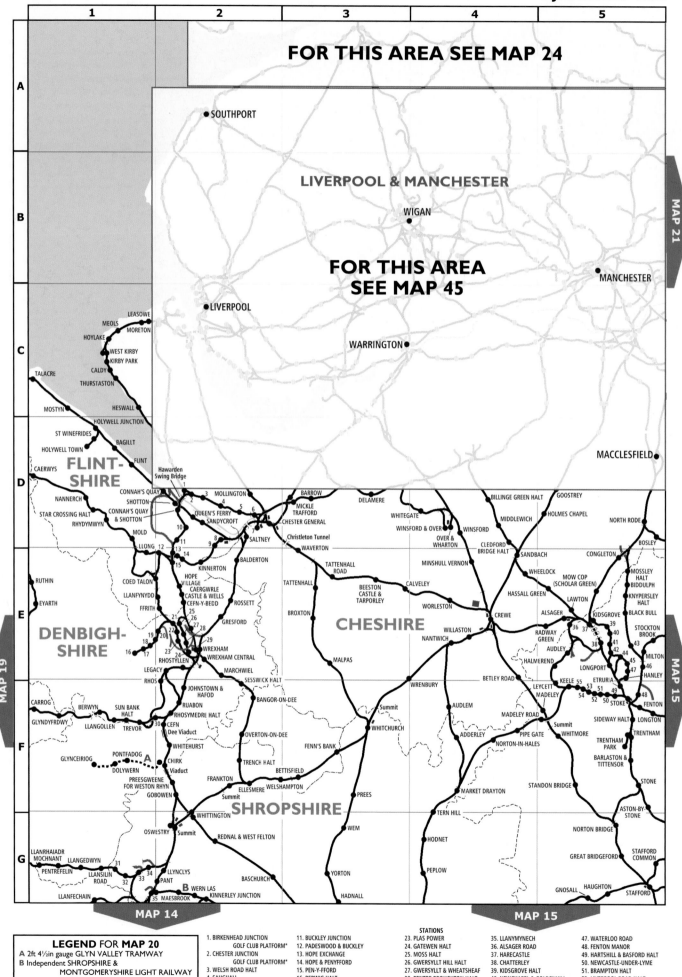

FOR THIS AREA SEE MAP 24

LIVERPOOL & MANCHESTER

WIGAN

FOR THIS AREA
SEE MAP 45

MANCHESTER

SOUTHPORT

LIVERPOOL

WARRINGTON

MACCLESFIELD

MAP 21

LEASOWE
MEOLS
MORETON
HOYLAKE
WEST KIRBY
KIRBY PARK
CALDY
THURSTASTON
TALACRE
HESWALL
MOSTYN

HOLYWELL JUNCTION
ST WINEFRIDES
BAGILLT
HOLYWELL TOWN
FLINT
CAERWYS

FLINT-SHIRE
NANNERCH
STAR CROSSING HALT
RHYDYMWYN
Hawarden
Swing Bridge
CONNAH'S QUAY
SHOTTON
CONNAH'S QUAY
& SHOTTON
MOLD
LLONG
RUTHIN
COED TALON
LLANFYNYDD
FFRITH
EYARTH

DENBIGH-SHIRE

MAP 19

QUEEN'S FERRY
SANDYCROFT
SALTNEY

MOLLINGTON
BARROW
MICKLE
TRAFFORD
CHESTER GENERAL
Christleton Tunnel
WAVERTON
DELAMERE
WHITEGATE
WINSFORD & OVER
OVER &
WHARTON
MIDDLEWICH
WINSFORD
BILLINGE GREEN HALT
GOOSTREY
HOLMES CHAPEL
NORTH RODE

KINNERTON
BALDERTON
HOPE
VILLAGE
CAERGWRLE
CASTLE & WELLS
CEFN-Y-BEDD
ROSSETT
GRESFORD
WREXHAM
WREXHAM CENTRAL
TATTENHALL
ROAD
TATTENHALL
BROXTON
BEESTON
CASTLE &
TARPORLEY
CALVELEY
MINSHULL VERNON
WORLESTON
WILLASTON
NANTWICH
CREWE

SANDBACH
WHEELOCK
HASSALL GREEN
RADWAY
GREEN
ALSAGER
MOW COP
(SCHOLAR GREEN)
LAWTON
AUDLEY
HALMEREND
KEELE
LEYCETT
MADELEY
BETLEY ROAD
MADELEY ROAD
PIPE GATE
NORTON-IN-HALES

CONGLETON
BOSLEY
MOSSLEY
HALT
BIDDULPH
KNYPERSLEY
HALT
BLACK BULL
KIDSGROVE
STOCKTON
BROOK
MILTON
HANLEY
ETRURIA
STOKE
FENTON
LONGTON
TRENTHAM
SIDEWAY HALT
LONGPORT
CLEDFORD
BRIDGE HALT

CHESHIRE

MALPAS
WRENBURY
AUDLEM
ADDERLEY
WHITMORE
Summit
TRENTHAM
PARK
BARLASTON &
TITTENSOR
STONE

LEGACY
RHOS
JOHNSTOWN &
HAFOD
RUABON
RHOSYMEDRE HALT
CEFN
Dee Viaduct
TREVOR
LLANGOLLEN
GLYNDYFRDWY
CARROG
BERWYN
SUN BANK
HALT
GLYNCEIRIOG
PONTFADOG
DOLYWERN
PREESGWEENE
FOR WESTON RHYN
GOBOWEN
WHITTINGTON
OSWESTRY Summit

RHOSTYLLEN
MARCHWIEL
SESSWICK HALT
BANGOR-ON-DEE
OVERTON-ON-DEE
WHITEHURST
CHIRK
Viaduct
FRANKTON
TRENCH HALT
BETTISFIELD
ELLESMERE WELSHAMPTON
FENN'S BANK
Summit
WHITCHURCH
PREES
WEM
YORTON
HADNALL
REDNAL & WEST FELTON
BASCHURCH

SHROPSHIRE

MARKET DRAYTON
TERN HILL
HODNET
PEPLOW

STANDON BRIDGE
NORTON BRIDGE
GREAT BRIDGEFORD
GNOSALL
HAUGHTON
STAFFORD
ASTON-BY-STONE
STAFFORD
COMMON

MAP 15

LLANRHAIADR
MOCHNANT
LLANGEDWYN
PENTREFELIN
LLANSILIN
ROAD
PANT
LLANFECHAIN
LLYNCLYS
MAESBROOK
WERN LAS
KINNERLEY JUNCTION

MAP 14

MAP 15

FOR THIS AREA SEE MAP 24
FOR THIS AREA SEE MAP 45
MAP 21
MAP 19
MAP 15
MAP 14

LEGEND FOR **MAP 20**
A 2ft 4½in gauge GLYN VALLEY TRAMWAY
B Independent SHROPSHIRE &
MONTGOMERYSHIRE LIGHT RAILWAY

STATIONS

1. BIRKENHEAD JUNCTION
   GOLF CLUB PLATFORM*
2. CHESTER JUNCTION
   GOLF CLUB PLATFORM*
3. WELSH ROAD HALT
4. SAUGHALL
5. BLACON
6. CHESTER LIVERPOOL ROAD
7. CHESTER NORTHGATE
8. SALTNEY FERRY
9. BROUGHTON & BRETTON
10. HAWARDEN

11. BUCKLEY JUNCTION
12. PADESWOOD & BUCKLEY
13. HOPE EXCHANGE
14. HOPE & PENYFFORD
15. PEN-Y-FFORD
16. BERWIG HALT
17. VICARAGE CROSSING HALT
18. COED POETH
19. PENTRESAESON FOR BWLCHGWYN HALT
20. BRYMBO WEST CROSSING HALT
21. BRYMBO
22. THE LODGE HALT

23. PLAS POWER
24. GATEWEN HALT
25. MOSS HALT
26. GWERSYLLT HILL HALT
27. GWERSYLLT & WHEATSHEAF
28. PENTRE BROUGHTON HALT
29. WREXHAM EXCHANGE
30. ACREFAIR
31. GLANYRAFON
32. LLANYBLODWELL
33. BLODWELL JUNCTION
34. PORTHYWAEN

35. LLANYMYNECH
36. ALSAGER ROAD
37. HARECASTLE
38. CHATTERLEY
39. KIDSGROVE HALT
40. NEWCHAPEL & GOLDENHILL
41. PITTS HILL
42. TUNSTALL
43. FORD GREEN
44. BURSLEM
45. COBRIDGE
46. BUCKNALL & NORTHWOOD

47. WATERLOO ROAD
48. FENTON MANOR
49. HARTSHILL & BASFORD HALT
50. NEWCASTLE-UNDER-LYME
51. BRAMPTON HALT
52. LIVERPOOL ROAD HALT
53. KNUTTON HALT
54. CROWN STREET HALT
55. SILVERDALE

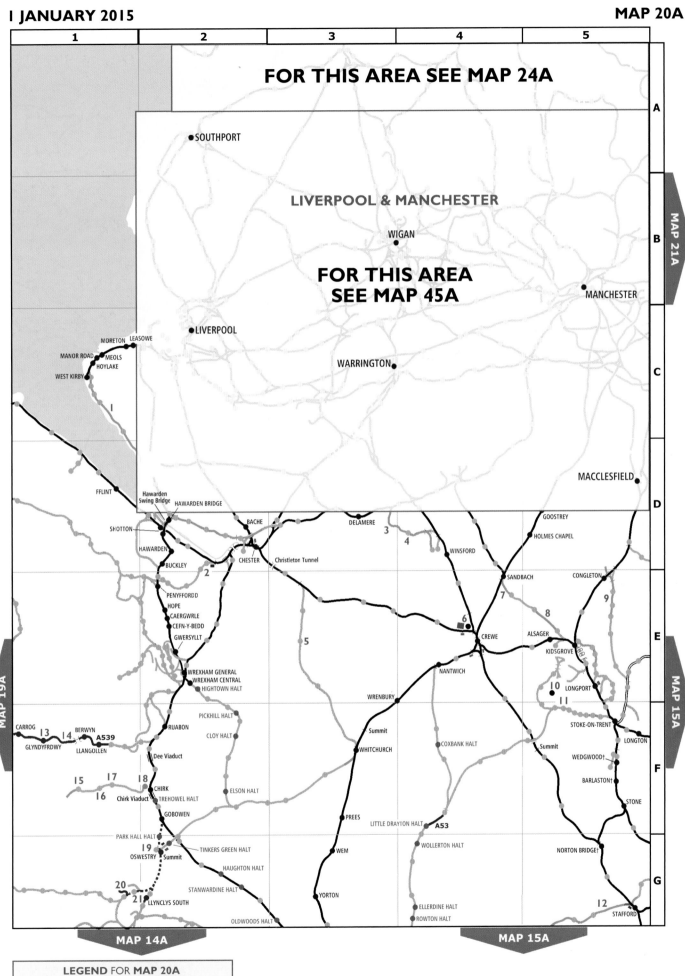

FOR THIS AREA SEE MAP 24A

SOUTHPORT

LIVERPOOL & MANCHESTER

WIGAN

FOR THIS AREA
SEE MAP 45A

MANCHESTER

LIVERPOOL

WARRINGTON

MACCLESFIELD

MORETON LEASOWE
MANOR ROAD MEOLS
HOYLAKE
WEST KIRBY

1

GOOSTREY
HOLMES CHAPEL

FFLINT
Hawarden
Swing Bridge
HAWARDEN BRIDGE
SHOTTON
HAWARDEN
BUCKLEY
BACHE
DELAMERE
3
4
WINSFORD
CHESTER Christleton Tunnel
2
PENYFFORDD
HOPE
CAERGWRLE
CEFN-Y-BEDD
GWERSYLLT
SANDBACH
CONGLETON
7
8
9
6
CREWE ALSAGER
KIDSGROVE
WREXHAM GENERAL
WREXHAM CENTRAL
HIGHTOWN HALT
NANTWICH
5
WRENBURY
10 LONGPORT
11
CARROG 13 BERWYN
GLYNDYFRDWY 14 A539
LLANGOLLEN
PICKHILL HALT
RUABON
CLOY HALT
Summit
WHITCHURCH
COXBANK HALT
Summit
STOKE-ON-TRENT
LONGTON
WEDGWOOD†
15 17 18
16 CHIRK
Chirk Viaduct TREHOWEL HALT
Dee Viaduct
ELSON HALT
BARLASTON†
STONE
GOBOWEN
PREES
LITTLE DRAYTON HALT A53
PARK HALL HALT
19 Summit TINKERS GREEN HALT
OSWESTRY
HAUGHTON HALT
WEM
WOLLERTON HALT
NORTON BRIDGE†
20
21 LLYNCLYS SOUTH
STANWARDINE HALT
YORTON
ELLERDINE HALT
ROWTON HALT
12
STAFFORD
OLDWOODS HALT

MAP 21A

MAP 19A

MAP 15A

MAP 14A

MAP 15A

A
B
C
D
E
F
G

1 2 3 4 5

LEGEND FOR MAP 20A
FOR THE LEGEND TO THIS MAP,
PLEASE SEE PAGE vii

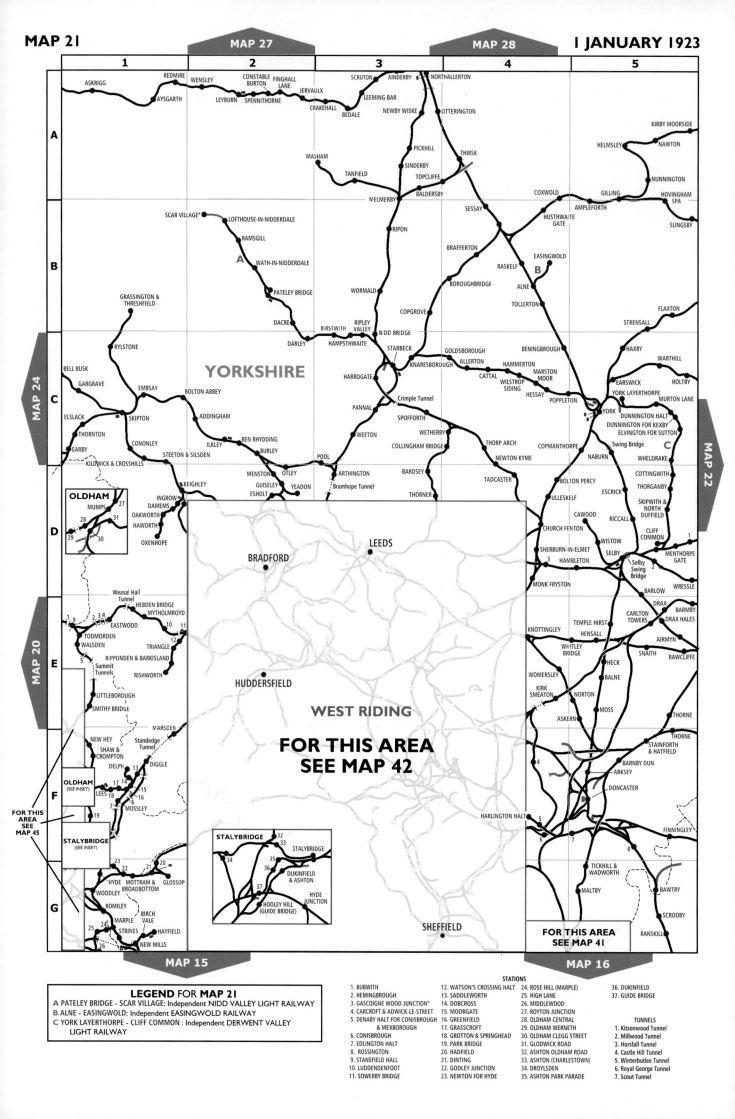

MAP 21 — 1 JANUARY 1923

LEGEND FOR MAP 21
A PATELEY BRIDGE - SCAR VILLAGE: Independent NIDD VALLEY LIGHT RAILWAY
B ALNE - EASINGWOLD: Independent EASINGWOLD RAILWAY
C YORK LAYERTHORPE - CLIFF COMMON: Independent DERWENT VALLEY LIGHT RAILWAY

STATIONS
1. BUBWITH
2. HEMINGBROUGH
3. GASCOIGNE WOOD JUNCTION*
4. CARCROFT & ADWICK-LE-STREET
5. DENABY HALT FOR CONISBROUGH & MEXBOROUGH
6. CONISBROUGH
7. EDLINGTON HALT
8. ROSSINGTON
9. STANSFIELD HALL
10. LUDDENDENFOOT
11. SOWERBY BRIDGE
12. WATSON'S CROSSING HALT
13. SADDLEWORTH
14. DOBCROSS
15. MOORGATE
16. GREENFIELD
17. GRASSCROFT
18. GROTTON & SPRINGHEAD
19. PARK BRIDGE
20. HADFIELD
21. DINTING
22. GODLEY JUNCTION
23. NEWTON FOR HYDE
24. ROSE HILL (MARPLE)
25. HIGH LANE
26. MIDDLEWOOD
27. ROYTON JUNCTION
28. OLDHAM CENTRAL
29. OLDHAM WERNETH
30. OLDHAM CLEGG STREET
31. GLODWICK ROAD
32. ASHTON OLDHAM ROAD
33. ASHTON (CHARLESTOWN)
34. DROYLSDEN
35. ASHTON PARK PARADE
36. DUKINFIELD
37. GUIDE BRIDGE

TUNNELS
1. Kitsonwood Tunnel
2. Millwood Tunnel
3. Horsfall Tunnel
4. Castle Hill Tunnel
5. Winterbutlee Tunnel
6. Royal George Tunnel
7. Scout Tunnel

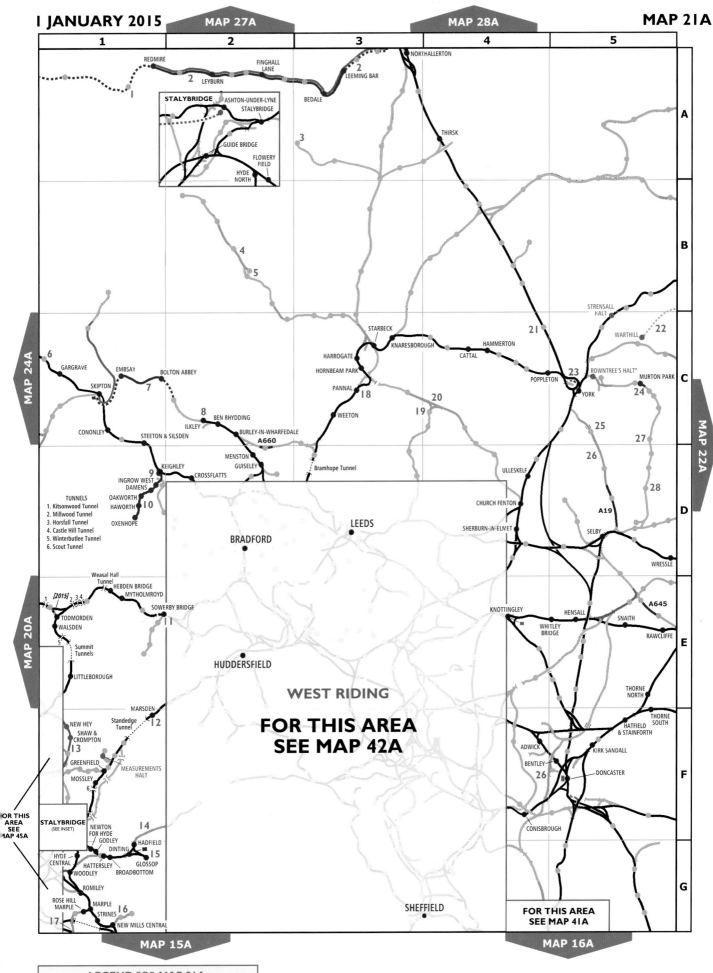

MAP 27A
MAP 28A
MAP 24A
MAP 22A
MAP 20A
MAP 15A
MAP 16A

STALYBRIDGE
ASHTON-UNDER-LYNE
STALYBRIDGE
GUIDE BRIDGE
FLOWERY FIELD
HYDE NORTH

REDMIRE
FINGHALL LANE
LEYBURN
LEEMING BAR
BEDALE
NORTHALLERTON
THIRSK

TUNNELS
1. Kitsonwood Tunnel
2. Millwood Tunnel
3. Horsfall Tunnel
4. Castle Hill Tunnel
5. Winterbutlee Tunnel
6. Scout Tunnel

GARGRAVE
EMBSAY
BOLTON ABBEY
SKIPTON
CONONLEY
STEETON & SILSDEN
ILKLEY
BEN RHYDDING
BURLEY-IN-WHARFEDALE
A660
KEIGHLEY
INGROW WEST
DAMENS
OAKWORTH
HAWORTH
OXENHOPE
CROSSFLATTS
MENSTON
GUISELEY
Bramhope Tunnel

STARBECK
KNARESBOROUGH
HARROGATE
HAMMERTON
HORNBEAM PARK
CATTAL
PANNAL
POPPLETON
WEETON

STRENSALL HALT
WARTHILL
ROWNTREE'S HALT*
MURTON PARK
YORK

ULLESKELF
CHURCH FENTON
SHERBURN-IN-ELMET
A19
SELBY
WRESSLE

Weasal Hall Tunnel
[2015]
HEBDEN BRIDGE
MYTHOLMROYD
SOWERBY BRIDGE
TODMORDEN
WALSDEN
Summit Tunnels
LITTLEBOROUGH
MARSDEN
Standedge Tunnel
NEW HEY
SHAW & CROMPTON
GREENFIELD
MEASUREMENTS HALT
MOSSLEY
STALYBRIDGE (SEE INSET)
NEWTON FOR HYDE
GODLEY
DINTING
HADFIELD
GLOSSOP
BROADBOTTOM
HYDE CENTRAL
HATTERSLEY
WOODLEY
ROMILEY
ROSE HILL MARPLE
MARPLE
STRINES
NEW MILLS CENTRAL

KNOTTINGLEY
HENSALL
A645
WHITLEY BRIDGE
SNAITH
RAWCLIFFE
THORNE NORTH
THORNE SOUTH
HATFIELD & STAINFORTH
ADWICK
KIRK SANDALL
BENTLEY
DONCASTER
CONISBROUGH

BRADFORD
LEEDS
HUDDERSFIELD
WEST RIDING

FOR THIS AREA SEE MAP 42A

SHEFFIELD

OR THIS AREA SEE MAP 45A

FOR THIS AREA SEE MAP 41A

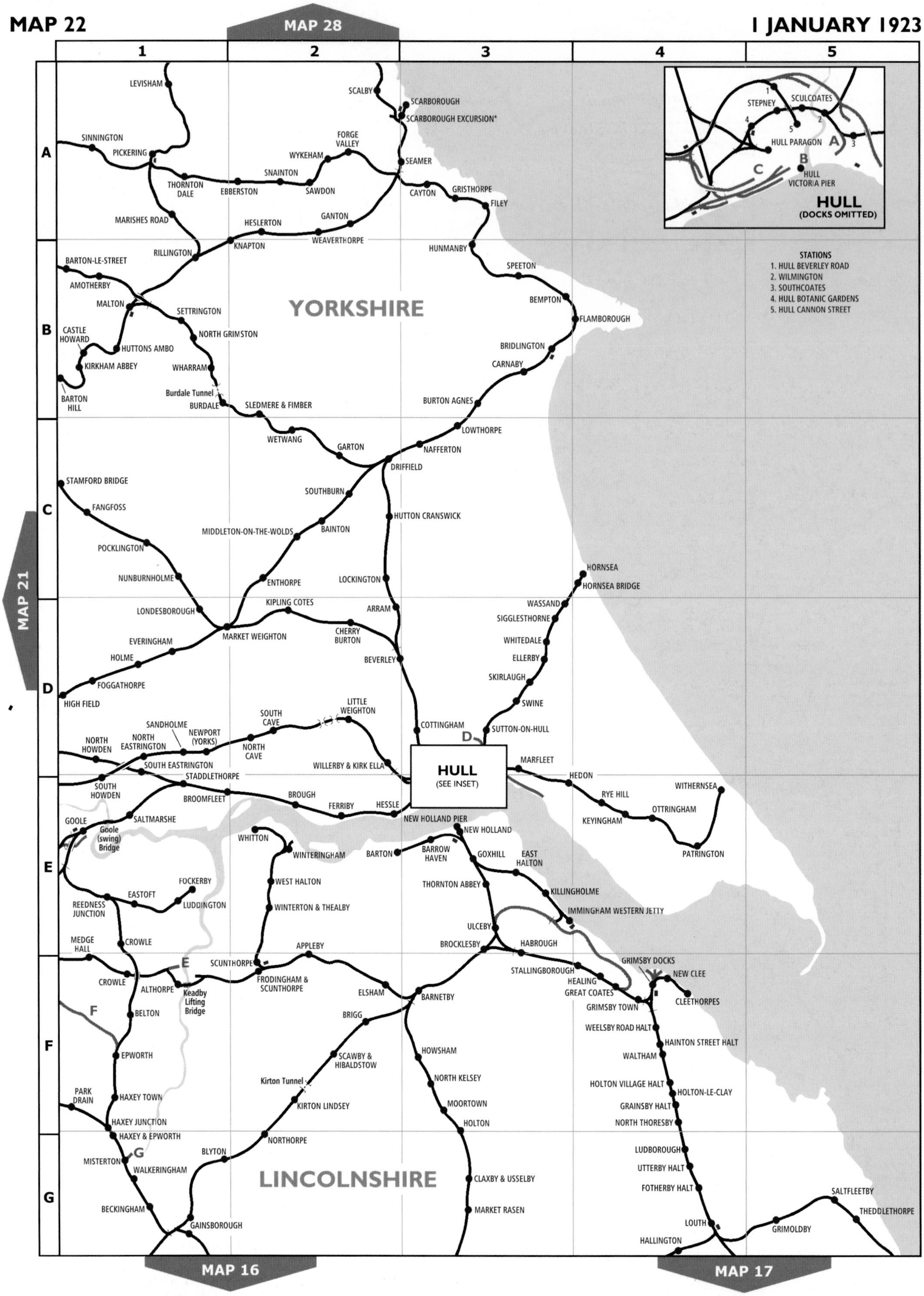

MAP 22 **MAP 28** **1 JANUARY 1923**

1 2 3 4 5

Inset (top right):
STEPNEY · SCULCOATES · HULL PARAGON · HULL VICTORIA PIER
HULL (DOCKS OMITTED)

STATIONS
1. HULL BEVERLEY ROAD
2. WILMINGTON
3. SOUTHCOATES
4. HULL BOTANIC GARDENS
5. HULL CANNON STREET

A

LEVISHAM · SINNINGTON · PICKERING · SCALBY · SCARBOROUGH · SCARBOROUGH EXCURSION* · FORGE VALLEY · WYKEHAM · SEAMER · THORNTON DALE · EBBERSTON · SAWDON · SNAINTON · CAYTON · GRISTHORPE · MARISHES ROAD · HESLERTON · GANTON · FILEY · WEAVERTHORPE

B

BARTON-LE-STREET · RILLINGTON · KNAPTON · HUNMANBY · SPEETON · AMOTHERBY · SETTRINGTON · BEMPTON · MALTON · NORTH GRIMSTON · FLAMBOROUGH · CASTLE HOWARD · HUTTONS AMBO · WHARRAM · BRIDLINGTON · KIRKHAM ABBEY · CARNABY · BURDALE TUNNEL · BARTON HILL · BURDALE · SLEDMERE & FIMBER · BURTON AGNES

YORKSHIRE

C

STAMFORD BRIDGE · WETWANG · GARTON · LOWTHORPE · FANGFOSS · NAFFERTON · DRIFFIELD · SOUTHBURN · POCKLINGTON · MIDDLETON-ON-THE-WOLDS · BAINTON · HUTTON CRANSWICK · NUNBURNHOLME · ENTHORPE · LOCKINGTON · HORNSEA · HORNSEA BRIDGE

D

LONDESBOROUGH · KIPLING COTES · ARRAM · WASSAND · SIGGLESTHORNE · EVERINGHAM · MARKET WEIGHTON · CHERRY BURTON · WHITEDALE · HOLME · BEVERLEY · ELLERBY · FOGGATHORPE · SKIRLAUGH · HIGH FIELD · SWINE · SANDHOLME · NORTH EASTRINGTON · NEWPORT (YORKS) · SOUTH CAVE · LITTLE WEIGHTON · COTTINGHAM · SUTTON-ON-HULL · NORTH HOWDEN · NORTH CAVE · SOUTH EASTRINGTON · STADDLETHORPE · WILLERBY & KIRK ELLA

HULL (SEE INSET) · MARFLEET · HEDON

E

SOUTH HOWDEN · BROOMFLEET · BROUGH · FERRIBY · HESSLE · RYE HILL · WITHERNSEA · GOOLE · SALTMARSHE · NEW HOLLAND PIER · KEYINGHAM · OTTRINGHAM · Goole (swing) Bridge · WHITTON · NEW HOLLAND · PATRINGTON · WINTERINGHAM · BARTON · BARROW HAVEN · GOXHILL · EAST HALTON · FOCKERBY · WEST HALTON · THORNTON ABBEY · EASTOFT · LUDDINGTON · KILLINGHOLME · REEDNESS JUNCTION · WINTERTON & THEALBY · IMMINGHAM WESTERN JETTY · MEDGE HALL · CROWLE · APPLEBY · ULCEBY · BROCKLESBY · HABROUGH

F

CROWLE · SCUNTHORPE · GRIMSBY DOCKS · ALTHORPE · Keadby Lifting Bridge · FRODINGHAM & SCUNTHORPE · STALLINGBOROUGH · NEW CLEE · BELTON · ELSHAM · BARNETBY · HEALING · GREAT COATES · EPWORTH · BRIGG · GRIMSBY TOWN · CLEETHORPES · WEELSBY ROAD HALT · HOWSHAM · HAINTON STREET HALT · SCAWBY & HIBALDSTOW · WALTHAM · PARK DRAIN · HAXEY TOWN · Kirton Tunnel · NORTH KELSEY · HOLTON VILLAGE HALT · HOLTON-LE-CLAY · KIRTON LINDSEY · MOORTOWN · GRAINSBY HALT · HAXEY JUNCTION · HOLTON · NORTH THORESBY

G

HAXEY & EPWORTH · BLYTON · NORTHORPE · LUDBOROUGH · MISTERTON · UTTERBY HALT · WALKERINGHAM · FOTHERBY HALT · SALTFLEETBY · BECKINGHAM · CLAXBY & USSELBY · THEDDLETHORPE · **LINCOLNSHIRE** · GAINSBOROUGH · MARKET RASEN · LOUTH · GRIMOLDBY · HALLINGTON

MAP 16 **MAP 17**

MAP 21

LEGEND FOR MAP 22
A Drypool branch
B Ferry service from NEW HOLLAND PIER
C Dock & pier branches
D Stoneferry branch
E Keadby branch
F Hatfield Moor branch
G Stockwith branch

1 SCARBOROUGH TO WHITBY RAIL TRAIL. discoveryyorkshirecoast.com
2 1ft 8in gauge NORTH BAY RAILWAY. www.nbr.org.uk
3 NORTH YORKSHIRE MOORS RAILWAY. www.nymr.co.uk
4 HUNMANBY: Holiday accommodation available in the former station building. www.oldwaitingrooms.co.uk
5 SLEDMERE & FIMBER: Site cleared as the Fimber Picnic Site; also base for the YORKSHIRE WOLDS RAILWAY

preservation group. www.yorkshirewoldsrailway.org.uk
6 CASTLE HOWARD: Holiday accommodation available in the former station building. www.castlehowardstation.com
7 Former 1ft 6in gauge SAND HUTTON LIGHT RAILWAY
8 STAMFORD BRIDGE: Site now a park; station buildings now the Old Station Club
9 FANGFOSS: Now part of Fangfoss Caravan Park. www.fangfosspark.co.uk

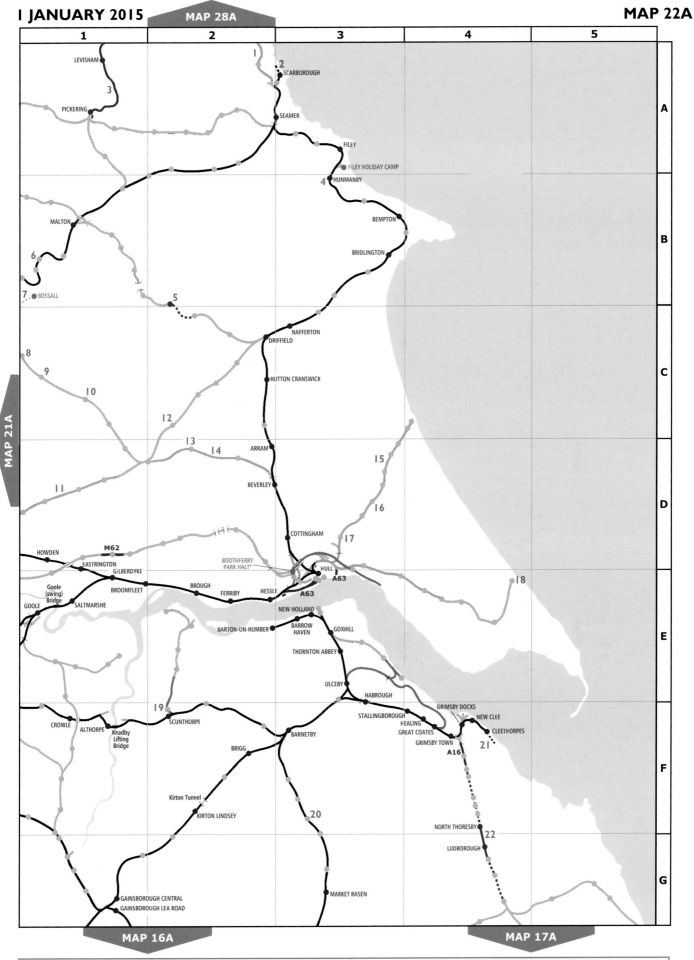

MAP 28A
MAP 21A
MAP 16A
MAP 17A

LEGEND FOR MAP 22A

10 **POCKLINGTON:** Station building and train shed now Pocklington School sports hall

11 BUBWITH RAIL TRAIL. walkingtheriding.eastriding.gov.uk

12 **ENTHORPE:** Holiday accommodation available in converted LNER box vans. www.thewagons.co.uk

13 **KIPLING COTES:** Signal box now an information centre for the HUDSON WAY; goods shed now a furniture shop

14 HUDSON WAY. my.viewranger.com

15 HORNSEA RAIL TRAIL / Part of the TRANS PENNINE TRAIL. www.gps-routes.co.uk

16 **SKIRLAUGH:** Site cleared as a car park and picnic area

17 **SUTTON-ON-HULL:** Site cleared as a children's play area

18 **WITHERNSEA:** Site cleared as a market place

19 **SCUNTHORPE:** Trips over the complex steelworks system are operated by the APPLEBY FRODINGHAM RAILWAY PRESERVATION SOCIETY. www.afrps.co.uk

20 **MOORTOWN:** Now the Station House B&B. www.moortownstation.com

21 1ft 3in gauge CLEETHORPES COAST LIGHT RAILWAY. www.cleethorpescoastlightrailway.co.uk

22 LINCOLNSHIRE WOLDS RAILWAY. www.lincolnshirewoldsrailway.co.uk

MAP 23   **1 JANUARY 1923**

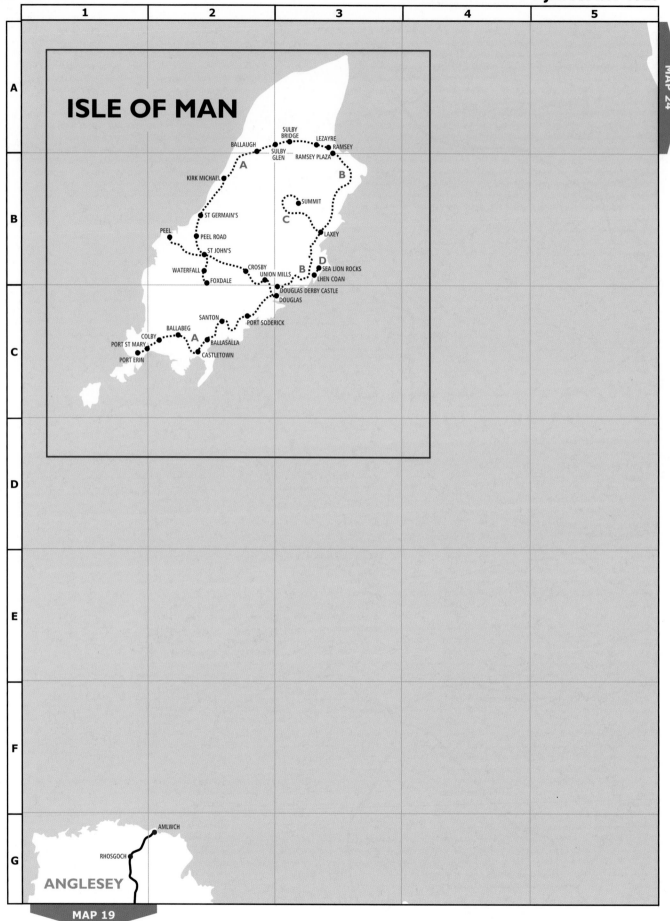

ISLE OF MAN

SULBY BRIDGE
BALLAUGH
SULBY GLEN
LEZAYRE
RAMSEY
RAMSEY PLAZA
KIRK MICHAEL
A
B
SUMMIT
ST GERMAIN'S
C
PEEL
PEEL ROAD
LAXEY
ST JOHN'S
WATERFALL
CROSBY
UNION MILLS
D
SEA LION ROCKS
FOXDALE
B
LHEN COAN
DOUGLAS DERBY CASTLE
DOUGLAS
SANTON
PORT SODERICK
COLBY
BALLABEG
A
PORT ST MARY
BALLASALLA
PORT ERIN
CASTLETOWN

MAP 24

AMLWCH
RHOSGOCH
ANGLESEY

MAP 19

LEGEND FOR **MAP 23**
A 3ft gauge ISLE OF MAN RAILWAY
B 3ft gauge MANX ELECTRIC RAILWAY
C 3ft 6in gauge SNAEFELL MOUNTAIN RAILWAY
D 2ft gauge GROUDLE GLEN RAILWAY

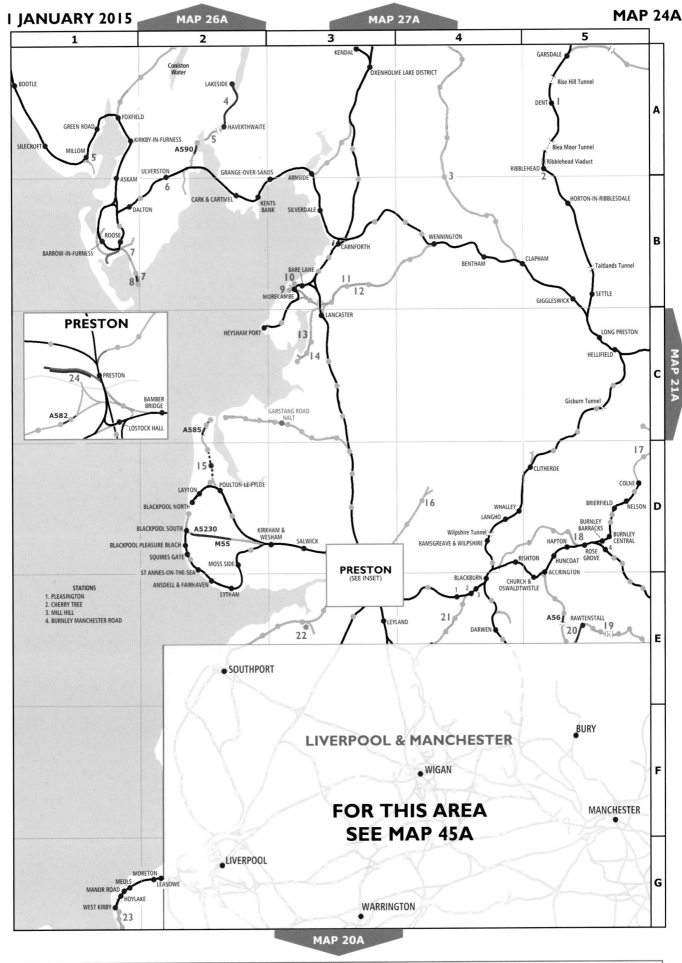

1 JANUARY 2015

MAP 24A

MAP 26A   **MAP 27A**

MAP 21A

MAP 20A

BOOTLE
GARSDALE
Rise Hill Tunnel
DENT
Coniston Water
LAKESIDE
4
FOXFIELD
GREEN ROAD
SILECROFT
MILLOM
5
KIRKBY-IN-FURNESS
5
HAVERTHWAITE
A590
Blea Moor Tunnel
Ribblehead Viaduct
RIBBLEHEAD
2
ULVERSTON
GRANGE-OVER-SANDS
ASKAM
6
DALTON
CARK & CARTMEL
KENTS BANK
ARNSIDE
SILVERDALE
HORTON-IN-RIBBLESDALE
ROOSE
7
BARROW-IN-FURNESS
8
7
CARNFORTH
WENNINGTON
BENTHAM
CLAPHAM
Taitlands Tunnel
BARE LANE
10
11
SETTLE
MORECAMBE
9
12
GIGGLESWICK
LANCASTER
LONG PRESTON
HEYSHAM PORT
13
HELLIFIELD
14
Gisburn Tunnel

PRESTON
24
PRESTON
BAMBER BRIDGE
A582
LOSTOCK HALL

GARSTANG ROAD HALT
17
A585
CLITHEROE
COLNE
15
WHALLEY
BRIERFIELD
NELSON
LAYTON
POULTON-LE-FYLDE
16
LANGHO
BURNLEY BARRACKS
BLACKPOOL NORTH
Wilpshire Tunnel
HAPTON
18
BURNLEY CENTRAL
BLACKPOOL SOUTH
A5230
KIRKHAM & WESHAM
Wilpshire
RAMSGREAVE & WILPSHIRE
ROSE GROVE
BLACKPOOL PLEASURE BEACH
M55
SALWICK
RISHTON
HUNCOAT
SQUIRES GATE
MOSS SIDE
ACCRINGTON
ST ANNES-ON-THE-SEA
PRESTON (SEE INSET)
BLACKBURN
ANSDELL & FAIRHAVEN
1
2
CHURCH & OSWALDTWISTLE
LYTHAM
3
STATIONS
1. PLEASINGTON
2. CHERRY TREE
3. MILL HILL
4. BURNLEY MANCHESTER ROAD
LEYLAND
21
A56
RAWTENSTALL
DARWEN
20
19
22

SOUTHPORT

LIVERPOOL & MANCHESTER
BURY

WIGAN

FOR THIS AREA SEE MAP 45A
MANCHESTER

MORETON
MEOLS
LEASOWE
MANOR ROAD
LIVERPOOL
HOYLAKE
WEST KIRBY
23
WARRINGTON

LEGEND FOR MAP 24A

now a tourist information office and The Platform entertainment venue
10 **MORECAMBE HARBOUR** (closed 1904): Now a café
11 **HALTON**: Now a rowing club boathouse
12 Part of the LUNE VALLEY RAMBLE. www.ldwa.org.uk
13 Part of the LANCASHIRE COASTAL WAY. www.ldwa.org.uk
14 **CONDER GREEN**: Site cleared as a car park and picnic area
15 **THORNTON**: Base of the POULTON & WYRE RAILWAY

SOCIETY. pwrs.org
16 **LONGRIDGE**: Now a heritage and visitor centre. www.longridgestation.co.uk
17 **FOULRIDGE**: Station building re-erected at INGROW WEST on the KEIGHLEY & WORTH VALLEY RAILWAY. www.kwvr.co.uk
18 PADIHAM GREENWAY. www.lancashire.gov.uk
19 Parts of the IRWELL SCULPTURE TRAIL. www.irwellsculpturetrail.co.uk

20 **EAST LANCASHIRE RAILWAY**. www.eastlancsrailway.org.uk
21 **WITHNELL**: Site now a nature reserve
22 WEST LANCASHIRE LIGHT RAILWAY: Collection of industrial narrow gauge equipment with a 2ft gauge operational line. www.wllr.net
23 WIRRAL WAY. www.discovercheshire.co.uk
24 **RIBBLE STEAM RAILWAY** and museum. www.ribblesteam.org.uk

MAP 25

1 JANUARY 1923

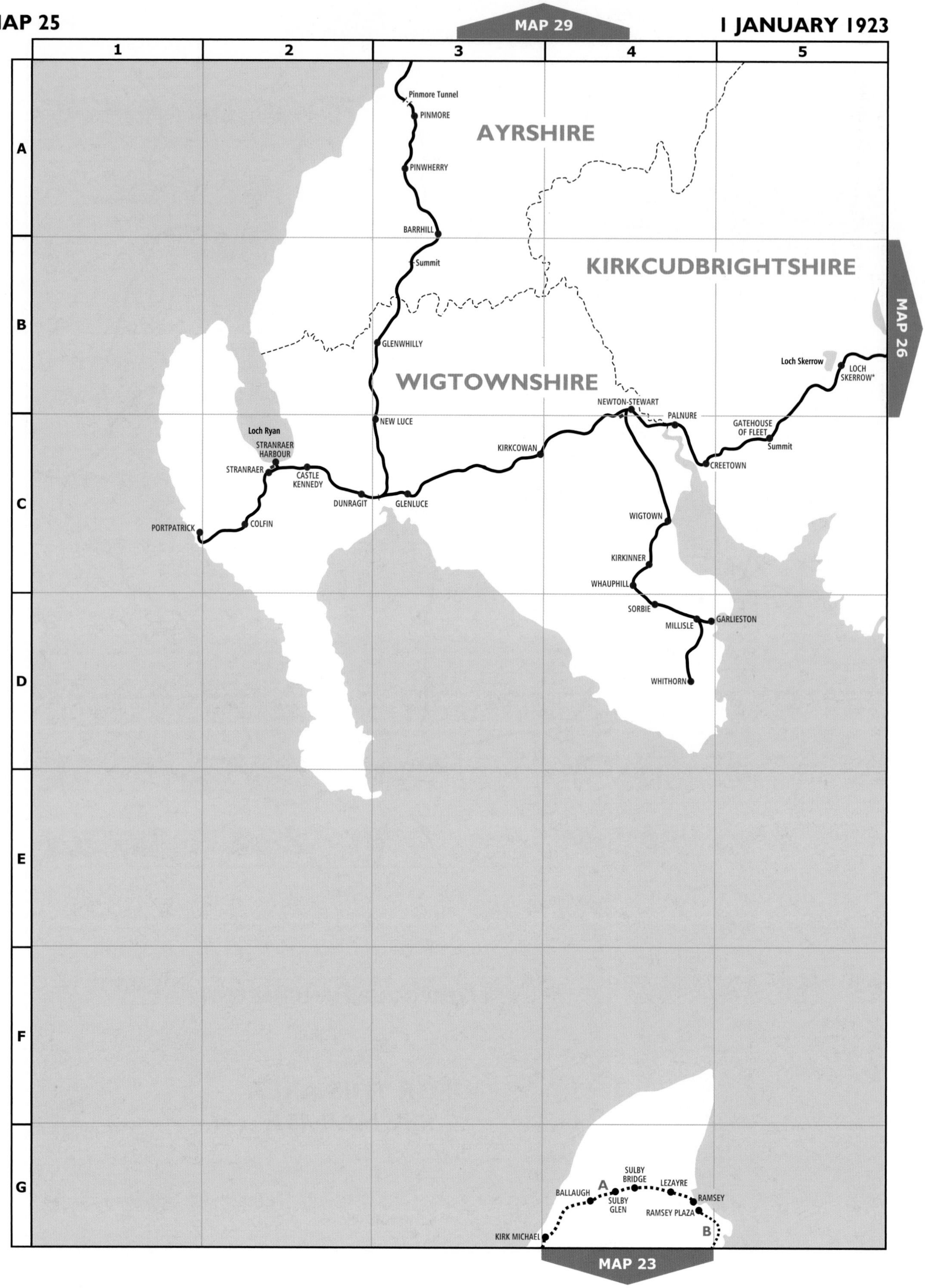

MAP 29
1
2
3
4
5
A
B
C
D
E
F
G
Pinmore Tunnel
PINMORE
AYRSHIRE
PINWHERRY
BARRHILL
Summit
KIRKCUDBRIGHTSHIRE
MAP 26
GLENWHILLY
WIGTOWNSHIRE
Loch Skerrow
LOCH SKERROW*
NEWTON-STEWART
PALNURE
GATEHOUSE OF FLEET
Summit
NEW LUCE
Loch Ryan
STRANRAER HARBOUR
STRANRAER
CASTLE KENNEDY
DUNRAGIT
GLENLUCE
KIRKCOWAN
CREETOWN
PORTPATRICK
COLFIN
WIGTOWN
KIRKINNER
WHAUPHILL
SORBIE
MILLISLE
GARLIESTON
WHITHORN
SULBY BRIDGE
A
LEZAYRE
BALLAUGH
SULBY GLEN
RAMSEY
RAMSEY PLAZA
B
KIRK MICHAEL
MAP 23

LEGEND FOR MAP 25
A 3ft gauge ISLE OF MAN RAILWAY
B 3ft gauge MANX ELECTRIC RAILWAY

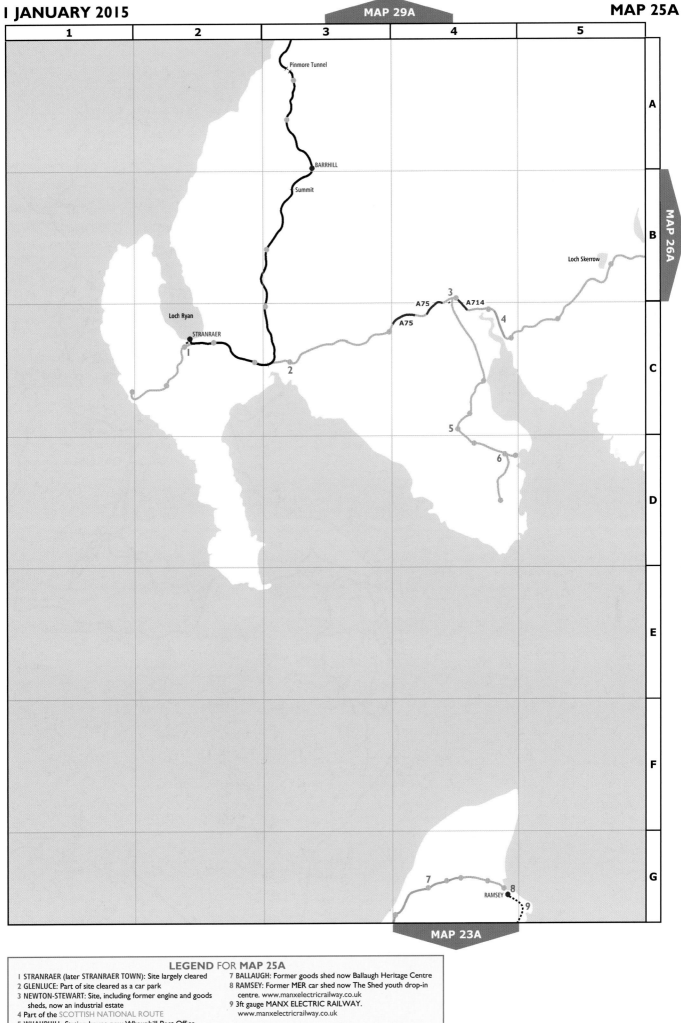

MAP 26A

MAP 23A

Pinmore Tunnel

BARRHILL

Summit

Loch Ryan

STRANRAER

A75

A75

A714

Loch Skerrow

RAMSEY

LEGEND FOR MAP 25A

1 STRANRAER (later STRANRAER TOWN): Site largely cleared
2 GLENLUCE: Part of site cleared as a car park
3 NEWTON-STEWART: Site, including former engine and goods
  sheds, now an industrial estate
4 Part of the SCOTTISH NATIONAL ROUTE
5 WHAUPHILL: Station house now Whauphill Post Office
6 MILLISLE: Station house now holiday accommodation.
  www.kilfillanholidaycottage.co.uk

7 BALLAUGH: Former goods shed now Ballaugh Heritage Centre
8 RAMSEY: Former MER car shed now The Shed youth drop-in
  centre. www.manxelectricrailway.co.uk
9 3ft gauge MANX ELECTRIC RAILWAY.
  www.manxelectricrailway.co.uk

MAP 26

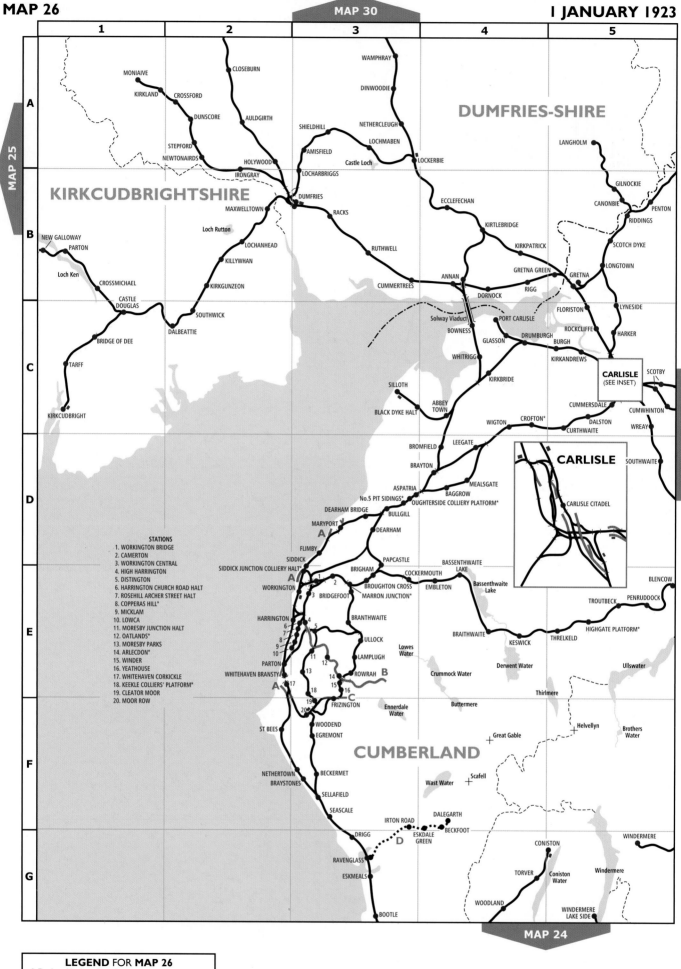

MAP 30

DUMFRIES-SHIRE

KIRKCUDBRIGHTSHIRE

CUMBERLAND

CARLISLE

CARLISLE
(SEE INSET)

CARLISLE CITADEL

STATIONS
1. WORKINGTON BRIDGE
2. CAMERTON
3. WORKINGTON CENTRAL
4. HIGH HARRINGTON
5. DISTINGTON
6. HARRINGTON CHURCH ROAD HALT
7. ROSEHILL ARCHER STREET HALT
8. COPPERAS HILL*
9. MICKLAM
10. LOWCA
11. MORESBY JUNCTION HALT
12. OATLANDS*
13. MORESBY PARKS
14. ARLECDON*
15. WINDER
16. YEATHOUSE
17. WHITEHAVEN CORKICKLE
18. KEEKLE COLLIERS' PLATFORM*
19. CLEATOR MOOR
20. MOOR ROW

LEGEND FOR **MAP 26**
A Dock and harbour branches
B Kelton Fell branch
C Eskett branch
D 1ft 3in gauge RAVENGLASS & ESKDALE RAILWAY

MAP 24

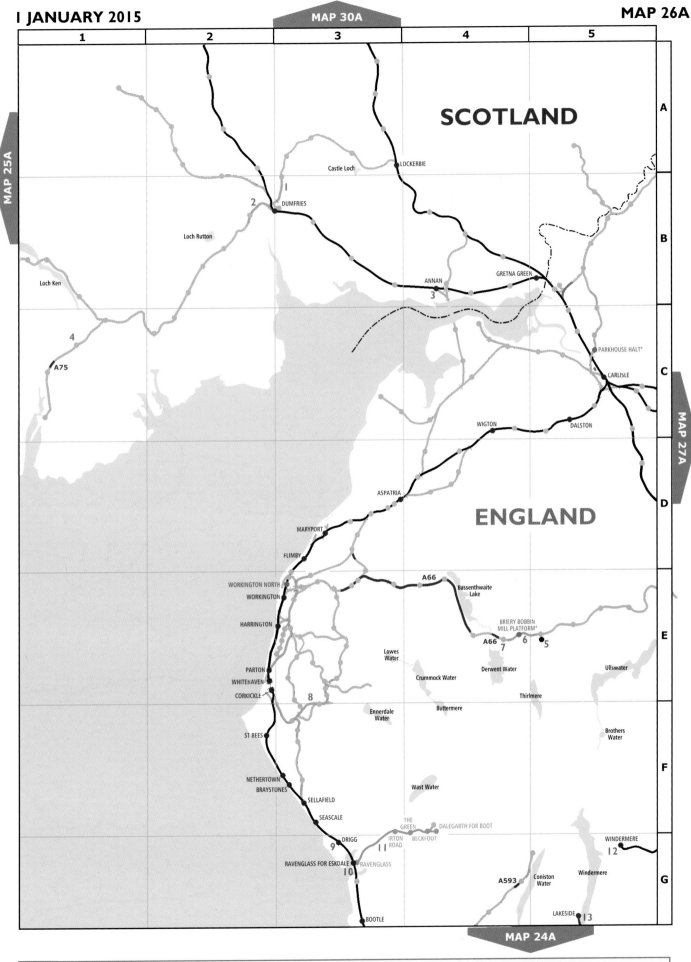

SCOTLAND

ENGLAND

LOCKERBIE
Castle Loch
DUMFRIES
Loch Rutton
Loch Ken
A75
ANNAN
GRETNA GREEN
PARKHOUSE HALT*
CARLISLE
WIGTON
DALSTON
ASPATRIA
MARYPORT
FLIMBY
WORKINGTON NORTH
WORKINGTON
HARRINGTON
A66
Bassenthwaite Lake
BRIERY BOBBIN MILL PLATFORM*
A66
Lowes Water
Crummock Water
Derwent Water
Thirlmere
Ullswater
PARTON
WHITEHAVEN
CORKICKLE
Ennerdale Water
Buttermere
Brothers Water
ST BEES
NETHERTOWN
BRAYSTONES
Wast Water
SELLAFIELD
SEASCALE
THE GREEN
BECKFOOT
DALEGARTH FOR BOOT
IRTON ROAD
WINDERMERE
DRIGG
RAVENGLASS FOR ESKDALE
RAVENGLASS
A593
Coniston Water
Windermere
BOOTLE
LAKESIDE

LEGEND FOR MAP 26A

1 CALEDONIAN CYCLE ROUTE. www.walkjogrun.net
2 MAXWELLTOWN RAILWAY PATH. www.railwaypaths.org.uk
3 ANNAN: Station building now the Station House pub
4 BRIDGE OF DEE: Holiday accommodation available in converted carriage. www.traincarriageholidays.co.uk
5 THRELKELD QUARRY & MINING MUSEUM with a 2ft gauge operational line. www.threlkeldquarryandminingmuseum.co.uk

6 KESWICK RAILWAY FOOTPATH. www.visitcumbria.com
7 KESWICK: Now part of the Keswick Hotel. www.thekeswickhotel.co.uk
8 WHITEHAVEN & ROWRAH RAILWAY PATH. www.visitcumbria.com
9 DRIGG: Original station building now a craft shop and café
10 RAVENGLASS FOR ESKDALE: Station building now the Ratty Arms pub. www.rattyarmspub.co.uk

11 1ft 3in gauge RAVENGLASS & ESKDALE RAILWAY and RAVENGLASS RAILWAY MUSEUM. ravenglass-railway.co.uk
12 WINDERMERE: Former station building now part of a supermarket
13 LAKESIDE & HAVERTHWAITE RAILWAY. www.lakesiderailway.co.uk

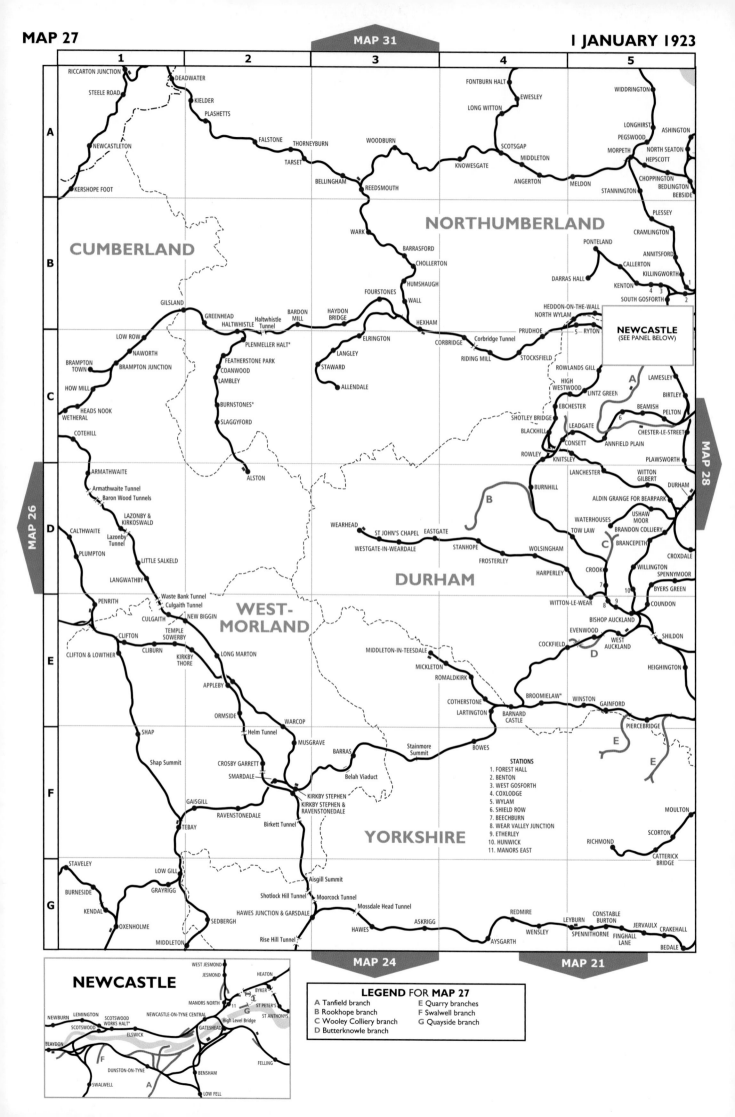

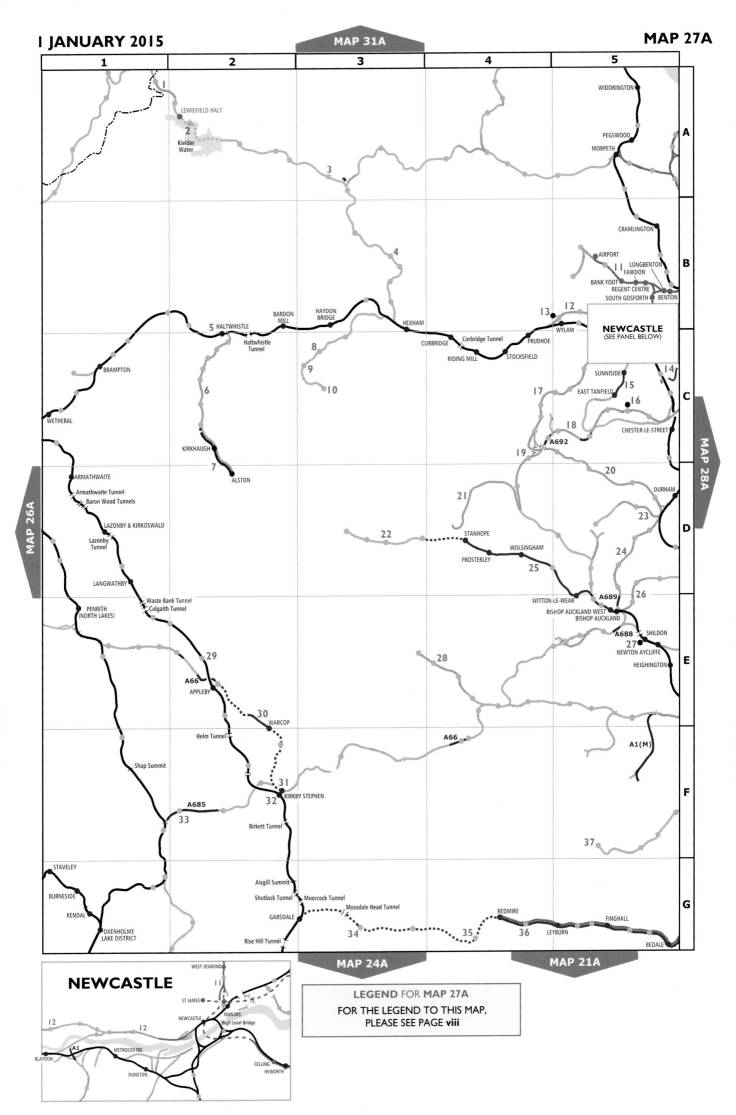

MAP 26A

MAP 28A

MAP 24A

MAP 21A

1　2　3　4　5

A
B
C
D
E
F
G

WIDDRINGTON
PEGSWOOD
MORPETH
CRAMLINGTON
AIRPORT
LONGBENTON
FAWDON
BANK FOOT
REGENT CENTRE
SOUTH GOSFORTH
BENTON

NEWCASTLE
(SEE PANEL BELOW)

LEWIEFIELD HALT
Kielder
Water

BARDON
MILL
HAYDON
BRIDGE
HALTWHISTLE
Haltwhistle
Tunnel
HEXHAM
CORBRIDGE
Corbridge Tunnel
RIDING MILL
STOCKSFIELD
PRUDHOE
WYLAM
SUNNISIDE
EAST TANFIELD
CHESTER-LE-STREET
A692
A692
DURHAM

BRAMPTON

WETHERAL
KIRKHAUGH
ALSTON
ARMATHWAITE
Armathwaite Tunnel
Baron Wood Tunnels
LAZONBY & KIRKOSWALD
Lazonby
Tunnel
LANGWATHBY
Waste Bank Tunnel
Culgaith Tunnel
PENRITH
(NORTH LAKES)

STANHOPE
FROSTERLEY
WOLSINGHAM
WITTON-LE-WEAR
A689
BISHOP AUCKLAND WEST
BISHOP AUCKLAND
A688
SHILDON
NEWTON AYCLIFFE
HEIGHINGTON

A66
APPLEBY
WARCOP
Helm Tunnel
Shap Summit
A685

A66

A1(M)

STAVELEY
BURNESIDE
KENDAL
OXENHOLME
LAKE DISTRICT

KIRKBY STEPHEN
Birkett Tunnel

Aisgill Summit
Shotlock Tunnel
Moorcock Tunnel
Mossdale Head Tunnel
GARSDALE
Rise Hill Tunnel

REDMIRE
LEYBURN
FINGHALL
BEDALE

NEWCASTLE

WEST JESMOND
ST JAMES
NEWCASTLE
MANORS
High Level Bridge
METROCENTRE
BLAYDON
A1
DUNSTON
FELLING
HEWORTH

LEGEND FOR MAP 27A
FOR THE LEGEND TO THIS MAP,
PLEASE SEE PAGE viii

MAP 28   1 JANUARY 1923

STATIONS
1. SEATON DELAVAL
2. BACKWORTH
3. WALKER
4. WALLSEND
5. HOWDON-ON-TYNE
6. PERCY MAIN
7. NORTH SHIELDS
8. WALKER GATE
9. CARVILLE
10. POINT PLEASANT
11. WILLINGTON QUAY
12. HEBBURN
13. JARROW
14. TYNE DOCK
15. HIGH SHIELDS
16. SOUTH SHIELDS
17. BROCKLEY WHINS
18. WASHINGTON
19. PALLION
20. MILLFIELD
21. LEAMSIDE
22. SHERBURN HOUSE
23. MIDDLESBROUGH
24. CARGO FLEET

YORKSHIRE

MAP 27

MAP 21

MAP 22

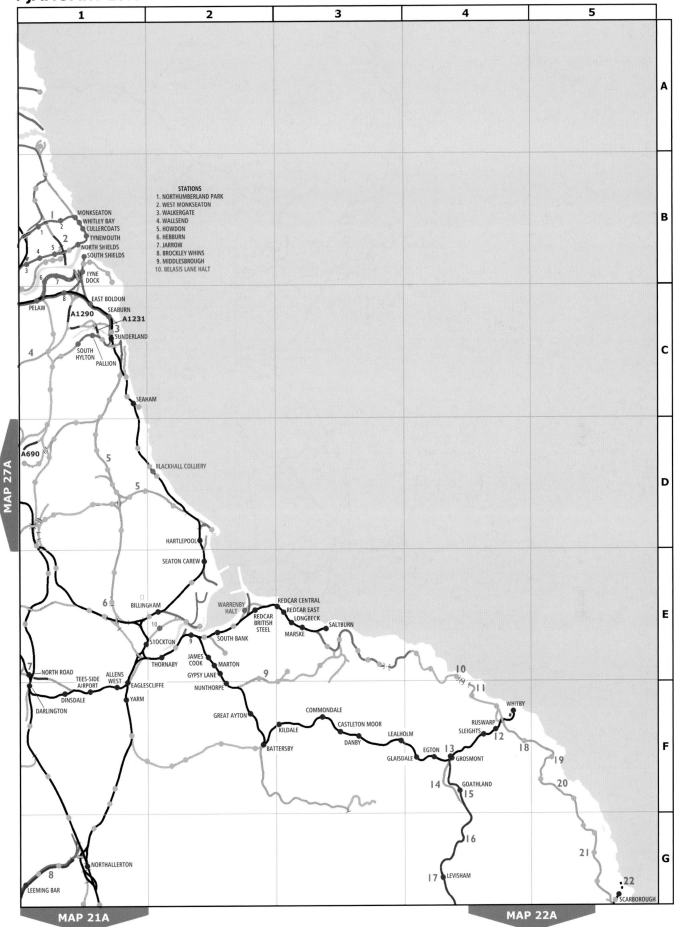

1   **2**   **3**   **4**   **5**

A

B

C

D

E

F

G

STATIONS
1. NORTHUMBERLAND PARK
2. WEST MONKSEATON
3. WALKERGATE
4. WALLSEND
5. HOWDON
6. HEBBURN
7. JARROW
8. BROCKLEY WHINS
9. MIDDLESBROUGH
10. BELASIS LANE HALT

MONKSEATON
WHITLEY BAY
CULLERCOATS
TYNEMOUTH
NORTH SHIELDS
SOUTH SHIELDS
TYNE DOCK
EAST BOLDON
PELAW
A1290
SEABURN
A1231
SUNDERLAND
SOUTH HYLTON
PALLION
SEAHAM
A690
BLACKHALL COLLIERY
HARTLEPOOL
SEATON CAREW
BILLINGHAM
WARRENBY HALT
REDCAR CENTRAL
REDCAR EAST
REDCAR BRITISH STEEL
LONGBECK
MARSKE
SALTBURN
SOUTH BANK
STOCKTON
JAMES COOK
MARTON
THORNABY
GYPSY LANE
NUNTHORPE
NORTH ROAD
TEES-SIDE AIRPORT
ALLENS WEST
EAGLESCLIFFE
DINSDALE
YARM
DARLINGTON
GREAT AYTON
COMMONDALE
KILDALE
CASTLETON MOOR
BATTERSBY
DANBY
LEALHOLM
EGTON
GLAISDALE
GROSMONT
GOATHLAND
WHITBY
RUSWARP
SLEIGHTS
LEVISHAM
NORTHALLERTON
LEEMING BAR
SCARBOROUGH

MAP 27A

MAP 21A   MAP 22A

LEGEND FOR MAP 28A

10 KETTLENESS: Now a scout centre and hostel

11 Part of the CLEVELAND WAY. www.clevelandway.co.uk

12 RUSWARP: Holiday accommodation available in former station building. www.sykescottages.co.uk

13 GROSMONT: Holiday accommodation available in former station house. www.nymr.co.uk

14 HISTORIC RAIL TRAIL. www.wonderfulwhitby.co.uk

15 GOATHLAND: Holiday accommodation available in a camping

coach. www.nymr.co.uk

16 NORTH YORKSHIRE MOORS RAILWAY. www.nymr.co.uk

17 LEVISHAM: Holiday accommodation available in a camping coach. www.nymr.co.uk

18 HAWSKER: Holiday accommodation available in a converted carriage, and a cycle-hire business. www.trailways.info

19 ROBIN HOOD'S BAY: Holiday accommodation available in station building. www.stationwaitingrooms.co.uk

20 SCARBOROUGH TO WHITBY RAIL TRAIL. www.discoveryorkshirecoast.com

21 CLOUGHTON: Holiday accommodation available (including a camping coach and former goods shed); also tearoom. www.cloughtonstation.co.uk

22 1ft 8in gauge NORTH BAY RAILWAY. www.nbr.org.uk

MAP 29

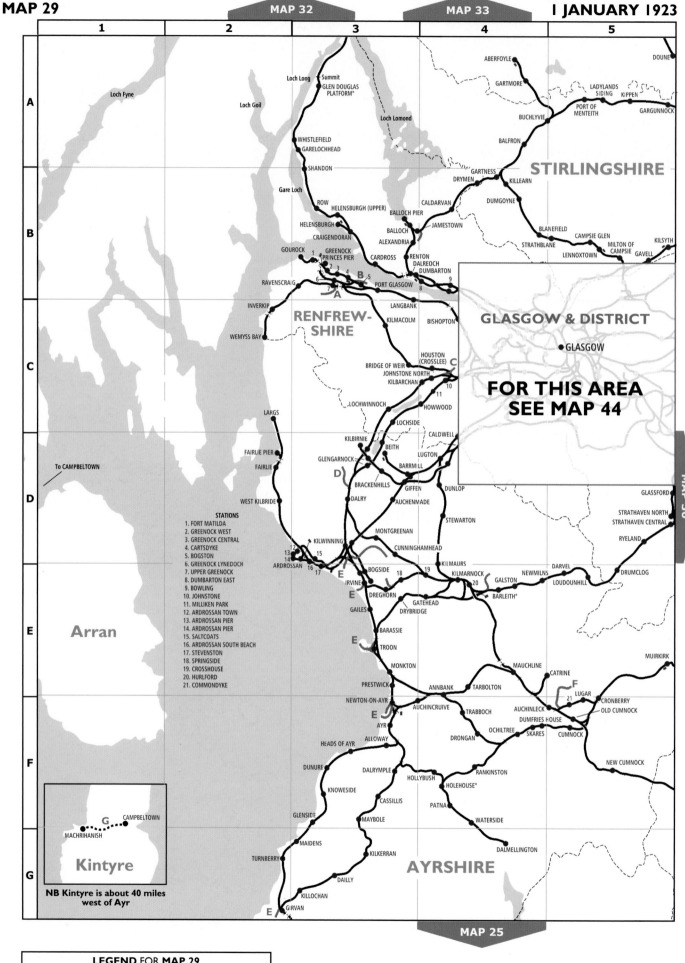

MAP 32 MAP 33 1 JANUARY 1923

STATIONS
1. FORT MATILDA
2. GREENOCK WEST
3. GREENOCK CENTRAL
4. CARTSDYKE
5. BOGSTON
6. GREENOCK LYNEDOCH
7. UPPER GREENOCK
8. DUMBARTON EAST
9. BOWLING
10. JOHNSTONE
11. MILLIKEN PARK
12. ARDROSSAN TOWN
13. ARDROSSAN PIER
14. ARDROSSAN PIER
15. SALTCOATS
16. ARDROSSAN SOUTH BEACH
17. STEVENSTON
18. SPRINGSIDE
19. CROSSHOUSE
20. HURLFORD
21. COMMONDYKE

GLASGOW & DISTRICT

• GLASGOW

FOR THIS AREA
SEE MAP 44

NB Kintyre is about 40 miles
west of Ayr

Kintyre

Arran

MAP 25

MAP 30

LEGEND FOR MAP 29
A Overton branch
B Inch branch
C Linwood branch
D Swinlees branch
E Harbour branches
F Gilmilnscroft branch
G 2ft 3in gauge CAMPBELTOWN & MACHRIHANISH LIGHT RAILWAY

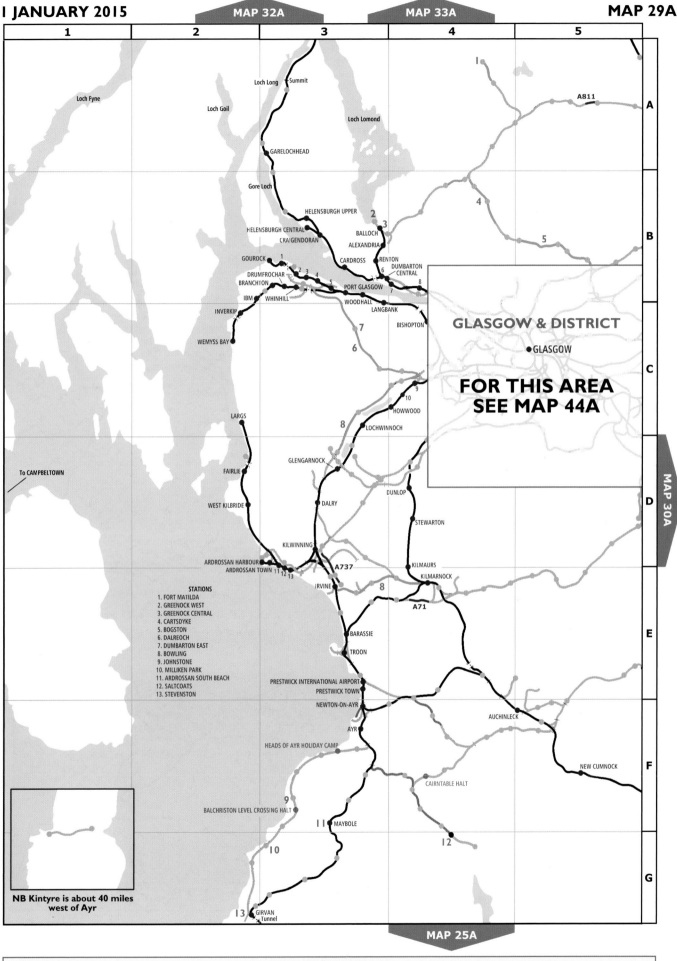

1 2 3 4 5

A811

A

Loch Fyne

Loch Long Summit

Loch Goil

Loch Lomond

GARELOCHHEAD

B

4

5

Gore Loch

HELENSBURGH UPPER

2

3

HELENSBURGH CENTRAL

BALLOCH

CRAIGENDORAN

ALEXANDRIA

GOUROCK

1

CARDROSS

RENTON

DUMBARTON CENTRAL

6

DRUMFROCHAR

2 3 4

BRANCHTON

5

PORT GLASGOW

IBM WHINHILL

7

8

WOODHALL

LANGBANK

INVERKIP

BISHOPTON

C

WEMYSS BAY

7

6

GLASGOW & DISTRICT

•Glasgow

9

LARGS

10

HOWWOOD

**FOR THIS AREA
SEE MAP 44A**

8

LOCHWINNOCH

To CAMPBELTOWN

FAIRLIE

GLENGARNOCK

DUNLOP

D

MAP 30A

WEST KILBRIDE

DALRY

STEWARTON

KILWINNING

ARDROSSAN HARBOUR

KILMAURS

ARDROSSAN TOWN

11

12 13

A737

KILMARNOCK

IRVINE

8

STATIONS
1. FORT MATILDA
2. GREENOCK WEST
3. GREENOCK CENTRAL
4. CARTSDYKE
5. BOGSTON
6. DALREOCH
7. DUMBARTON EAST
8. BOWLING
9. JOHNSTONE
10. MILLIKEN PARK
11. ARDROSSAN SOUTH BEACH
12. SALTCOATS
13. STEVENSTON

A71

BARASSIE

E

TROON

PRESTWICK INTERNATIONAL AIRPORT

PRESTWICK TOWN

NEWTON-ON-AYR

AUCHINLECK

AYR

HEADS OF AYR HOLIDAY CAMP

NEW CUMNOCK

F

CAIRNTABLE HALT

9

BALCHRISTON LEVEL CROSSING HALT

11 MAYBOLE

12

13

GIRVAN
Tunnel

10

G

NB Kintyre is about 40 miles
west of Ayr

MAP 25A

LEGEND FOR **MAP 29A**

1 ABERFOYLE: Site cleared as a car park

2 BALLOCH PIER: Station trackbed now a car park

3 BALLOCH: Former station buildings now a tourist information office

4 Part of the WEST HIGHLAND WAY. www.west-highland-way.co.uk

5 Part of the JOHN MUIR WAY. www.walkhighlands.co.uk

6 PAISLEY & CLYDE CYCLE PATH. www.sustrans.org.uk

7 KILMACOLM: Now the Pullman Diner

8 Parts of the National Cycle Network. www.sustrans.org.uk

9 KNOWESIDE: Site now a caravan park

10 MAIDENS: Site now a caravan park

11 MAYBOLE: Part of the station building now a convenience store

12 DUNASKIN: SCOTTISH INDUSTRIAL RAILWAY CENTRE. www.arpg.org.uk

13 GIRVAN: Also home to the STRANRAER TO AYR LINE SUPPORT ASSOCIATION. www.saylsa.org.uk

MAP 30   **MAP 33**   **MAP 34**   **1 JANUARY 1923**

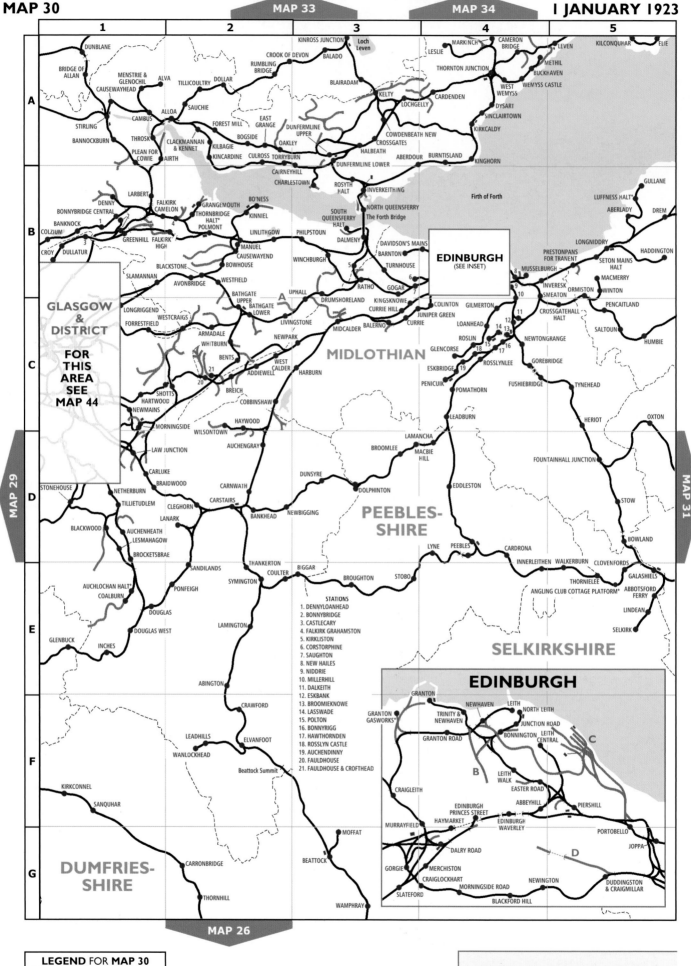

MAP 29 · MAP 31

STATIONS
1. DENNYLOANHEAD
2. BONNYBRIDGE
3. CASTLECARY
4. FALKIRK GRAHAMSTON
5. KIRKLISTON
6. CORSTORPHINE
7. SAUGHTON
8. NEW HAILES
9. NIDDRIE
10. MILLERHILL
11. DALKEITH
12. ESKBANK
13. BROOMIEKNOWE
14. LASSWADE
15. POLTON
16. BONNYRIGG
17. HAWTHORNDEN
18. ROSSLYN CASTLE
19. AUCHENDINNY
20. FAULDHOUSE
21. FAULDHOUSE & CROFTHEAD

EDINBURGH

LEGEND FOR MAP 30
A Former Bangour Asylum branch
B Scotland Street branch
C South Leith branches
D St Leonard's branch

1 DEVON WAY. www.tillicoultry.org.uk
2 WEST FIFE CYCLE WAY. www.edinburghbicycle.com
3 Part of the FIFE COASTAL PATH. www.fifecoastalpath.co.uk
4 LEVEN: Kirkland marshalling yard now the operating base of
  the KINGDOM OF FIFE RAILWAY PRESERVATION
  SOCIETY. www.roskotheque.com
5 KINGHORN: Now a studio and art gallery.
  www.kinghorngallery.co.uk

MAP 26

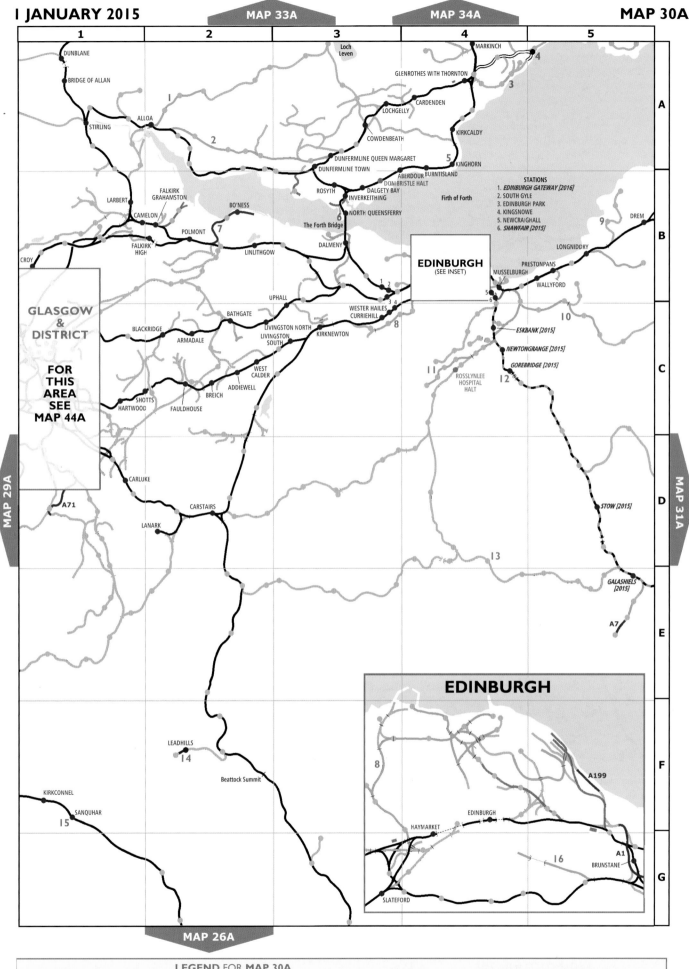

STATIONS
1. *EDINBURGH GATEWAY [2016]*
2. SOUTH GYLE
3. EDINBURGH PARK
4. KINGSNOWE
5. NEWCRAIGHALL
6. *SHAWFAIR [2015]*

EDINBURGH
(SEE INSET)

GLASGOW & DISTRICT

FOR THIS AREA SEE MAP 44A

EDINBURGH

LEGEND FOR MAP 30A

6 NORTH QUEENSFERRY: Station building now a café and heritage centre

7 BO'NESS & KINNEIL RAILWAY and THE MUSEUM OF SCOTTISH RAILWAYS. www.bkrailway.co.uk

8 Parts of the WATER OF LEITH WALKWAY. www.wateroflieth.org.ok

9 ABERLADY: Site now a caravan park. www.aberladycaravanpark.co.uk

10 PENTCAITLAND RAILWAY WALK. www.eastlothian.gov.uk

11 GOREBRIDGE: Former station building now the Porters pub

12 PENICUICK TO MUSSELBURGH CYCLE-WALKWAY. www.midlothian.gov.uk

13 CARDRONA: Now the village store and tea room; the signal box is a newsagents

14 2ft gauge LEADHILLS & WANLOCKHEAD RAILWAY. www.leadhillsrailway.co.uk

15 SANQUHAR: Holiday accommodation available in former station building. www.sanquharstation.co.uk

16 INNOCENT RAILWAY PATH. www.edinburghguide.com

MAP 31

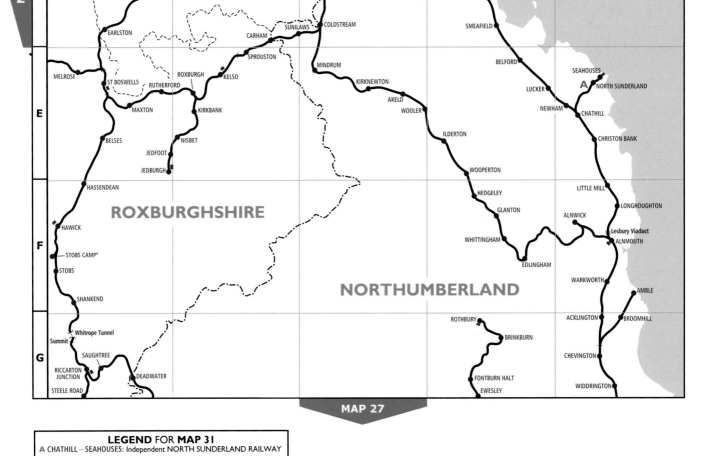

Isle of May

Bass Rock

A

B

NORTH BERWICK
DIRLETON
EAST FORTUNE
DUNBAR
EAST LINTON
INNERWICK
COCKBURNSPATH

EAST LOTHIAN

GIFFORD

Penmanshiel Tunnel
Summit
GRANTSHOUSE
RESTON
EYEMOUTH
BURNMOUTH
AYTON
CHIRNSIDE

C

EDROM
DUNS
BERWICK
Royal Border Bridge
TWEEDMOUTH

BERWICKSHIRE

MARCHMONT
VELVET HALL
SCREMERSTON

LAUDER
NORHAM
GOSWICK
Holy Island

GORDON
GREENLAW
TWIZELL
BEAL

D

EARLSTON
SUNILAWS
COLDSTREAM
SMEAFIELD
CARHAM

MELROSE
SPROUSTON
MINDRUM
BELFORD
SEAHOUSES
A NORTH SUNDERLAND
ST BOSWELLS
ROXBURGH
KELSO
KIRKNEWTON
LUCKER
RUTHERFORD
AKELD
NEWHAM
CHATHILL

E

MAXTON
KIRKBANK
WOOLER
CHRISTON BANK
BELSES
NISBET
ILDERTON
JEDFOOT
JEDBURGH
WOOPERTON

HASSENDEAN
HEDGELEY
LITTLE MILL

ROXBURGHSHIRE
GLANTON
ALNWICK
LONGHOUGHTON
Lesbury Viaduct

HAWICK
WHITTINGHAM
ALNMOUTH
STOBS CAMP*
STOBS
EDLINGHAM

NORTHUMBERLAND

WARKWORTH
AMBLE
SHANKEND

F

Whitrope Tunnel
ROTHBURY
ACKLINGTON
BROOMHILL
Summit
BRINKBURN
SAUGHTREE
CHEVINGTON
RICCARTON JUNCTION
DEADWATER
FONTBURN HALT
STEELE ROAD
EWESLEY
WIDDRINGTON

G

MAP 30
MAP 27

LEGEND FOR **MAP 31**
A CHATHILL – SEAHOUSES: Independent NORTH SUNDERLAND RAILWAY

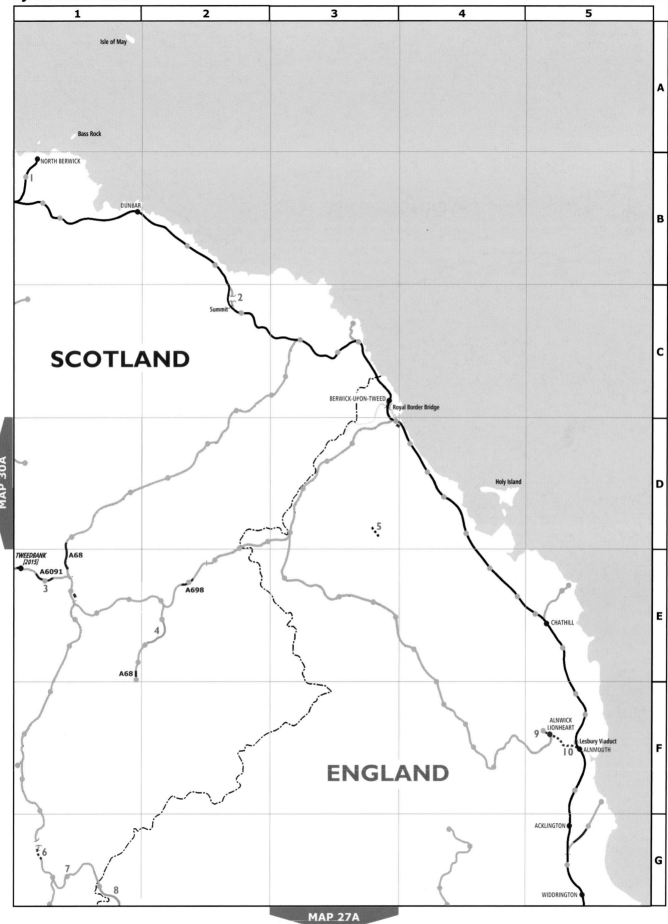

LEGEND FOR MAP 31A

1 DIRLETON: Now Station House B&B. www.privatestay.com
2 Penmanshiel Tunnel: Now bypassed
3 MELROSE: Now Melrose Station Crafts Centre
4 Part of the BORDERS ABBEYS WAY.
   www.bordersabbeysway.fsnet.co.uk
5 1ft 3in gauge HEATHERSLAW LIGHT RAILWAY
   heatherslawlightrailway.co.uk

6 Former Whitrope siding: Home to the WHITROPE
   HERITAGE CENTRE. wrha.org.uk
7 SAUGHTREE: Now a B&B. saughtreestation.weebly.com
8 Part of the KIELDER FOREST BORDER RAILWAY TRAIL.
   www.visitkielder.com
9 ALNWICK: Home to Barter Books bookshop.
   www.barterbooks.co.uk
10 ALN VALLEY RAILWAY. www.alnvalleyrailway.co.uk

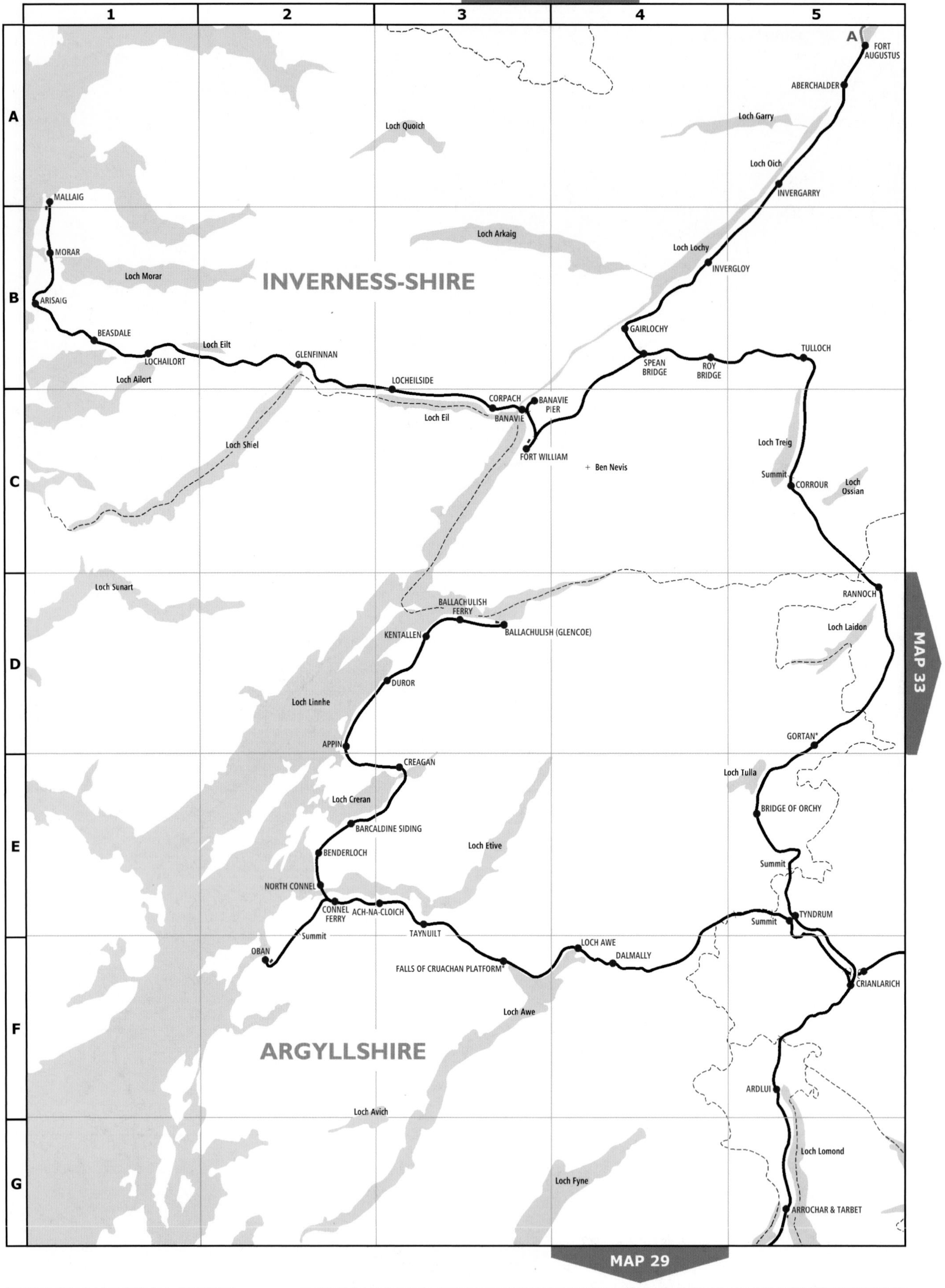

MAP 32

MAP 35

	1	2	3	4	5

A

A
FORT
AUGUSTUS

ABERCHALDER

Loch Quoich

Loch Garry

Loch Oich

INVERGARRY

MALLAIG

MORAR

Loch Arkaig

INVERNESS-SHIRE

Loch Lochy

INVERGLOY

ARISAIG

Loch Morar

B

BEASDALE

Loch Eilt

GLENFINNAN

GAIRLOCHY

LOCHAILORT

Loch Ailort

LOCHEILSIDE

SPEAN
BRIDGE

ROY
BRIDGE

TULLOCH

CORPACH
BANAVIE
PIER

Loch Eil
BANAVIE

Loch Shiel

FORT WILLIAM

+ Ben Nevis

Loch Treig

Summit
CORROUR

Loch
Ossian

C

Loch Sunart

BALLACHULISH
FERRY

RANNOCH

Loch Laidon

KENTALLEN

BALLACHULISH (GLENCOE)

D

DUROR

Loch Linnhe

GORTAN*

APPIN

CREAGAN

Loch Tulla

BRIDGE OF ORCHY

Loch Creran

BARCALDINE SIDING

Loch Etive

Summit

E

BENDERLOCH

NORTH CONNEL

CONNEL
FERRY
ACH-NA-CLOICH

TYNDRUM

Summit

Summit
TAYNUILT

OBAN

LOCH AWE
DALMALLY

CRIANLARICH

FALLS OF CRUACHAN PLATFORM*

Loch Awe

F

ARGYLLSHIRE

ARDLUI

Loch Avich

Loch Lomond

Loch Fyne

G

ARROCHAR & TARBET

MAP 29

MAP 33

LEGEND FOR **MAP 32**
A Former pier branch

1 MORAR: Home to West Word community newspaper
2 GLENFINNAN: Home to the GLENFINNAN STATION
  MUSEUM with a dining car and holiday accommodation
  available in a converted sleeping car.
  www.glenfinnanstationmuseum.co.uk
3 Part of the GREAT GLEN WAY. www.greatglenway.com
4 INVERGARRY: Part of site now a Forestry Commission car
  park, part being restored as a static museum.

www.stationproject.org.uk
5 GAIRLOCHY: Site part of the Gairlochy Holiday Park.
  www.theghp.co.uk
6 SPEAN BRIDGE: Former station building now a restaurant.
  www.oldstationrestaurant.co.uk
7 TULLOCH: Former station building now an outdoor activities
  hostel. www.stationlodge.co.uk

MAP 33A

MAP 29A

MALLAIG
MORAR
Loch Morar
ARISAIG
BEASDALE
LOCHAILORT
Loch Ailort
Loch Eilt
GLENFINNAN
LOCHEILSIDE
LOCH EIL OUTWARD BOUND
Loch Eil
CORPACH
BANAVIE
FORT WILLIAM
Loch Shiel
+ Ben Nevis

Loch Quoich
Loch Arkaig
Loch Garry
Loch Oich
Loch Lochy
Loch Lochy

SPEAN BRIDGE
ROY BRIDGE
TULLOCH
Loch Treig
Summit
CORROUR
Loch Ossian
RANNOCH
Loch Laidon
Loch Tulla
BRIDGE OF ORCHY
Summit
UPPER TYNDRUM
TYNDRUM LOWER
CRIANLARICH
ARDLUI
Loch Lomond
ARROCHAR & TARBET

Loch Sunart
Loch Linnhe
A828
Loch Creran
Loch Etive
CONNEL FERRY
Summit
OBAN
TAYNUILT
FALLS OF CRUACHAN
LOCH AWE
DALMALLY
Loch Awe
Loch Avich
Loch Fyne

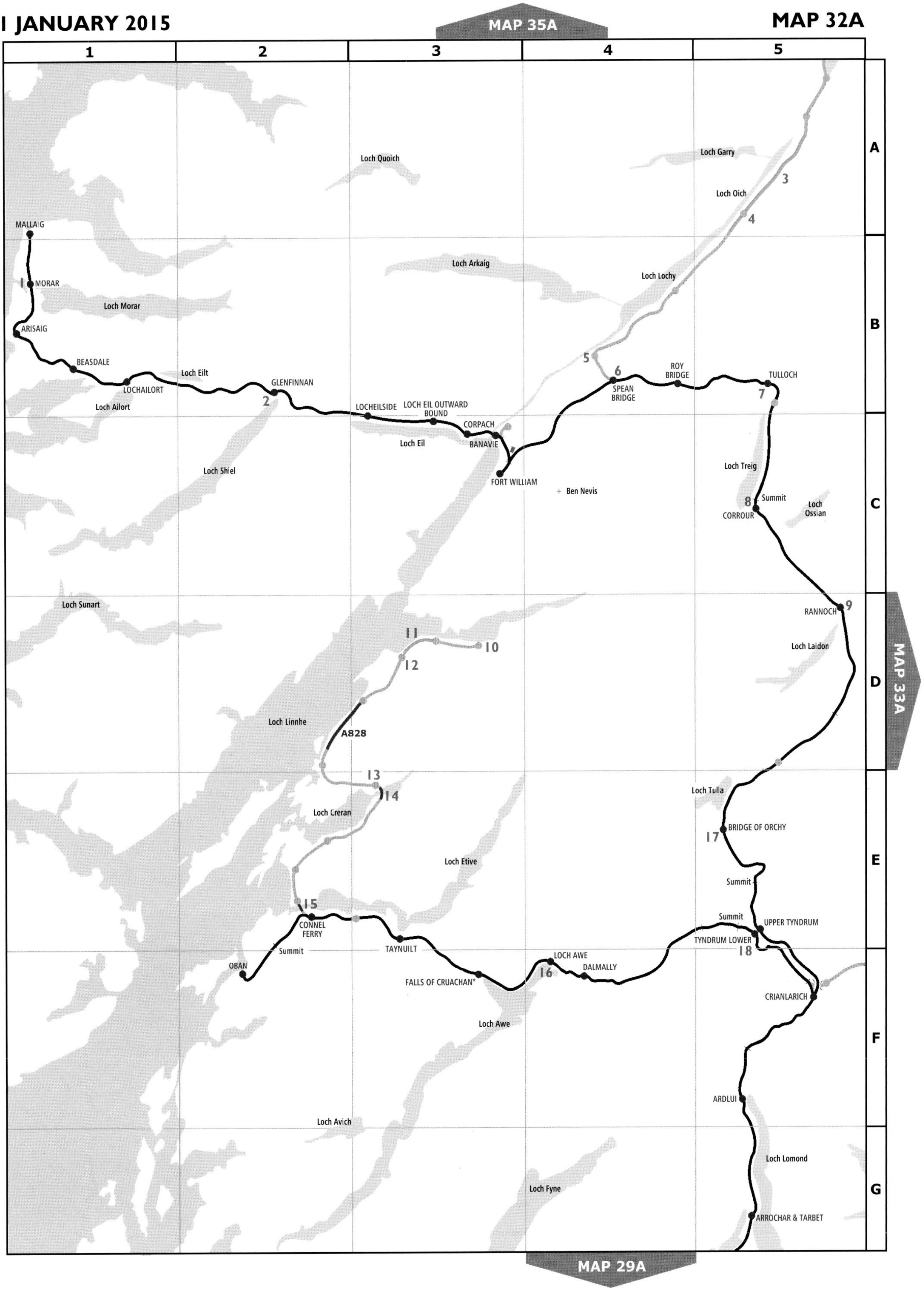

LEGEND FOR MAP 32A

8 CORROUR: Former station building now a restaurant and holiday accommodation. www.corrour-station-house-restaurant.co.uk
9 RANNOCH: Former station building now a tearoom, gift shop and visitor centre
10 BALLACHULISH (GLENCOE): Station building now Ballachulish Medical Practice

11 Part of NATIONAL CYCLE NETWORK. www.sustrans.org.uk
12 KENTALLEN: Now part of hotel. www.hollytreehotel.co.uk
13 CREAGAN: Station building and converted railway cottages now part of a caravan park. www.appinholidayhomes.co.uk
14 Creagan Viaduct: Rebuilt as A828 roadbridge
15 Connel Bridge: Now in use as A828 roadbridge

16 LOCH AWE: Holiday accommodation available in a converted carriage. www.scotlandrailholiday.com
17 BRIDGE OF ORCHY: Former station building now a West Highland Way bunkhouse. www.westhighlandwaysleeper.co.uk
18 TYNDRUM LOWER: Former goods yard now a campsite and hostel. www.tyndrumbytheway.com

MAP 33

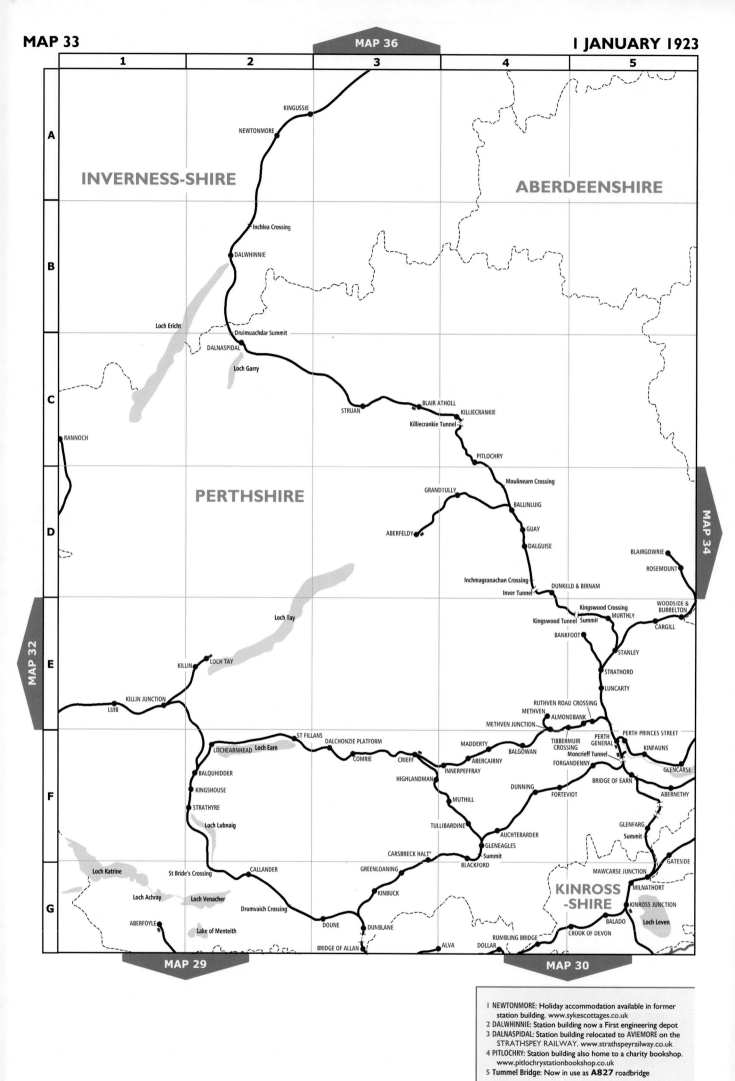

MAP 36

MAP 34

MAP 32

| 1 | 2 | 3 | 4 | 5 |

INVERNESS-SHIRE

ABERDEENSHIRE

A

KINGUSSIE
NEWTONMORE

B

Inchlea Crossing
DALWHINNIE
Loch Ericht
Druimuachdar Summit
DALNASPIDAL
Loch Garry

C

RANNOCH
STRUAN
BLAIR ATHOLL
KILLIECRANKIE
Killiecrankie Tunnel
PITLOCHRY

PERTHSHIRE

Moulinearn Crossing
GRANDTULLY
BALLINLUIG

D

ABERFELDY
GUAY
DALGUISE

BLAIRGOWRIE
ROSEMOUNT

Inchmagranachan Crossing
DUNKELD & BIRNAM
Inver Tunnel
WOODSIDE & BURRELTON

Kingswood Crossing
Kingswood Tunnel Summit MURTHLY
CARGILL

Loch Tay
BANKFOOT
STANLEY
STRATHORD

E

KILLIN LOCH TAY
LUNCARTY

KILLIN JUNCTION
RUTHVEN ROAD CROSSING
LUIB
METHVEN ALMONDBANK
METHVEN JUNCTION
PERTH PRINCES STREET

ST FILLANS
DALCHONZIE PLATFORM
MADDERTY
TIBBERMUIR CROSSING
PERTH GENERAL
LOCHEARNHEAD Loch Earn
BALGOWAN
KINFAUNS
COMRIE CRIEFF
ABERCAIRNY
Moncrieff Tunnel
BALQUHIDDER
INNERPEFFRAY
FORGANDENNY
GLENCARSE

F

HIGHLANDMAN
DUNNING
KINGSHOUSE
FORTEVIOT
BRIDGE OF EARN
STRATHYRE
MUTHILL
ABERNETHY
Loch Lubnaig
TULLIBARDINE
GLENFARG
AUCHTERARDER Summit
CARSBRECK HALT*
GLENEAGLES
Loch Katrine
St Bride's Crossing CALLANDER
GREENLOANING
Summit
GATESIDE
BLACKFORD
MAWCARSE JUNCTION

G

Loch Achray Loch Venacher
KINBUCK
MILNATHORT
Drumvaich Crossing
KINROSS -SHIRE
KINROSS JUNCTION
ABERFOYLE Lake of Menteith
DOUNE DUNBLANE
BALADO Loch Leven
RUMBLING BRIDGE
CROOK OF DEVON
BRIDGE OF ALLAN ALVA DOLLAR

MAP 29

MAP 30

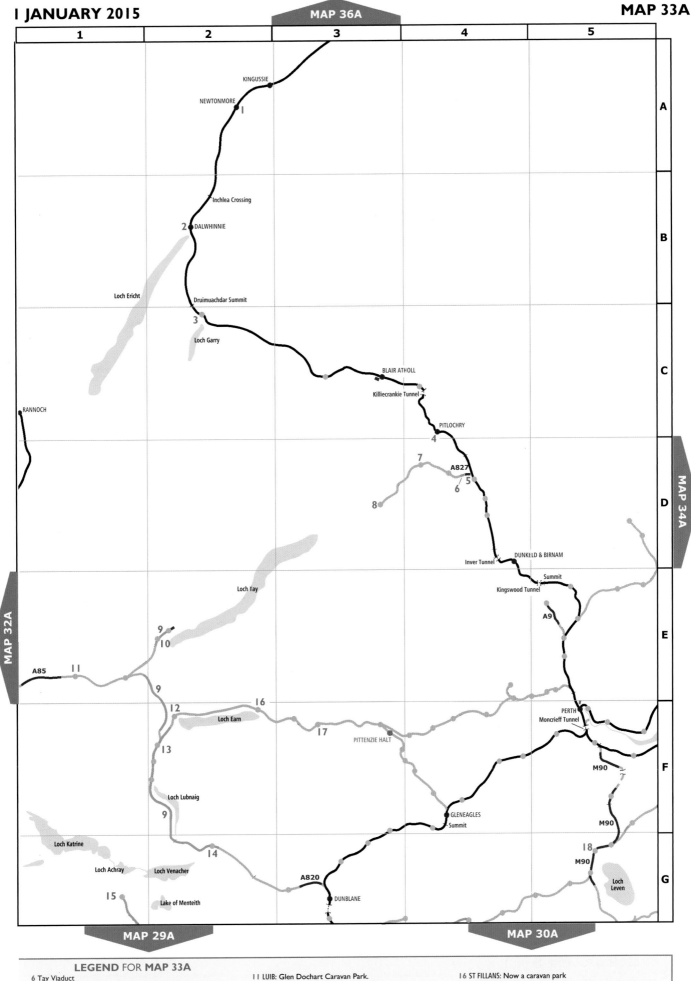

MAP 34A

MAP 32A

MAP 29A

MAP 30A

KINGUSSIE
NEWTONMORE
1
Inchlea Crossing
2 DALWHINNIE
Loch Ericht
Druimuachdar Summit
3
Loch Garry
BLAIR ATHOLL
Killiecrankie Tunnel
PITLOCHRY
4
RANNOCH
7
A827
5
6
8
DUNKELD & BIRNAM
Inver Tunnel
Summit
Loch Tay
Kingswood Tunnel
A9
9
10
A85 11
9
12
16
Loch Earn
17
PITTENZIE HALT
PERTH
Moncrieff Tunnel
13
Loch Lubnaig
M90
9
M90
Loch Katrine
14
GLENEAGLES
Summit
18
Loch Achray
Loch Venacher
M90
Loch Leven
15
Lake of Menteith
A820
DUNBLANE

LEGEND FOR MAP 33A

6 Tay Viaduct
7 GRANDTULLY: Scottish Canoe Association campsite.
   www.canoescotland.org
8 ABERFELDY: Site cleared as car park. 1939 Barclay saddle tank
   on track section outside Dewar's distillery
9 Part of the ROB ROY WAY. www.robroyway.com
10 KILLIN: Site cleared as car park

11 LUIB: Glen Dochart Caravan Park.
   www.glendochart-caravanpark.co.uk
12 LOCHEARNHEAD: Station building now Lochearnhead Scout
   Station
13 BALQUHIDDER: In Balquhidder Braes Holiday Park.
   www.balquhidderbraes.co.uk
14 CALLANDER: Site cleared as car park
15 ABERFOYLE: Site cleared as car park

16 ST FILLANS: Now a caravan park
17 COMRIE: In Comrie Holiday Park. www.comriecaravans.co.uk
18 MILNATHORT: Part of station platforms and trackbed now a
   footbridge over the North Queich rivulet

MAP 34

MAP 37

1 JANUARY 1923

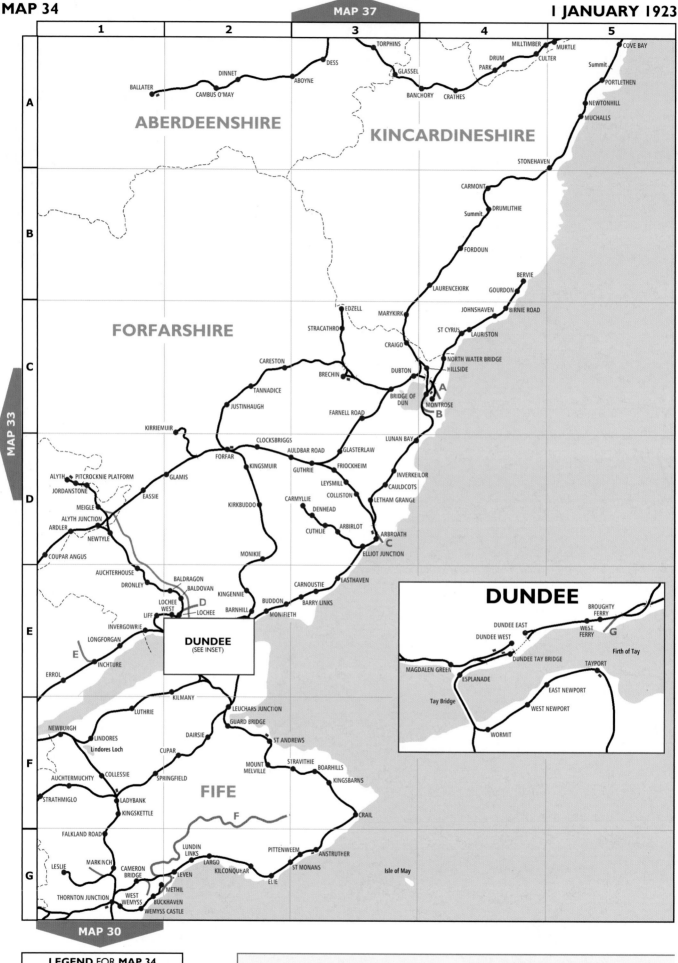

MAP 33

MAP 30

DUNDEE

ABERDEENSHIRE

KINCARDINESHIRE

FORFARSHIRE

FIFE

BALLATER
DINNET
CAMBUS O'MAY
ABOYNE
DESS
GLASSEL
TORPHINS
BANCHORY
CRATHES
MILLTIMBER
DRUM
PARK
CULTER
MURTLE
COVE BAY
Summit
PORTLETHEN
NEWTONHILL
MUCHALLS
STONEHAVEN
CARMONT
Summit
DRUMLITHIE
FORDOUN
BERVIE
LAURENCEKIRK
GOURDON
JOHNSHAVEN
BIRNIE ROAD
MARYKIRK
ST CYRUS
LAURISTON
EDZELL
STRACATHRO
CRAIGO
NORTH WATER BRIDGE
HILLSIDE
DUBTON
A
MONTROSE
B
CARESTON
BRECHIN
BRIDGE OF DUN
TANNADICE
JUSTINHAUGH
FARNELL ROAD
LUNAN BAY
KIRRIEMUIR
CLOCKSBRIGGS
AULDBAR ROAD
GLASTERLAW
ALYTH PITCROCKNIE PLATFORM
FORFAR
KINGSMUIR
GUTHRIE
FRIOCKHEIM
JORDANSTONE
GLAMIS
LEYSMILL
INVERKEILOR
MEIGLE
EASSIE
CAULDCOTS
ALYTH JUNCTION
KIRKBUDDO
CARMYLLIE
COLLISTON
LETHAM GRANGE
ARDLER
DENHEAD
NEWTYLE
CUTHLIE
ARBIRLOT
ARBROATH
COUPAR ANGUS
MONIKIE
C
ELLIOT JUNCTION
AUCHTERHOUSE
BALDRAGON
BALDOVAN
CARNOUSTIE
EASTHAVEN
DRONLEY
KINGENNIE
LOCHEE WEST
D
LIFF
LOCHEE
BARNHILL
BUDDON
BARRY LINKS
INVERGOWRIE
MONIFIETH
LONGFORGAN
E
DUNDEE (SEE INSET)
INCHTURE
ERROL
KILMANY
LUTHRIE
LEUCHARS JUNCTION
NEWBURGH
GUARD BRIDGE
LINDORES
DAIRSIE
ST ANDREWS
Lindores Loch
CUPAR
AUCHTERMUCHTY
COLLESSIE
SPRINGFIELD
MOUNT MELVILLE
STRAVITHIE
BOARHILLS
STRATHMIGLO
LADYBANK
KINGSBARNS
KINGSKETTLE
F
FALKLAND ROAD
CRAIL
LUNDIN LINKS
PITTENWEEM
LESLIE
MARKINCH
LARGO
ANSTRUTHER
CAMERON BRIDGE
KILCONQUHAR
ST MONANS
LEVEN
ELIE
Isle of May
THORNTON JUNCTION
METHIL
WEST WEMYSS
BUCKHAVEN
WEMYSS CASTLE

DUNDEE

DUNDEE EAST
DUNDEE WEST
BROUGHTY FERRY
WEST FERRY
G
MAGDALEN GREEN
DUNDEE TAY BRIDGE
Firth of Tay
TAYPORT
ESPLANADE
EAST NEWPORT
Tay Bridge
WEST NEWPORT
WORMIT

LEGEND FOR MAP 34
A North Harbour branch
B South Harbour branch
C Harbour branch
D Maryfield branch
E Former INCHTURE TRAMWAY [CR]
F Lochty branch
G Pier branch

1 BALLATER: Now tourist information office and visitor centre. www.royal-deeside.org.uk
2 Parts of the DEESIDE WAY (CULTER – CRATHES not continuous). www.cyclegrampian.co.uk
3 ABOYNE: Now shops; tunnel west of station used as a shooting range
4 BANCHORY: Site cleared as a park and car park; engine shed now a garden equipment centre
5 ROYAL DEESIDE RAILWAY. www.deeside-railway.co.uk
6 LAURISTON: Site now a caravan park
7 MONTROSE: Former Caledonian Railway station building and site now a nursing home and garden
8 CALEDONIAN RAILWAY. www.caledonianrailway.com
9 KIRRIEMUIR: Site landscaped with trackbed now a footpath

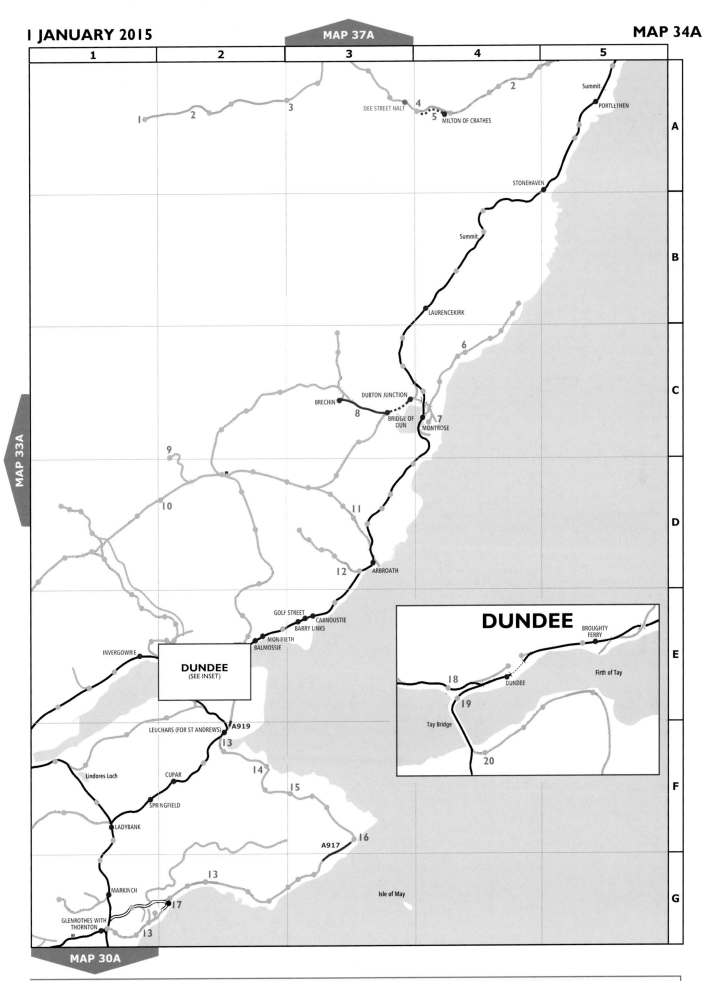

1   2   3   4   5

MAP 33A

MAP 30A

A
B
C
D
E
F
G

Summit
PORTLETHEN
STONEHAVEN
Summit
LAURENCEKIRK
DEE STREET HALT
MILTON OF CRATHES
6
DUBTON JUNCTION
BRECHIN
BRIDGE OF DUN
MONTROSE
ARBROATH
GOLF STREET
CARNOUSTIE
BARRY LINKS
MONIFIETH
BALMOSSIE
INVERGOWRIE
DUNDEE (SEE INSET)
LEUCHARS (FOR ST ANDREWS)
A919
Lindores Loch
CUPAR
SPRINGFIELD
LADYBANK
MARKINCH
GLENROTHES WITH THORNTON
A917
Isle of May

DUNDEE
BROUGHTY FERRY
Firth of Tay
18
19
DUNDEE
Tay Bridge
20

LEGEND FOR MAP 34A

10 GLAMIS: Site now used by the Strathmore Vintage Vehicle Club. www.svvc.co.uk

11 Part of the ST VIGEANS NATURE TRAIL. www.walkscotland.com

12 Part of the ELLIOT NATURE TRAIL. www.walkscotland.com

13 Part of the FIFE COASTAL PATH. www.fifecoastalpath.co.uk

14 ST ANDREWS (closed 1867): Station building now incorporated into the Old Course Hotel. www.oldcoursehotel.co.uk

ST ANDREWS (closed 1969): Site cleared as a car park

15 STRAVITHIE: Now a guest house, complete with converted carriage accommodation. www.theoldstation.co.uk

16 CRAIL: Station building now part of a garden centre

17 LEVEN: Kirkland marshalling yard now the operating base of the KINGDOM OF FIFE RAILWAY PRESERVATION SOCIETY. www.roskotheque.com

18 MAGDALEN GREEN: Station building now a café/restaurant. www.bridgeviewstation.com

19 ESPLANADE: Now the Tay Bridge maintenance centre

20 WORMIT: Former station building rebuilt at BO'NESS on the BO'NESS & KINNEIL RAILWAY. srps.org.uk

MAP 35   **1 JANUARY 1923**

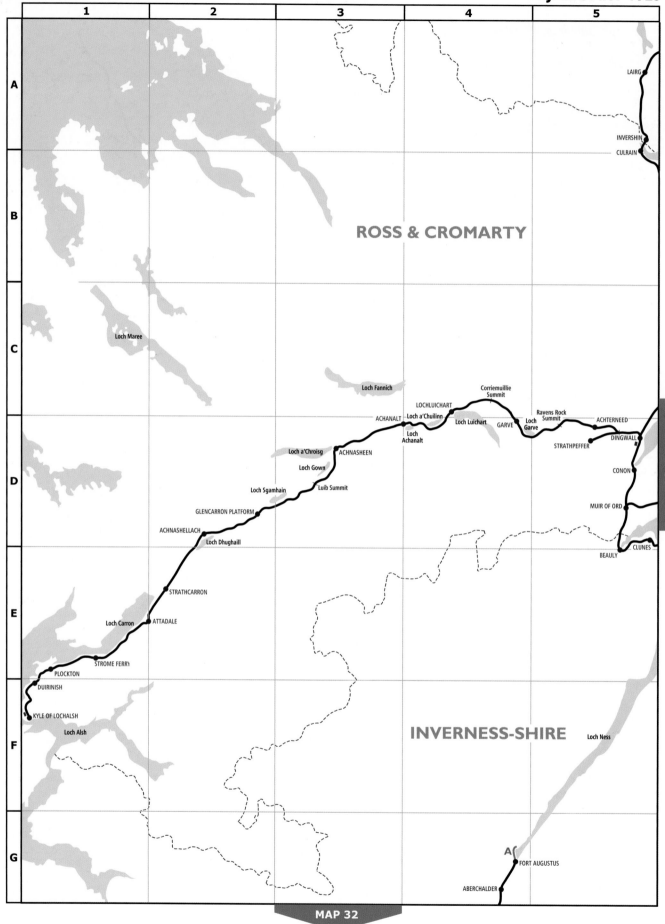

ROSS & CROMARTY

INVERNESS-SHIRE

MAP 36

MAP 32

LAIRG
INVERSHIN
CULRAIN

Loch Maree

Loch Fannich
Corriemuillie Summit
LOCHLUICHART
Loch a'Chuilinn
ACHANALT
Loch Achanalt
Loch Luichart
GARVE
Loch Garve
Ravens Rock Summit
ACHTERNEED
DINGWALL
STRATHPEFFER
CONON
Loch a'Chroisg
ACHNASHEEN
Loch Gown
Loch Sgamhain
Luib Summit
MUIR OF ORD
GLENCARRON PLATFORM
CLUNES
ACHNASHELLACH
Loch Dhughaill
BEAULY

STRATHCARRON
Loch Carron
ATTADALE
STROME FERRY
PLOCKTON
DUIRINISH
KYLE OF LOCHALSH
Loch Alsh
Loch Ness

A
FORT AUGUSTUS
ABERCHALDER

LEGEND FOR **MAP 35**
A Former pier branch

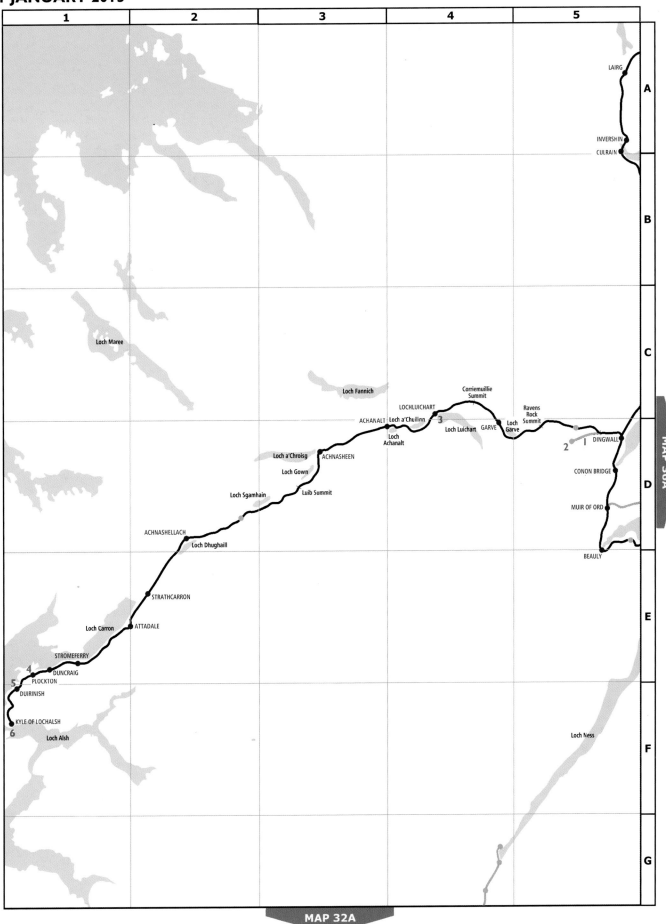

MAP 36A

MAP 32A

MAP 36
MAP 38

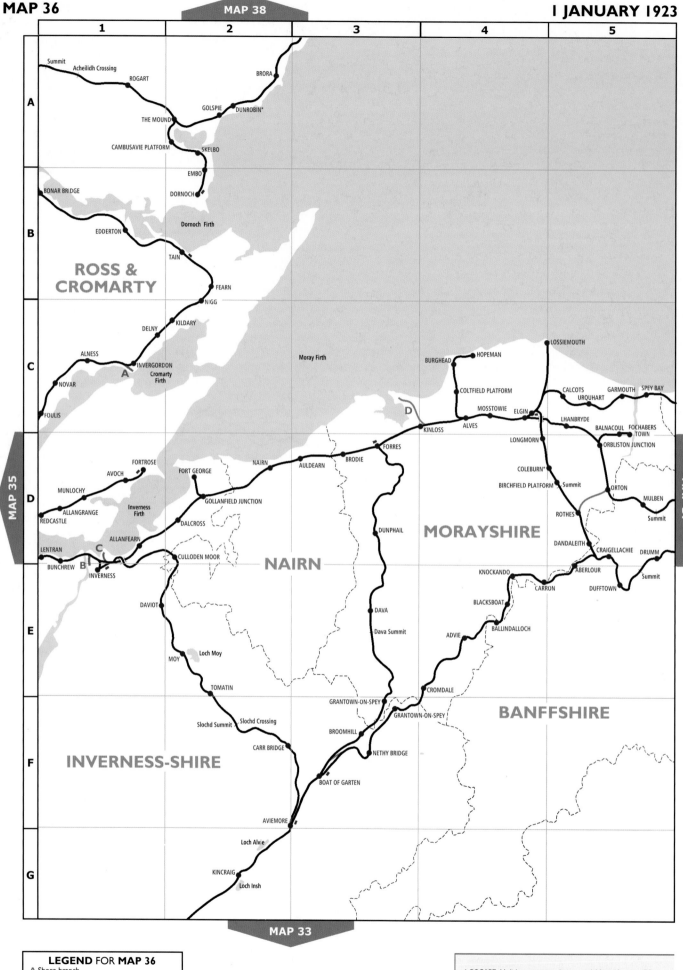

MAP 35

MAP 37

MAP 33

ROSS & CROMARTY

MORAYSHIRE

NAIRN

BANFFSHIRE

INVERNESS-SHIRE

Summit
Acheilidh Crossing
ROGART
BRORA
GOLPIE
DUNROBIN*
THE MOUND
SKELBO
CAMBUSAVIE PLATFORM
EMBO
DORNOCH
BONAR BRIDGE
EDDERTON
TAIN
Dornoch Firth
FEARN
NIGG
KILDARY
DELNY
ALNESS
INVERGORDON
NOVAR
Cromarty Firth
FOULIS
Moray Firth
LOSSIEMOUTH
BURGHEAD
HOPEMAN
COLTFIELD PLATFORM
CALCOTS
GARMOUTH
SPEY BAY
URQUHART
MOSSTOWIE
ELGIN
LHANBRYDE
BALNACOUL
FOCHABERS TOWN
KINLOSS
ALVES
LONGMORN
ORBLISTON JUNCTION
FORRES
COLEBURN*
FORTROSE
AVOCH
FORT GEORGE
NAIRN
AULDEARN
BRODIE
BIRCHFIELD PLATFORM
Summit
ORTON
MUNLOCHY
GOLLANFIELD JUNCTION
MULBEN
ALLANGRANGE
Inverness Firth
DALCROSS
ROTHES
Summit
REDCASTLE
DUNPHAIL
DANDALEITH
CRAIGELLACHIE
DRUMM
LENTRAN
ALLANFEARN
CULLODEN MOOR
KNOCKANDO
ABERLOUR
BUNCHREW
INVERNESS
DAVA
BLACKSBOAT
CARRON
DUFFTOWN
Summit
DAVIOT
DAVA
Dava Summit
ADVIE
BALLINDALLOCH
MOY
Loch Moy
CROMDALE
TOMATIN
GRANTOWN-ON-SPEY
GRANTOWN-ON-SPEY
Slochd Summit
Slochd Crossing
BROOMHILL
CARR BRIDGE
NETHY BRIDGE
BOAT OF GARTEN
AVIEMORE
Loch Alvie
KINCRAIG
Loch Insh

LEGEND FOR MAP 36
A Shore branch
B Canal branch
C Harbour branch
D Former FINDHORN RAILWAY

1 ROGART: Holiday accommodation available in three ex-BR carriages. www.sleeperzzz.com
2 DORNOCH: Station building now a chiropractic clinic
3 TAIN: Permission granted for conversion of former station building into a restaurant
4 DAVA WAY. www.davaway.org.uk
5 HOPEMAN: Station building now office for caravan park on station site

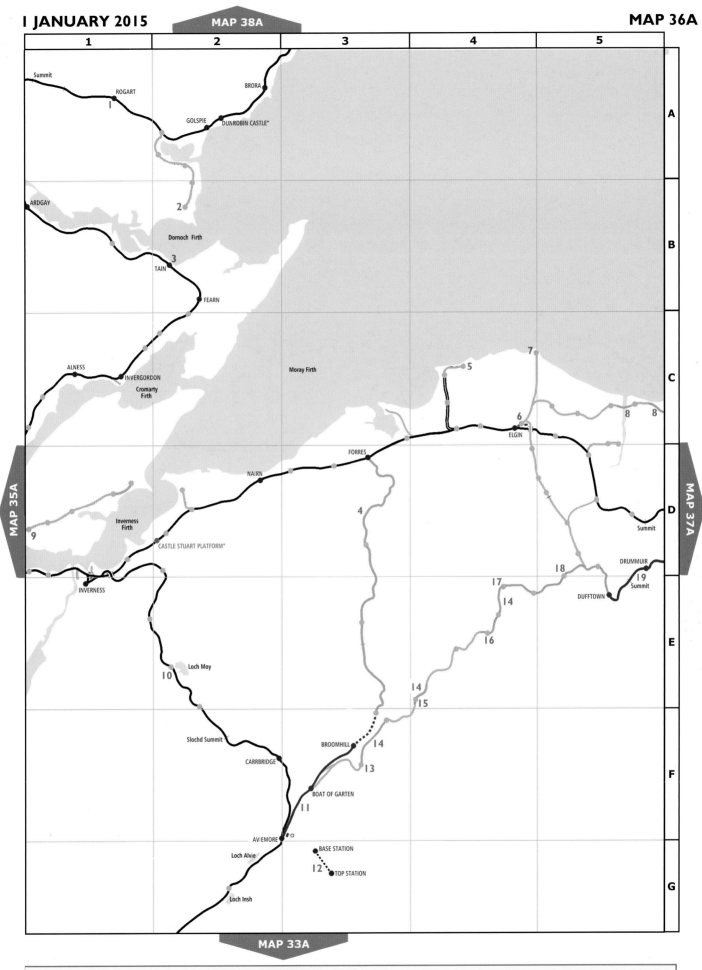

Summit
ROGART
BRORA
GOLSPIE
DUNROBIN CASTLE*
ARDGAY
Dornoch Firth
TAIN
FEARN
ALNESS
INVERGORDON
Cromarty Firth
Moray Firth
ELGIN
FORRES
NAIRN
Inverness Firth
CASTLE STUART PLATFORM*
INVERNESS
Loch Moy
Summit
DRUMMUIR
Summit
DUFFTOWN
Slochd Summit
BROOMHILL
CARRBRIDGE
BOAT OF GARTEN
AVIEMORE
Loch Alvie
BASE STATION
TOP STATION
Loch Insh

LEGEND FOR MAP 36A

6 ELGIN (later ELGIN EAST): Station building now offices
7 LOSSIEMOUTH: Site cleared as car park and garden centre
8 Part of the MORAY COAST TRAIL. www.morayways.org.uk
9 REDCASTLE: Station building now a training station for young
   adults with learning disabilities. www.nansenhighland.co.uk
10 MOY: Holiday accommodation in former station building.
    www.holidayatmoy.com
11 STRATHSPEY RAILWAY. www.strathspeyrailway.co.uk

12 2m gauge CAIRNGORM FUNICULAR RAILWAY.
    www.cairngormmountain.com
13 NETHY BRIDGE: Station building now an outdoor leisure
    activities bunkhouse. www.nethy.org
14 Part of the SPEYSIDE WAY. www.speysideway.org
15 CROMDALE: Holiday accommodation available in a converted
    carriage. www.cromdalestation.co.uk

16 BALLINDALLOCH: Station building now an outdoor leisure
    activities hostel. www.ldwa.org.uk
17 KNOCKANDO: Renamed TAMDHU for use as Tamdhu
    Distillery visitor centre (currently empty)
18 ABERLOUR: Tearoom and tourist information office
19 KEITH & DUFFTOWN RAILWAY.
    www.keith-dufftown-railway.co.uk

MAP 37

	1	2	3	4	5
A					
B					
C					
D					
E					
F					
G					

MAP 36

MAP 34

FINDOCHTY
PORTKNOCKIE
PORTESSIE
CULLEN
BUCKIE
TOCHIENEAL
GLASSAUGH
PORTSOY
BANFF GOLF CLUB HOUSE HALT
BRIDGEFOOT HALT
BANFF
MACDUFF
ORDENS PLATFORM*
PORT GORDON
BUCKPOOL
LADYSBRIDGE
BANFF BRIDGE
BANFFSHIRE
TILLYNAUGHT
CORNHILL
KING EDWARD
GLENBARRY
KEITH
KNOCK
PLAIDY
KEITH TOWN
GRANGE
TURRIFF
AUCHINDACHY
CAIRNIE JUNCTION
ROTHIEMAY
AUCHTERLESS
HUNTLY
FYVIE
ROTHIE-NORMAN
GARTLY
WARTLE
Summit
WARDHOUSE
KENNETHMONT
INSCH
OYNE
FINGASK PLATFORM
OLDMELDRUM
PITCAPLE
INVERAMSAY
LETHENTY
ABERDEENSHIRE
INVERURIE
ALFORD
KINTORE
WHITEHOUSE
MONYMUSK
KENMAY
KINALDIE
PITMEDDEN
PARKHILL
TILLYFOURIE
DYCE
STONEYWOOD
BANKHEAD
WOODSIDE
BUCKSBURN
DON STREET
PERSLEY
KITTYBREWSTER
HUTCHEON STREET
SCHOOLHILL
ABERDEEN JOINT
HOLBURN STREET
RUTHRIESTON
LUMPHANAN
CULTS
PITFODELS
TORPHINS
BIELDSIDE
MILLTIMBER
WEST CULTS
CULTER
MURTLE
COVE BAY
DINNET
ABOYNE
DESS
GLASSEL
DRUM
PARK
Summit
PORTLETHEN

FRASERBURGH
KIRKTON BRIDGE PLATFORM
PHILORTH BRIDGE HALT
PHILORTH HALT*
CAIRNBULG
RATHEN
ST COMBS
LONMAY
MORMOND
STRICHEN
BRUCKLAY
MINTLAW
NEWSEAT
MAUD JUNCTION
LONGSIDE
INVERUGIE
PETERHEAD
A
AUCHNAGATT
BODDAM
LONGHAVEN
ARNAGE
HATTON
BULLERS O' BUCHAN PLATFORM
PITLURG
CRUDEN BAY
ELLON
AUCHMACOY
ESSLEMONT
LOGIERIEVE
UDNY
Summit
NEWMACHAR
B

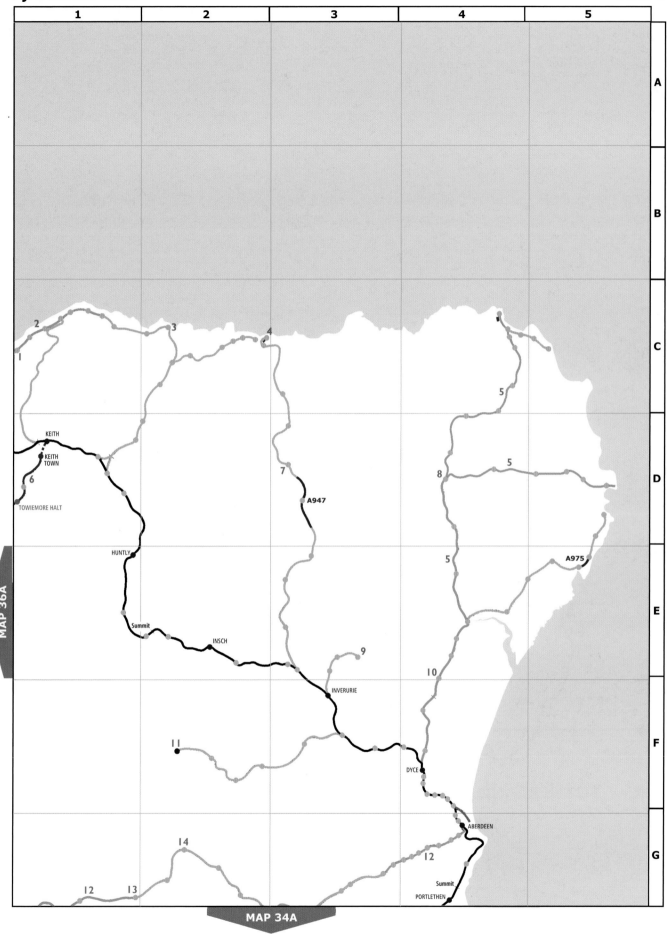

MAP 36A

MAP 34A

LEGEND FOR MAP 37A

1 PORT GORDON (later PORTGORDON): Part of site now a bowling club green

2 Part of the MORAY COAST TRAIL. www.morayways.org.uk

3 PORTSOY: Station building now Portsoy scout hut

4 MACDUFF: Station buildings now home to Seaway Marine boat-builders and chandlery

5 FORMARTINE AND BUCHAN WAY. www.cyclegrampian.co.uk

6 KEITH & DUFFTOWN RAILWAY. www.keith-dufftown-railway.co.uk

7 TURRIFF: Site now a caravan park. www.turriffcaravanpark.com

8 MAUD JUNCTION: Home to MAUD RAILWAY MUSEUM. www.friendsofmaud.org.uk

9 OLDMELDRUM: Station building re-erected at MILTON OF CRATHES on the ROYAL DEESIDE RAILWAY. www.deeside-railway.co.uk

10 UDNY: Former goods yard now a football pitch

11 ALFORD: Terminus of 2ft gauge ALFORD VALLEY RAILWAY. www.alfordvalleyrailway.org.uk

12 Parts of the DEESIDE WAY. www.cyclegrampian.co.uk

13 ABOYNE: Now shops; tunnel west of station used as a shooting range

14 LUMPHANAN: Site cleared as a car park

MAP 38

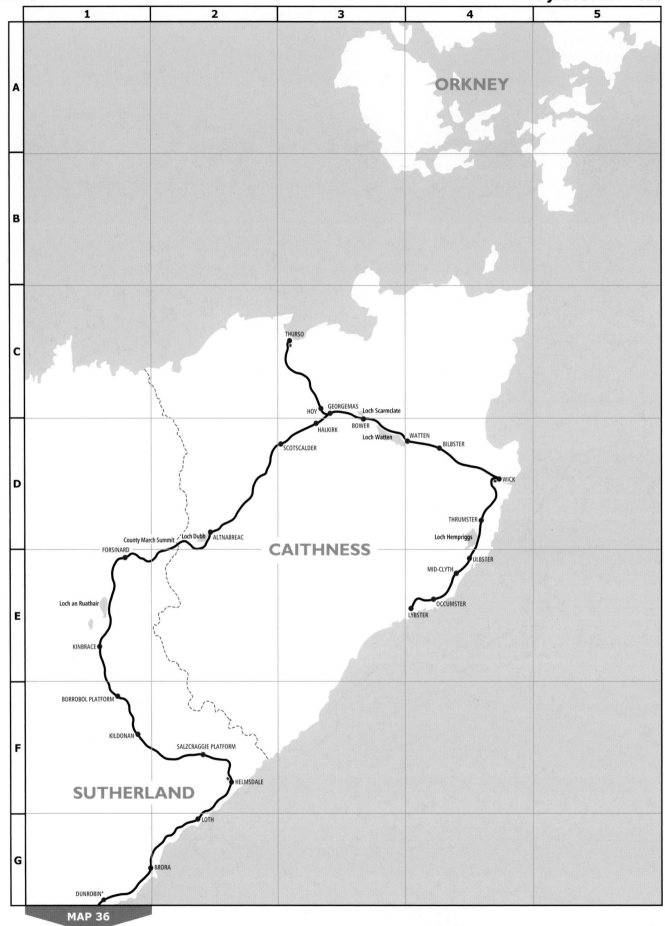

ORKNEY

THURSO

GEORGEMAS
HOY   Loch Scarmclate
HALKIRK   BOWER
SCOTSCALDER   Loch Watten   WATTEN
  BILBSTER

WICK

THRUMSTER

County March Summit   Loch Dubh   ALTNABREAC   Loch Hempriggs
FORSINARD   CAITHNESS   ULBSTER
  MID-CLYTH

Loch an Ruathair

  OCCUMSTER
  LYBSTER

KINBRACE

BORROBOL PLATFORM

KILDONAN   SALZCRAGGIE PLATFORM

SUTHERLAND   HELMSDALE

  LOTH

  BRORA

DUNROBIN*

MAP 36

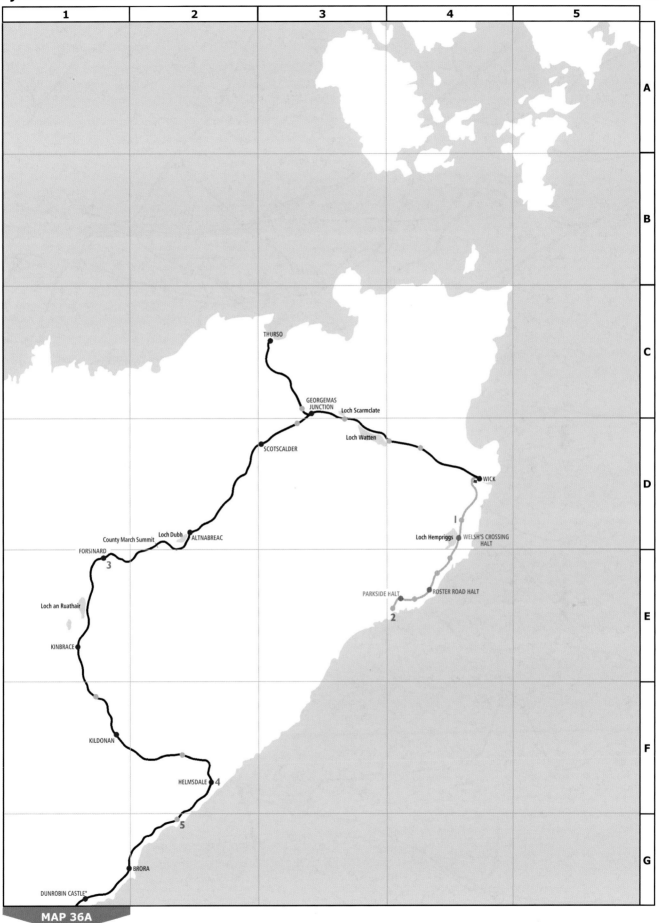

THURSO

GEORGEMAS JUNCTION
Loch Scarmclate
Loch Watten
SCOTSCALDER

WICK

County March Summit
Loch Dubh
ALTNABREAC
FORSINARD
3

Loch Hempriggs
WELSH'S CROSSING HALT

Loch an Ruathair

PARKSIDE HALT
ROSTER ROAD HALT
2

KINBRACE

KILDONAN

HELMSDALE
4

5

BRORA

DUNROBIN CASTLE*

MAP 36A

STATIONS
1. WEST HAMPSTEAD
2. WEST END LANE
3. SOUTH HAMPSTEAD
4. ST QUINTIN PARK & WORMWOOD SCRUBBS
5. WESTBOURNE PARK
6. ROYAL OAK
7. BISHOP'S ROAD

TO SIMPLIFY THE MAP, TUBE RAILWAYS ARE OMITTED AND METROPOLITAN AND DISTRICT COVERED SECTIONS ARE SHOWN AS SURFACE LINES

LEGEND FOR **MAP 39**
A Mitre Bridge branch
B Former Hammersmith & Chiswick passenger branch
C Battersea Wharf branch
D Chelsea Dock siding

1 2 3 4 5

A B C D E F G

BELMONT

HARROW & WEALDSTONE

KENTON

HENDON

HARROW-ON-THE-HILL

SOUTH KENTON

NORTH WEMBLEY

CRICKLEWOOD

WEST HAMPSTEAD THAMESLINK

FINCHLEY ROAD & FROGNAL

HAMPSTEAD HEATH

GOSPEL OAK

NORTHOLT PARK

SUDBURY HILL HARROW

SUDBURY & HARROW ROAD

WEMBLEY STADIUM

WEMBLEY STADIUM

WEST HAMPSTEAD

SOUTH RUISLIP

WEMBLEY CENTRAL

BRONDESBURY

HAVERSTOCK HILL Tunnel

GREENFORD

STONEBRIDGE PARK

BRONDESBURY PARK

KENSAL RISE

QUEENS PARK (LONDON)

KILBURN HIGH ROAD

SOUTH HAMPSTEAD

HARLESDEN

WILLESDEN JUNCTION

KENSAL GREEN

SOUTH GREENFORD

CASTLE BAR PARK

PARK ROYAL WEST

Kensal Green Tunnels

Lords Tunnel

MARYLEBONE

DRAYTON GREEN

EALING BROADWAY

ACTON MAIN LINE

PADDINGTON

BOND STREET [2017]

WEST EALING

ACTON CENTRAL 1

Tunnel

SOUTHALL

HANWELL

SOUTH ACTON

WHITE CITY

SHEPHERD'S BUSH

KENSINGTON OLYMPIA

VICTORIA

BRENTFORD

GUNNERSBURY

KEW BRIDGE

CHISWICK

WEST BROMPTON

2

SYON LANE

ISLEWORTH

KEW GARDENS

BARNES BRIDGE

3

IMPERIAL WHARF

BATTERSEA PARK

QUEENSTOWN ROAD

BARNES

BATTERSEA

HOUNSLOW

RICHMOND

NORTH SHEEN

MORTLAKE

CLAPHAM JUNCTION

WANDSWORTH TOWN

PUTNEY

WANDSWORTH COMMON

ST MARGARETS

WHITTON

TWICKENHAM

EARLSFIELD

BALHAM

STRAWBERRY HILL

WIMBLEDON PARK STAFF HALT*

FULWELL

HAYDONS ROAD

4

TOOTING

KEMPTON PARK

TEDDINGTON

WIMBLEDON

MERTON PARK

A24

MERTON ABBEY

HAMPTON

KINGSTON

HAMPTON WICK

NORBITON

WIMBLEDON CHASE

MORDEN ROAD

MITCHAM EASTFIELDS

5

HAMPTON COURT

BERRYLANDS

NEW MALDEN

RAYNES PARK

SOUTH MERTON

MITCHAM

THAMES DITTON

SURBITON

MOTSPUR PARK

MORDEN SOUTH

MITCHAM JUNCTION

HERSHAM

ESHER

HINCHLEY WOOD

MALDEN MANOR

WORCESTER PARK

ST HELIER

SUTTON COMMON

HACKBRIDGE

TO AVOID CONFUSION THE ONLY LONDON UNDERGROUND LINES SHOWN ARE CONVERSIONS FROM THE PRE-1923 NATIONAL NETWORK

LEGEND FOR **MAP 39A**

1 ACTON CENTRAL: Former station building now the Station House pub. www.thestationhousew3.com

2 OSTERLEY: Original station building (closed 1934) now the Osterley Bookshop

3 BARNES BRIDGE: Former ticket office now a physiotherapy and sports clinic

4 2ft gauge HAMPTON & KEMPTON WATERWORKS RAILWAY. www.hamptonkemptonrailway.org.uk

5 LONDON TRAMLINK. www.tfl.gov.uk

MAP 40

GREATER LONDON (EAST)

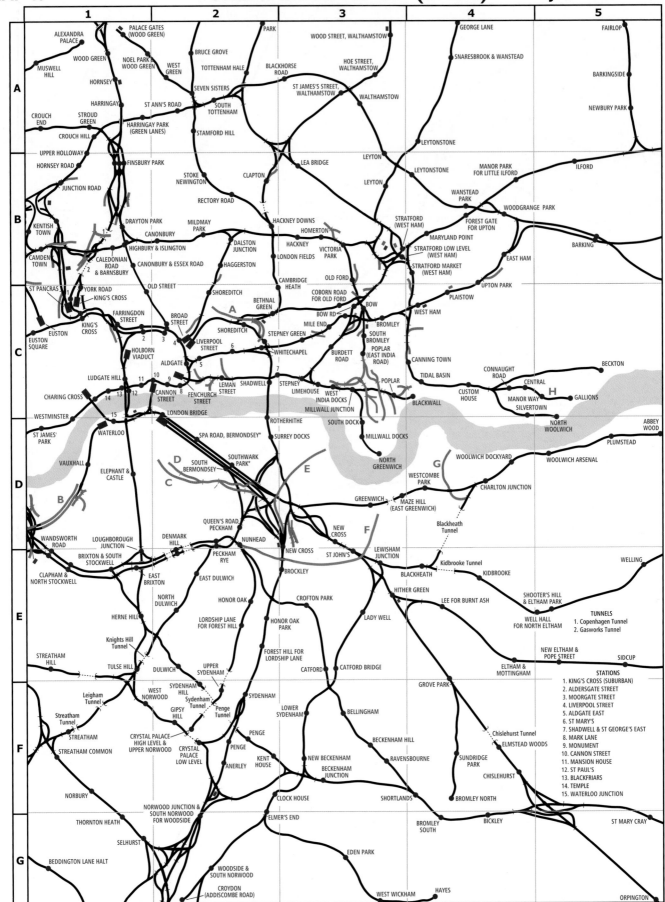

TO SIMPLIFY THE MAP, TUBE RAILWAYS ARE OMITTED AND METROPOLITAN AND DISTRICT COVERED SECTIONS ARE SHOWN AS SURFACE LINES

LEGEND FOR MAP 40

A Bishopsgate branch
B Nine Elms branch
C Bricklayers Arms branch
D Willow Walk branch
E Deptford Wharf branch
F Former Greenwich Park branch
G Angerstein Wharf branch

H CUSTOM HOUSE – GALLIONS services
worked by both the LNER and the
Port of London Authority

TUNNELS
1. Copenhagen Tunnel
2. Gasworks Tunnel

STATIONS
1. KING'S CROSS (SUBURBAN)
2. ALDERSGATE STREET
3. MOORGATE STREET
4. LIVERPOOL STREET
5. ALDGATE EAST
6. ST MARY'S
7. SHADWELL & ST GEORGE'S EAST
8. MARK LANE
9. MONUMENT
10. CANNON STREET
11. MANSION HOUSE
12. ST PAUL'S
13. BLACKFRIARS
14. TEMPLE
15. WATERLOO JUNCTION

TO AVOID CONFUSION THE ONLY LONDON UNDERGROUND LINES SHOWN ARE CONVERSIONS FROM THE PRE-1923 NATIONAL NETWORK

LEGEND FOR MAP 40A

1 ALEXANDRA PALACE (closed 1954): Former station building now a community centre

2 Part of the PARKLAND WALK. www.parkland-walk.org.uk

3 LONDON TRANSPORT MUSEUM. www.ltmuseum.co.uk

4 DOCKLANDS LIGHT RAILWAY. www.dlrlondon.co.uk

5 WATERLOO: Tunnels beneath station home to a multi-purpose arts/music/recreation venue. houseofvans.com

6 DENMARK HILL: Part of the station building rebuilt as the Phoenix pub after a 1980 fire. www.thephoenixwindsorwalk.co.uk

7 LEWISHAM ROAD (closed 1917): Former station building now a second-hand shop

8 LONDON TRAMLINK. www.tfl.gov.uk

Stations list

STATIONS
1. KIRKBY-IN-ASHFIELD
2. NEWSTEAD & ANNESLEY
3. BUTLER'S HILL
4. ILKESTON
5. ILKESTON TOWN
6. ILKESTON JUNCTION & COSSALL
7. KIMBERLEY
8. BULWELL COMMON
9. BASFORD & BULWELL
10. NOTTINGHAM ARKWRIGHT STREET
11. NOTTINGHAM LONDON ROAD HIGH LEVEL
12. NOTTINGHAM LONDON ROAD LOW LEVEL
13. NOTTINGHAM RACE COURSE*
14. NETHERFIELD
15. CARLTON & NETHERFIELD FOR GEDLING & COLWICK
16. GEDLING & CARLTON
17. BURTON JOYCE

CABLE-WORKED INCLINES
A. MIDDLETON INCLINE
B. SHEEP PASTURE INCLINE

Map labels

SHEFFIELD VICTORIA, SHEFFIELD MIDLAND, HEELEY, MILLHOUSES & ECCLESALL, BEAUCHIEF, DORE & TOTLEY, DARNALL FOR HANDSWORTH, WOODHOUSE MILL, WOODHOUSE, BEIGHTON, TREETON, DINNINGTON & LAUGHTON, WALESWOOD, ANSTON, KIVETON PARK, SHIREOAKS, KILLAMARSH, UPPERTHORPE & KILLAMARSH, WORKSOP

TOTLEY TUNNEL, BRADWAY TUNNEL, GRINDLEFORD, DRONFIELD, UNSTONE, BROOMHOUSE TUNNEL, WHITTINGTON, ECKINGTON & RENISHAW, BARROW HILL & STAVELEY WORKS, SPINK HILL FOR MOUNT ST MARY, STAVELEY TOWN, CLOWN, WHITWELL, ELMTON & CRESWELL, CRESWELL & WELBECK

SHEEPBRIDGE & WHITTINGTON MOOR, STAVELEY WORKS, SHEEPBRIDGE & BRIMINGTON, CHESTERFIELD CENTRAL, CHESTERFIELD MARKET PLACE, CHESTERFIELD, ARKWRIGHT TOWN, BOLSOVER, LANGWITH JUNCTION, LANGWITH, PALTERTON & SUTTON, SCARCLIFFE, SHIREBROOK, BOLSOVER TUNNEL, GRASSMOOR, SPRINGWOOD TUNNEL, GLAPWELL, WARSOP, EDWINSTOWE

ROWSLEY, HEATH, CLAY CROSS, CLAY CROSS TUNNEL, ROWTHORN & HARDWICK, PLEASLEY, DARLEY DALE, MATLOCK, HIGH TOR TUNNELS, MATLOCK BATH, WILLERSLEY TUNNEL, CROMFORD, PILSLEY, STRETTON, TIBSHELF TOWN, TIBSHELF & NEWTON, DOE HILL, WHITEBOROUGH, TEVERSALL, TEVERSALL, SKEGBY, MANSFIELD WOODHOUSE, MANSFIELD, SUTTON-IN-ASHFIELD, SUTTON, BLIDWORTH & RAINWORTH, FARNSFIELD

WIRKSWORTH, LEA WOOD TUNNEL, WHATSTANDWELL, WINGFIELD, WINGFIELD TUNNEL, ALFRETON & SOUTH NORMANTON, ALFRETON TUNNEL, WESTHOUSES & BLACKWELL, PINXTON & SELSTON, PINXTON, KIRKBY & PINXTON, KIRKBY-IN-ASHFIELD, HOLLIN WELL & ANNESLEY*, ANNESLEY, NEWSTEAD

AMBERGATE, IDRIDGEHAY, RIPLEY, BUTTERLEY, PYE BRIDGE, PYE HILL & SOMERCOTES, CODNOR PARK & IRONVILLE, CODNOR PARK & SELSTON FOR IRONVILLE & JACKSDALE, CROSSHILL & CODNOR, LINBY, HUCKNALL, HUCKNALL TOWN, BESTWOOD COLLIERY

SHOTTLE, BELPER, DENBY, KILBURN, MILFORD TUNNEL, HAZELWOOD, DUFFIELD, COXBENCH, LITTLE EATON, LANGLEY MILL, HEANOR [LMS], HEANOR [LNER], SHIPLEY GATE, MARLPOOL, EASTWOOD & LANGLEY MILL, NEWTHORPE, WATNALL, KIMBERLEY, AWSWORTH, BASFORD, BULWELL HALL HALT, BULWELL, BULWELL FOREST, DAYBROOK, NEW BASFORD, CARRINGTON, NOTTINGHAM VICTORIA

WEST HALLAM, TROWELL, RADFORD, STANTON GATE, NOTTINGHAM, BREADSALL, DERBY NOTTINGHAM ROAD, DERBY FRIARGATE, STAPLEFORD & SANDIACRE, BEESTON, EDWALTON, MICKLEOVER, DERBY, SPONDON, BORROWASH, DRAYCOTT, SAWLEY, LONG EATON, ATTENBOROUGH, RUDDINGTON, PEAR TREE & NORMANTON

Legend

LEGEND FOR MAP 41
A Cromford & High Peak line

1 **GRINDLEFORD:** Station building now the Grindleford Station Café
2 **SHEFFIELD SUPERTRAM.** www.supertram.com
3 **BARROW HILL:** Railway centre based on the restored roundhouse. www.barrowhill.org.uk
4 Part of the TRANS PENNINE TRAIL. www.transpenninetrail.org.uk
5 **WHITWELL:** Station building rebuilt at BUTTERLEY at the MIDLAND RAILWAY CENTRE
6 **ROWSLEY** (1st station, closed to passengers in 1862): Now shops in the Peak Village shopping complex
7 **PEAK RAIL.** www.peakrail.co.uk
8 Former 2ft gauge ASHOVER LIGHT RAILWAY. www.alrs.org.uk
9 Parts of the PLEASEY TRAILS. www.cycle-trails.co.uk

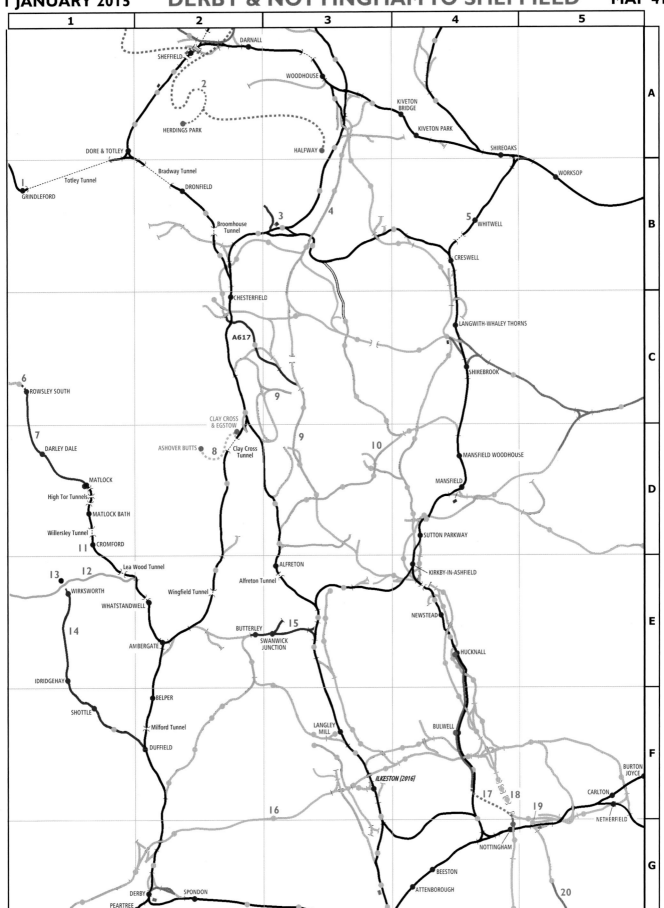

DARNALL
SHEFFIELD
WOODHOUSE
KIVETON BRIDGE
KIVETON PARK
SHIREOAKS
HERDINGS PARK
HALFWAY
DORE & TOTLEY
WORKSOP
1 GRINDLEFORD
Totley Tunnel
Bradway Tunnel
DRONFIELD
Broomhouse Tunnel
3
4
5 WHITWELL
CRESWELL
CHESTERFIELD
LANGWITH-WHALEY THORNS
A617
SHIREBROOK
6 ROWSLEY SOUTH
9
7 DARLEY DALE
CLAY CROSS & EGSTOW
8 ASHOVER BUTTS
Clay Cross Tunnel
9
10 MANSFIELD WOODHOUSE
MATLOCK
High Tor Tunnels
MATLOCK BATH
MANSFIELD
Willersley Tunnel
11 CROMFORD
SUTTON PARKWAY
Lea Wood Tunnel
ALFRETON
13   12
KIRKBY-IN-ASHFIELD
WIRKSWORTH
Wingfield Tunnel
Alfreton Tunnel
WHATSTANDWELL
NEWSTEAD
14
BUTTERLEY   15
SWANWICK JUNCTION
AMBERGATE
HUCKNALL
IDRIDGEHAY
BELPER
BULWELL
SHOTTLE
LANGLEY MILL
Milford Tunnel
BURTON JOYCE
DUFFIELD
17   18
CARLTON
ILKESTON [2016]
19
16
NETHERFIELD
NOTTINGHAM
BEESTON
ATTENBOROUGH
20
DERBY   SPONDON
PEARTREE

LEGEND FOR MAP 41A

10 Parts of the FIVE PITS TRAIL (part of the PHOENIX GREENWAYS network). www.derbyshire.gov.uk
11 CROMFORD: Holiday accommodation available in a former waiting room. www.cromfordstationwaitingroom.co.uk
12 HIGH PEAK TRAIL. www.peakdistrictinformation.com
13 1ft 6in gauge STEEPLE GRANGE LIGHT RAILWAY on the trackbed of a branch of the former CROMFORD & HIGH PEAK RAILWAY. www.steeplegrange.co.uk

14 ECCLESBOURNE VALLEY RAILWAY. www.e-v-r.com
15 MIDLAND RAILWAY – BUTTERLEY. Midland Railway-centred museum and presentation complex with operational railways of different gauges. www.midlandrailway-butterley.co.uk
16 WEST HALLAM: Now the Station House garden centre.
17 NOTTINGHAM EXPRESS TRANSIT. www.thetram.net

18 NOTTINGHAM VICTORIA: Clock tower survives in the Victoria Shopping Centre
19 NOTTINGHAM LONDON ROAD LOW LEVEL: Station building now a fitness centre
20 OLD DALBY TEST TRACK. www.old-dalby.com

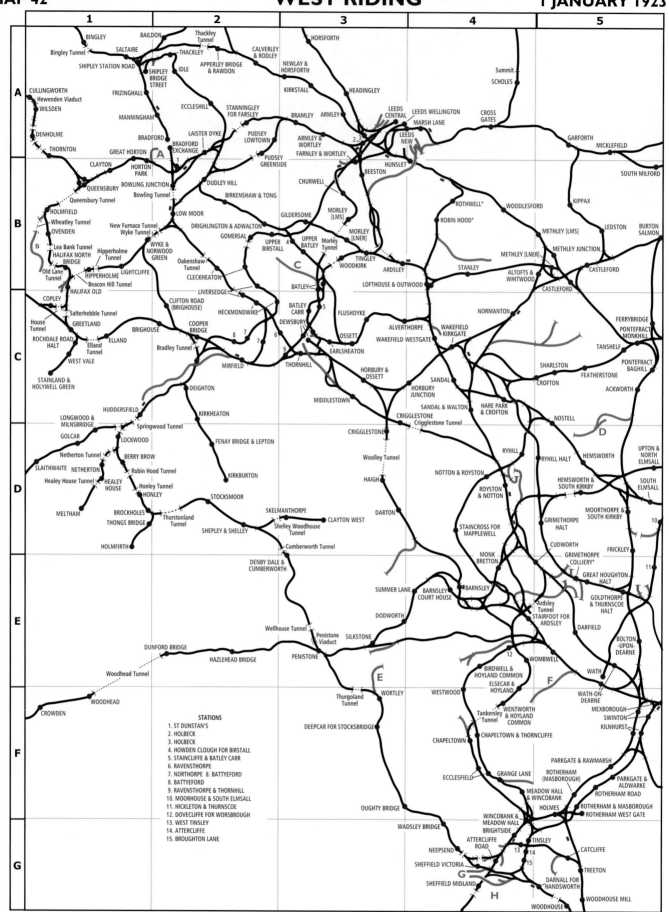

STATIONS
1. ST DUNSTAN'S
2. HOLBECK
3. HOLBECK
4. HOWDEN CLOUGH FOR BIRSTALL
5. STAINCLIFFE & BATLEY CARR
6. RAVENSTHORPE
7. NORTHORPE 8. BATTYEFORD
8. BATTYEFORD
9. RAVENSTHORPE & THORNHILL
10. MOORHOUSE & SOUTH ELMSALL
11. HICKLETON & THURNSCOE
12. DOVECLIFFE FOR WORSBROUGH
13. WEST TINSLEY
14. ATTERCLIFFE
15. BROUGHTON LANE

LEGEND FOR MAP 42
A City Road branch
B St Paul's branch
C Birstall branch
D Former BRACKENHILL LIGHT RAILWAY
E Thurgoland siding
F Elsecar branch
G Park branch
H City branch

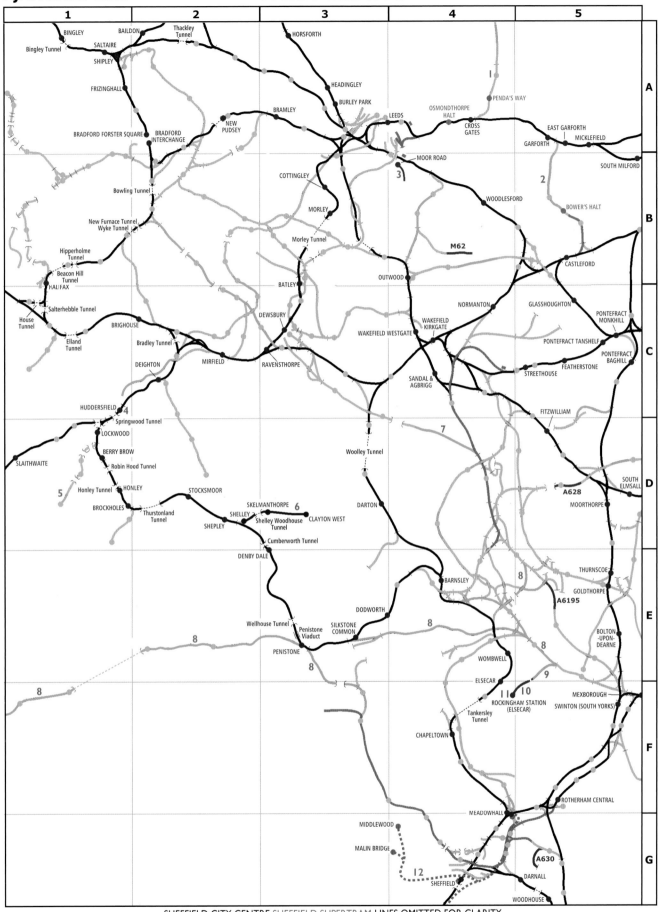

SHEFFIELD CITY CENTRE SHEFFIELD SUPERTRAM LINES OMITTED FOR CLARITY

LEGEND FOR MAP 42A

1 SCHOLES: Now the Buffers pub/restaurant.
www.thebuffers.co.uk

2 Part of the LEEDS COUNTRY WAY. www.leeds.gov.uk

3 MIDDLETON RAILWAY. www.middletonrailway.org.uk

4 HUDDERSFIELD: Station building now also home to the King's
Head and the Head of Steam pubs. www.theheadofsteam.co.uk

5 MELTHAM GREENWAY. www.kirklees.gov.uk

6 1ft 3in gauge KIRKLEES LIGHT RAILWAY.
www.kirkleeslightrailway.com

7 CHEVET BRANCH LINE. Local nature reserve

8 Parts of the TRANS PENNINE TRAIL.
www.transpenninetrail.org.uk

9 Part of the BARNSLEY BOUNDARY WALK. www.ldwa.org.uk

10 ELSECAR HERITAGE RAILWAY.
www.elsecarrailway.co.uk

11 ELSECAR: Earl Fitzwilliam's private station (closed 1910)
now part of the ELSECAR HERITAGE CENTRE.
www.elsecar-heritage-centre.co.uk

12 SHEFFIELD SUPERTRAM. www.supertram.com

MAP 43   1 JANUARY 1923

SOUTH WALES

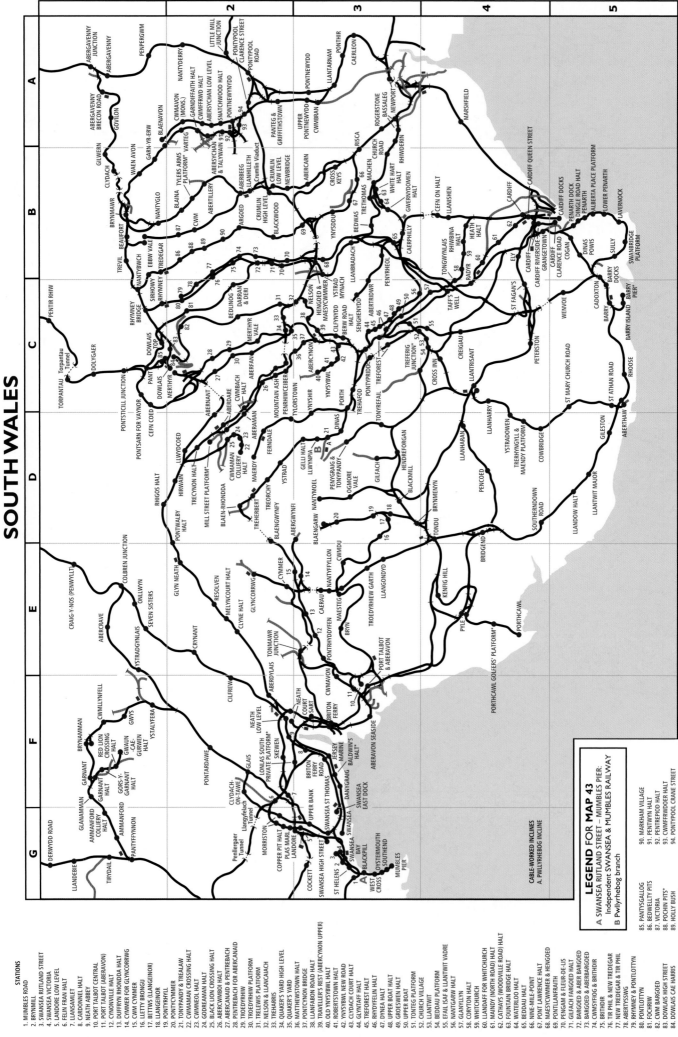

SOUTH WALES

ABERGAVENNY

PONTYPOOL & NEW INN
PONTYRHYDRUN HALT
CWMBRAN
NEWPORT
PYE CORNER
ROGERSTONE
RISCA & PONTYMISTER
A48
A4051

WAENFELIN HALT
FURNACE SIDINGS
BLAENAVON HIGH LEVEL
GARNDIFFAITH HALT
LLANHILLETH
SEBASTOPOL
A472
CELYNEN NORTH HALT
CELYNEN SOUTH HALT
NEWBRIDGE
CROSSKEYS
A467
A472
CARDIFF QUEEN STREET

EBBW VALE PARKWAY
A467
EBBW VALE TOWN [2015]
OAKDALE HALT
PENMAEN HALT
WYLLIE HALT
ENERGLYN & CHURCHILL PARK
ABER
CAERPHILLY
LISVANE & THORNHILL
LLANISHEN
HEATH HIGH LEVEL
HEATH LOW LEVEL
A48
CATHAYS
CARDIFF BAY
DINGLE ROAD
PENARTH

TILLWYN HALT
RHYMNEY
PONTLOTTYN
BRITHDIR
HENGOED
LLANBRADACH
A468
WHITCHURCH
RHIWBINA
CORYTON
TY GLAS
BIRCHGROVE
LLANDAF
RADYR
NINIAN PARK
CARDIFF CENTRAL
GRANGETOWN
COGAN
EASTBROOK
DINAS POWYS
CADOXTON
BARRY
BARRY DOCKS
BARRY ISLAND

A465
TIR-PHIL
BARGOED
GILFACH FARGOED
PENGAM
YSTRAD MYNACH
TRELEWIS HALT
PONTYPRIDD
A470
TREFOREST ESTATE
TAFF'S WELL
DANESCOURT
FAIRWATER
WAUN-GRON PARK

PANT
DOLYGAER
PONTSTICILL
PENTRE-BACH
OGILVIE VILLAGE HALT
TROED-Y-RHIW
MERTHYR VALE
QUAKERS YARD
ABERCYNON
TREHAFOD
PORTH
TREFOREST
TONTEG HALT
PONTYCLUN
A4232
RHOOSE CARDIFF INTERNATIONAL AIRPORT

TORPANTAU
MERTHYR TYDFIL
ABERDARE
A470
CWMBACH
FERNHILL
MOUNTAIN ASH
PENRHIWCEIBER
A4059
LLWYNYPIA
TONYPANDY
DINAS RHONDDA
LEWISTOWN HALT
COED ELY
LLANHARAN
PENCOED
ST ATHAN
LLANDOW WICK ROAD HALT
LLANTWIT MAJOR

TREHERBERT
YNYSWEN
TREORCHY
TON PENTRE
YSTRAD RHONDDA
WYNDHAM HALT
PONTYCYMER
MAESTEG
TONDU
SARN
WILDMILL
BRIDGEND

NORTH RHONDDA HALT
SOUTH PIT HALT
MAESTEG EWENNY ROAD
GARTH (MID GLAMORGAN)
PORT TALBOT PARKWAY
PYLE
M4
A4229

PANTYFFORDD HALT
DILLWYN PLATFORM
A4068
CWMTWRCH WELL HALT
CEFN COED COLLIERY HALT
A4067
PENSCYNOR HALT
CADOXTON TERRACE HALT
SKEWEN
NEATH
BRITON FERRY
BAGLAN
BAGLAN SANDS HALT

LLANDYBIE
AMMANFORD
PARCRHUN HALT
PANTYFFYNNON
PONT LLIW
LLANGYFELACH HALT
Llangyfelach Tunnel
LLANSAMLET
LLANDARCY PLATFORM
PENTREFELIN HALT
Penllergaer Tunnel
A4067
SWANSEA

LEGEND FOR MAP 43A

1 Part of the TAFF TRAIL. www.tafftrail.org.uk
2 DOLYGAER: Station building now the Dolygaer Mountain Centre. www.dolygaer-scouts.co.uk
3 1ft 11¾in gauge BRECON MOUNTAIN RAILWAY. www.breconmountainrailway.co.uk
4 TREVITHICK TRAIL: Trackbed of former PENYDARREN TRAMROAD. www.trevithicktrail.co.uk
5 PONTYPOOL & BLAENAVON RAILWAY. www.pontypool-and-blaenavon.co.uk
6 PONTYPOOL CRANE STREET: Station building dismantled for rebuilding at FURNACE SIDINGS on the PONTYPOOL & BLAENAVON RAILWAY
7 BARRY TOURIST RAILWAY. www.barrytouristrailway.co.uk
8 BARRY PIER: Tunnel to BARRY ISLAND now a shooting range.
9 PONTYCYMER: Base for the GARW VALLEY RAILWAY. www.garwvalleyrailway.co.uk
10 CYMMER: Station building now the Refreshment Rooms bar and restaurant. www.refreshmentrooms.co.uk
11 SWANSEA BIKE PATH. www.gps-routes.co.uk

GLASGOW & DISTRICT

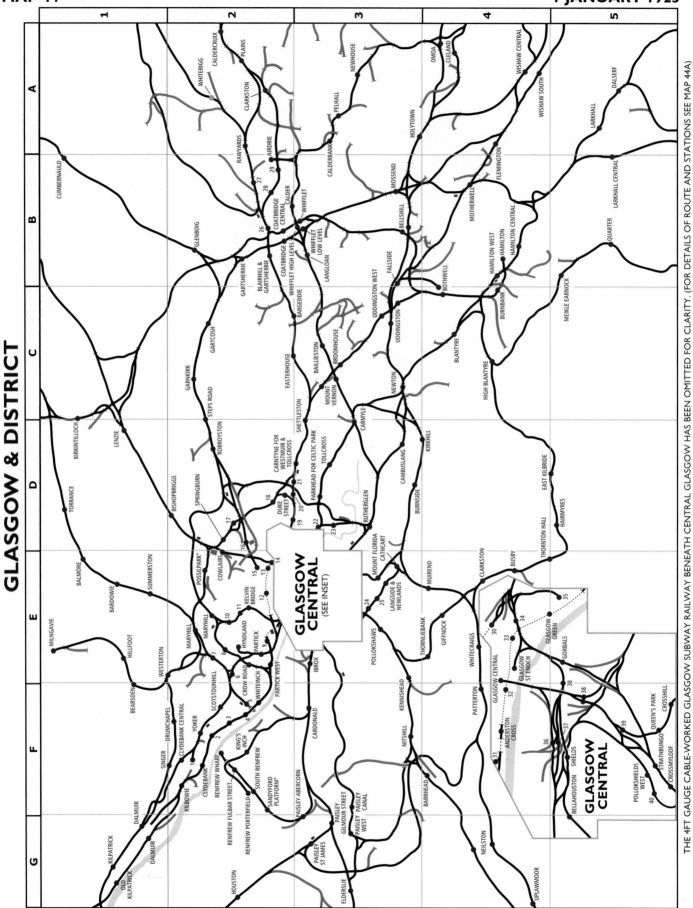

THE 4FT GAUGE CABLE-WORKED GLASGOW SUBWAY RAILWAY BENEATH CENTRAL GLASGOW HAS BEEN OMITTED FOR CLARITY. (FOR DETAILS OF ROUTE AND STATIONS SEE MAP 44A)

STATIONS

1. CLYDEBANK EAST
2. YOKER FOR RENFREW
3. SCOTSTOUN
4. SCOTSTOUN WEST
5. VICTORIA PARK, WHITEINCH
6. JORDANHILL
7. GREAT WESTERN ROAD
8. KELVINSIDE
9. PARTICK CENTRAL
10. KIRKLEE FOR NORTH KELVINSIDE
11. BOTANIC GARDENS
12. CHARING CROSS
13. GLASGOW QUEEN STREET LOW LEVEL
14. GLASGOW QUEEN STREET HIGH LEVEL
15. GLASGOW BUCHANAN STREET
16. ST ROLLOX
17. BARNHILL
18. ALEXANDRA PARK
19. BELLGROVE
20. DUKE STREET
21. PARKHEAD
22. BRIDGETON CROSS
23. DALMARNOCK
24. SHAWLANDS
25. POLLOKSHAWS EAST
26. COATBRIDGE SUNNYSIDE
27. COMMONHEAD (AIRDRIE NORTH)
28. COATDYKE
29. AIRDRIE SOUTH
30. HIGH STREET
31. STOBCROSS
32. GLASGOW CENTRAL LOW LEVEL
33. GLASGOW CROSS
34. GALLOWGATE*
35. BRIDGETON CROSS
36. POLLOKSHIELDS
37. SHIELDS ROAD
38. EGLINTON STREET
39. POLLOKSHIELDS EAST
40. MAXWELL PARK

GLASGOW & DISTRICT

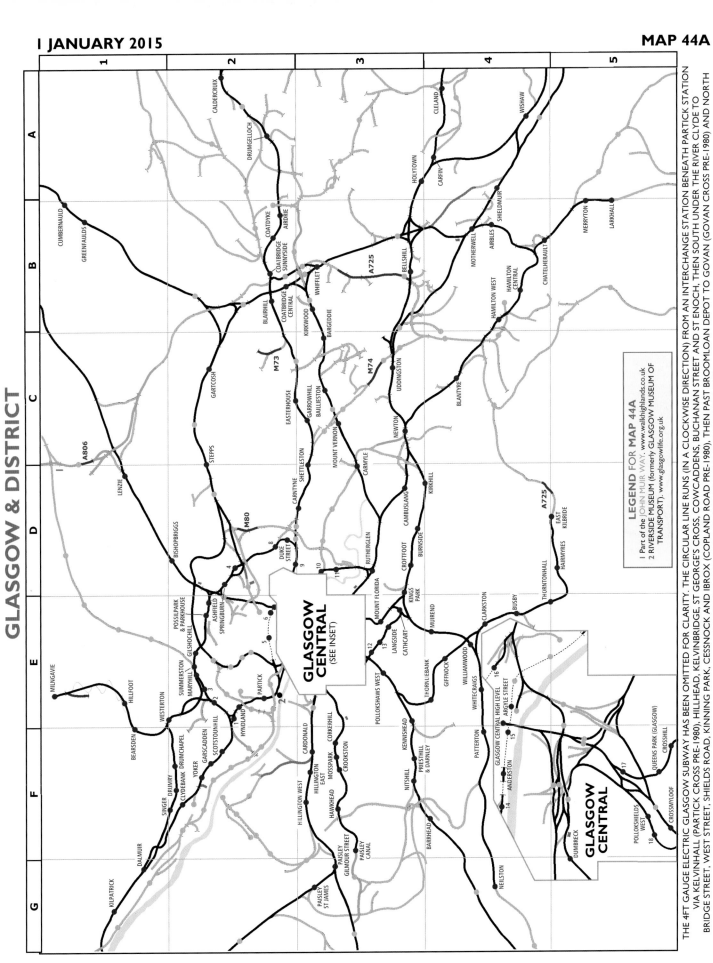

THE 4FT GAUGE ELECTRIC GLASGOW SUBWAY HAS BEEN OMITTED FOR CLARITY. THE CIRCULAR LINE RUNS (IN A CLOCKWISE DIRECTION) FROM AN INTERCHANGE STATION BENEATH PARTICK STATION VIA KELVINHALL (PARTICK CROSS PRE-1980), HILLHEAD, KELVINBRIDGE, ST GEORGE'S CROSS, COWCADDENS, BUCHANAN STREET AND ST ENOCH, THEN SOUTH UNDER THE RIVER CLYDE TO BRIDGE STREET, WEST STREET, SHIELDS ROAD, KINNING PARK, CESSNOCK AND IBROX (COPLAND ROAD PRE-1980), THEN PAST BROOMLOAN DEPOT TO GOVAN (GOVAN CROSS PRE-1980) AND NORTH UNDER THE CLYDE TO PARTICK (MERKLAND STREET PRE-1980).

LEGEND FOR MAP 44A

1 Part of the JOHN MUIR WAY. www.walkhighlands.co.uk
2 RIVERSIDE MUSEUM (formerly GLASGOW MUSEUM OF TRANSPORT). www.glasgowlife.org.uk

STATIONS

1. JORDANHILL
2. ANNIESLAND
3. KELVINDALE
4. BARNHILL
5. CHARING CROSS
6. GLASGOW QUEEN STREET LOW LEVEL
7. GLASGOW QUEEN STREET HIGH LEVEL
8. ALEXANDRA PARADE
9. BELLGROVE
10. BRIDGETON
11. DALMARNOCK
12. SHAWLANDS
13. POLLOKSHAWS EAST
14. EXHIBITION CENTRE
15. GLASGOW CENTRAL LOW LEVEL
16. HIGH STREET
17. POLLOKSHIELDS EAST
18. MAXWELL PARK

MAP 45   1 JANUARY 1923

Liverpool & Manchester

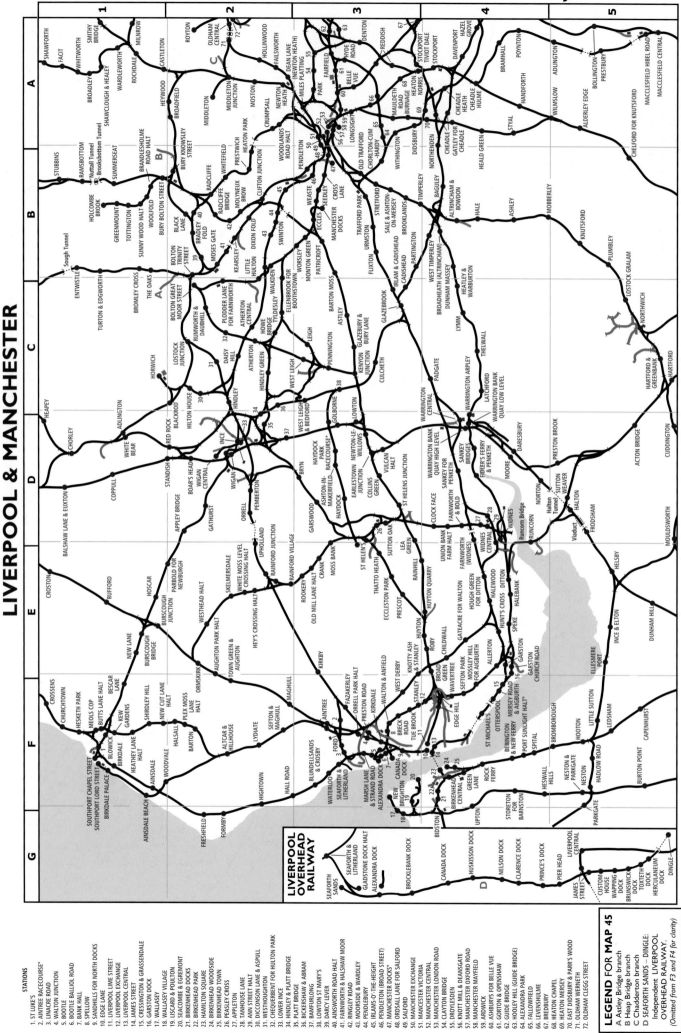

TO SIMPLIFY THE MAP OF THE LIVERPOOL OVERHEAD RAILWAY AND AVOID CONFUSION, DOCK AND GOODS LINES HAVE BEEN OMITTED

LIVERPOOL OVERHEAD RAILWAY

STATIONS

1. ST LUKE'S
2. AINTREE RACECOURSE*
3. LINACRE ROAD
4. WALTON JUNCTION
5. BOOTLE
6. BOOTLE BALLIOL ROAD
7. BANK HALL
8. SPELLOW
9. SANDHILLS FOR NORTH DOCKS
10. EDGE LANE
11. LIVERPOOL LIME STREET
12. LIVERPOOL EXCHANGE
13. LIVERPOOL CENTRAL
14. JAMES STREET
15. CRESSINGTON & GRASSENDALE
16. GARSTON DOCK
17. WALLASEY
18. WALLASEY VILLAGE
19. LISCARD & POULTON
20. SEACOMBE & EGREMONT
21. BIRKENHEAD DOCKS
22. BIRKENHEAD PARK
23. HAMILTON SQUARE
24. BIRKENHEAD WOODSIDE
25. BIRKENHEAD TOWN
26. PEASLEY CROSS
27. APPLETON
28. TANHOUSE LANE
29. ANN STREET HALT
30. DICCONSON LANE & ASPULL
31. WESTHOUGHTON
32. CHEQUERBENT FOR HULTON PARK
33. LOWER INCE
34. HINDLEY & PLATT BRIDGE
35. PLATT BRIDGE
36. BICKERSHAW & ABRAM
37. BAMFURLONG
38. LOWTON ST MARY'S
39. DARCY LEVER
40. AINSWORTH ROAD HALT
41. FARNWORTH & HALSHAW MOOR
42. RINGLEY ROAD
43. MOORSIDE & WARDLEY
44. PENDLEBURY
45. IRLAMS-O'-TH'-HEIGHT
46. PENDLETON (BROAD STREET)
47. MANCHESTER DOCKS*
48. ORDSALL LANE FOR SALFORD
49. SALFORD
50. MANCHESTER EXCHANGE
51. MANCHESTER VICTORIA
52. MANCHESTER CENTRAL
53. MANCHESTER LONDON ROAD
54. CLAYTON BRIDGE
55. DROYLSDEN
56. KNOTT MILL & DEANSGATE
57. MANCHESTER OXFORD ROAD
58. MANCHESTER MAYFIELD
59. ARDWICK
60. ASHBURYS FOR BELLE VUE
61. GORTON & OPENSHAW
62. GUIDE BRIDGE
63. HOOLEY HILL (GUIDE BRIDGE)
64. ALEXANDRA PARK
65. FALLOWFIELD
66. LEVENSHULME
67. BREDBURY
68. HEATON CHAPEL
69. HEATON MERSEY
70. EAST DIDSBURY & PARR'S WOOD
71. OLDHAM WERNETH
72. OLDHAM CLEGG STREET

LEGEND FOR MAP 45

A Astley Bridge branch
B Heap Bridge branch
C Chadderton branch
D SEAFORTH SANDS – DINGLE: Independent LIVERPOOL OVERHEAD RAILWAY.
(Omitted from F3 and F4 for clarity)

LIVERPOOL & MANCHESTER

MANCHESTER CITY CENTRE METROLINK LINES BETWEEN MANCHESTER PICCADILLY, VICTORIA AND CENTRAL OMITTED FOR CLARITY

Grid columns: 1, 2, 3, 4, 5
Grid rows: A, B, C, D, E, F, G

Station and place labels

SMITHY BRIDGE, MILNROW, ROCHDALE, ROCHDALE TOWN CENTRE, CASTLETON, HEYWOOD, MILLS HILL, MOSTON, BOWKER VALE, CRUMPSALL, NEWTON HEATH & MOSTON, HOLLINWOOD, FAILSWORTH, FAIRFIELD, BELLE VUE, RYDER BROW, REDDISH NORTH, DENTON, DAVENPORT, HAZEL GROVE, WOODSMOOR, POYNTON, ADLINGTON, PRESTBURY, MACCLESFIELD

RAMSBOTTOM, SUMMERSEAT, Brooksbottom Tunnel, Nuttall Tunnel, BURY INTERCHANGE, RADCLIFFE, WHITEFIELD, BESSES O' TH' BARN, PRESTWICH, HEATON PARK, CLIFTON, FARNWORTH, MOSES GATE, KEARSLEY, WALKDEN, MOORSIDE, SWINTON (MANCHESTER), PATRICROFT, ECCLES, HUMPHREY PARK, TRAFFORD PARK, URMSTON, STRETFORD, SALE, DANE ROAD, OLD TRAFFORD, CHORLTON, EAST DIDSBURY, GATLEY, HEALD GREEN, STYAL, CHEADLE HULME, BRAMHALL, HANDFORTH, WILMSLOW, ALDERLEY EDGE, CHELFORD

LONGSIGHT, MAULDETH ROAD, BURNAGE, REDDISH SOUTH, STOCKPORT, BREDBURY, M60, MANCHESTER AIRPORT, TIMPERLEY, NAVIGATION ROAD, ALTRINCHAM, HALE, ASHLEY, MOBBERLEY, KNUTSFORD, PLUMLEY, LOSTOCK GRALAM, NORTHWICH, GREENBANK, HARTFORD

Sough Tunnel, ENTWISTLE, A6099, BROMLEY CROSS, HALL I' TH' WOOD, BOLTON, LOSTOCK, HORWICH PARKWAY, DAISY HILL, HAG FOLD, ATHERTON, ATHERLEIGH, A579, GLAZEBROOK, IRLAM, CHASSEN ROAD, FLIXTON, CHASSEN ROAD, BROOKLANDS, BIRCHWOOD, PADGATE, WARRINGTON CENTRAL, WARRINGTON BANK QUAY, CUDDINGTON, ACTON BRIDGE

BLACKROD, WESTHOUGHTON, HINDLEY, INCE, WIGAN WALLGATE, WIGAN NORTH WESTERN, ADLINGTON, CHORLEY, BUCKSHAW PARKWAY, EUXTON BALSHAW LANE, CROSTON, RUFFORD, HOSCAR, BURSCOUGH BRIDGE, BURSCOUGH JUNCTION, NEW LANE, BESCAR LANE, APPLEY BRIDGE, GATHURST, ORRELL, PEMBERTON, BRYN, GARSWOOD, NEWTON-LE-WILLOWS, EARLESTOWN, ST HELENS JUNCTION, SANKEY FOR PENKETH, WARRINGTON, RUNCORN EAST, HALTON TUNNEL, FRODSHAM, HELSBY, MOULDSWORTH

UPHOLLAND, PARBOLD, RAINFORD, KIRKBY, FAZAKERLEY, WARBRECK, RICE LANE, KIRKDALE, OLD ROAN, AINTREE, MAGHULL, TOWN GREEN, AUGHTON PARK, ORMSKIRK, B5312, ST HELENS CENTRAL, THATTO HEATH, ECCLESTON PARK, PRESCOT, RAINHILL, HUYTON, ROBY, WAVERTREE TECHNOLOGY PARK, BROAD GREEN, EDGE HILL, MOSSLEY HILL, WEST ALLERTON, LIVERPOOL SOUTH PARKWAY, WHISTON, LEA GREEN, HOUGH GREEN, WIDNES, HALEWOOD, HUNTS CROSS, RUNCORN, Runcorn Bridge, Viaduct, ELLESMERE PORT, STANLOW & THORNTON, INCE & ELTON, HELSBY & ALVANLEY, CAPENHURST

SOUTHPORT, MEOLS COP, BIRKDALE, HILLSIDE, AINSDALE, FRESHFIELD, FORMBY, HIGHTOWN, HALL ROAD, BLUNDELLSANDS & CROSBY, WATERLOO, SEAFORTH & LITHERLAND, BOOTLE NEW STRAND, ORRELL PARK, SANDHILLS, NEW BRIGHTON, BIDSTON, UPTON, BIRKENHEAD CENTRAL, GREEN LANE, ROCK FERRY, ST MICHAELS, BRUNSWICK, AIGBURTH, CRESSINGTON, PORT SUNLIGHT, SPITAL, BEBINGTON, BROMBOROUGH RAKE, BROMBOROUGH, EASTHAM RAKE, HOOTON, LITTLE SUTTON, OVERPOOL, HESWALL, NESTON, NORTHWICH

LIVERPOOL OVERHEAD RAILWAY
SEAFORTH & LITHERLAND, GLADSTONE DOCK, JAMES STREET, LIVERPOOL CENTRAL

STATIONS
1. WALLASEY GROVE ROAD
2. WALLASEY VILLAGE
3. BIRKENHEAD NORTH
4. BIRKENHEAD PARK
5. CONWAY PARK
6. BIRKENHEAD HAMILTON SQUARE
7. BOOTLE ORIEL ROAD
8. BANK HALL
9. WALTON
10. MOORFIELDS
11. LIVERPOOL LIME STREET
12. LIVERPOOL CENTRAL
13. JAMES STREET
14. SALFORD CRESCENT
15. SALFORD CENTRAL
16. MANCHESTER VICTORIA
17. DEANSGATE
18. MANCHESTER OXFORD ROAD
19. MANCHESTER PICCADILLY
20. ARDWICK
21. ASHBURYS
22. GORTON
23. GUIDE BRIDGE
24. LEVENSHULME
25. HEATON CHAPEL
26. BRINNINGTON

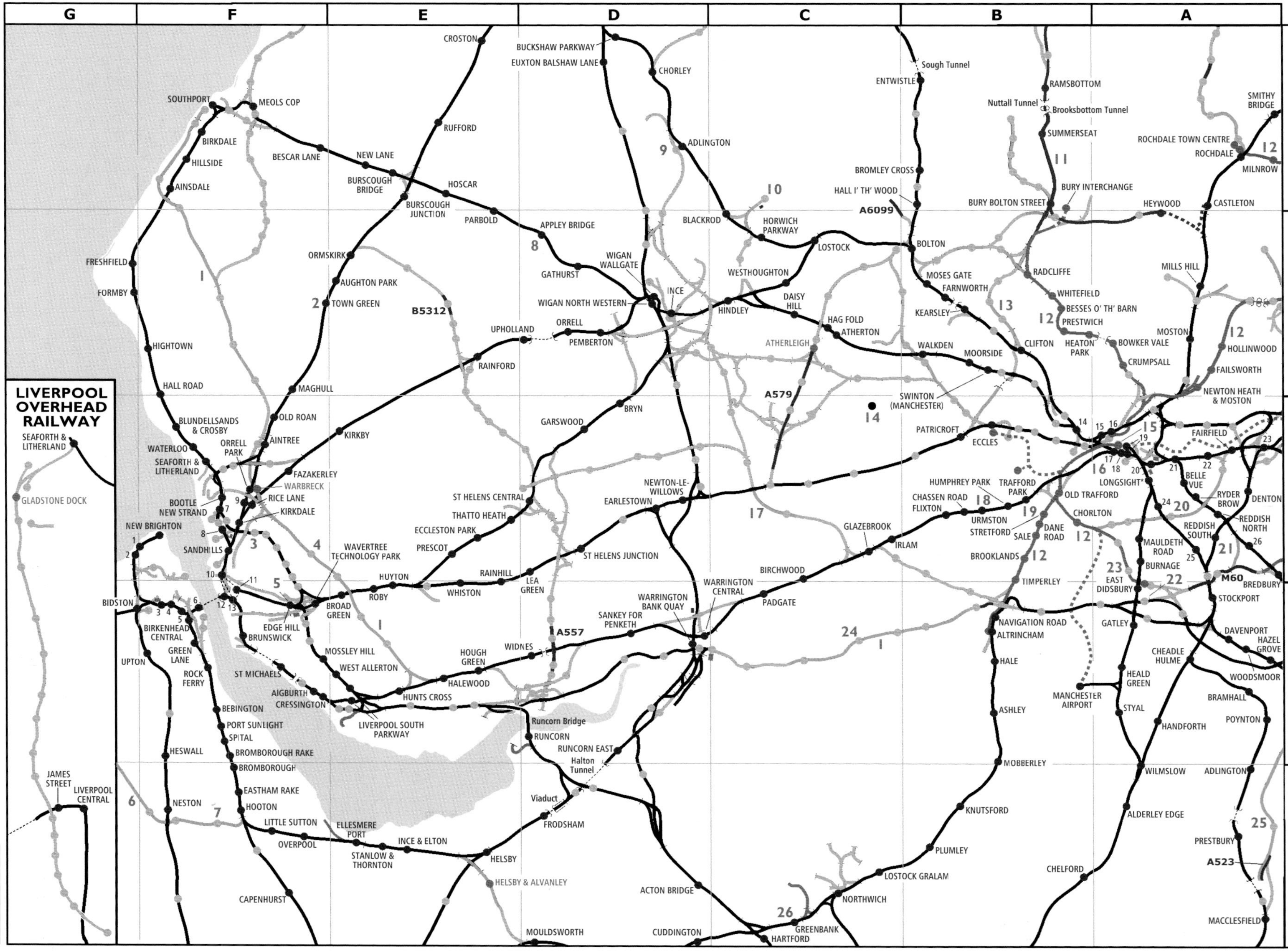

LEGEND FOR MAP 45A — FOR THE LEGEND TO THIS MAP, PLEASE SEE PAGE viii

LEGENDS

LEGEND FOR MAP 3A

1 WESTON-SUPER-MARE: First station site (closed 1866) now a commemorative garden
2 YATTON: Home to the Strawberry Line community café. www.strawberrylinecafe.co.uk
3 STRAWBERRY LINE. www.thestrawberryline.co.uk
4 SANDFORD: Now part of a retirement village
5 WINSCOMBE: Site cleared as the Old Station Millennium Green open community space
6 AXBRIDGE: Station building now a youth centre
7 BRISTOL & BATH RAILWAY PATH. www.bristolbathrailwaypath.org.uk
8 AVON VALLEY RAILWAY. www.avonvalleyrailway.org
9 WARMLEY: Down platform shelter now a food kiosk
10 BATH (later BATH GREEN PARK): Station building now a market/offices/events space
11 TWO TUNNELS GREENWAY. www.twotunnels.org.uk
12 MIDFORD: Being rebuilt by the NEW SOMERSET & DORSET RAILWAY. www.newsomersetanddorsetrailway.org
13 MIDSOMER NORTON (later MIDSOMER NORTON SOUTH): Operating base of the SOMERSET & DORSET RAILWAY HERITAGE TRUST. www.sdjr.co.uk
14 Part of Chilcompton Tunnel now a shooting range
15 EAST SOMERSET RAILWAY. www.eastsomersetrailway.com
16 GLASTONBURY: Former island platform canopy re-erected as the market car park shelter
17 2ft gauge GARTELL LIGHT RAILWAY. newglr.weebly.com
18 SHILLINGSTONE: Restored as the base of the SHILLINGSTONE RAILWAY PROJECT. www.shillingstone-railway-project.org.uk
19 YEOVIL JUNCTION: Former GWR transfer shed home to the YEOVIL RAILWAY CENTRE with visitor centre and art gallery. www.yeovilrailway.freeservers.com
20 Part of the STOP LINE WAY
21 LYME REGIS: Station building re-erected at ALRESFORD on the MID HANTS RAILWAY. www.watercressline.co.uk
22 BRIDPORT WEST BAY: Now the Station Café
23 TOLLER: Station building re-erected at TOTNES LITTLEHEMPSTON on the SOUTH DEVON RAILWAY. www.southdevonrailway.co.uk
24 PORTESHAM: Holiday accommodation available as Sleepers. www.railwaystationcottages.co.uk
25 RODWELL TRAIL. www.gps-routes.co.uk
26 WIMBORNE: Site used as a market place
27 Part of the CASTLEMAN TRAILWAY. www.dorsetforyou.com
28 BOURNEMOUTH WEST: Site cleared as a car park and part of the **A338** road
29 SWANAGE RAILWAY. www.swanagerailway.co.uk
30 CLIFTON DOWN: Original station building now the Roo Bar
31 BRISTOL HARBOUR RAILWAY. bristolharbourrailway.co.uk

LEGEND FOR MAP 4A

1 CHISELDON & MARLBOROUGH RAILWAY PATH. www.gps-routes.co.uk
2 LAMBOURN VALLEY WAY. www.ldwa.org.uk
3 READING: Former station building now the Three Guineas pub. www.three-guineas.co.uk
4 2ft gauge OLD KILN LIGHT RAILWAY. www.oldkilnlightrailway.com
5 HOLLYCOMBE WORKING STEAM MUSEUM with operational lines of different gauges. www.hollycombe.co.uk
6 MID HANTS RAILWAY. www.watercressline.co.uk
7 Part of the TEST WAY. www3.hants.gov.uk
8 HORSEBRIDGE: Now an events venue. horsebridgestation.co.uk
9 SALISBURY: Ex-GWR station site now occupied by SALISBURY depot
10 Part of the CASTLEMAN TRAILWAY. www.dorsetforyou.com/castlemantrailway
11 HURN: Station building now the Avon Causeway Inn. www.avoncauseway.co.uk
12 HOLMSLEY: Station building now a tearoom. www.stationhouseholmsley.com
13 Former TOTTON, HYTHE & FAWLEY LIGHT RAILWAY [SR]
14 SOUTHAMPTON TOWN FOR DOCKS: Station building now a casino
15 7¼in/10¼in gauge EASTLEIGH LAKESIDE STEAM RAILWAY. www.steamtrain.co.uk
16 Part of the PILGRIMS' TRAIL. www3.hants.gov.uk
17 MEON VALLEY TRAIL. www.gps-routes.co.uk
18 10¼in gauge ROYAL VICTORIA RAILWAY. www.royalvictoriarailway.co.uk
19 GOSPORT – FAREHAM now a bus lane. www3.hants.gov.uk
20 LEE-ON-THE-SOLENT: Station building now an amusement arcade
21 NORTH HAYLING: Site cleared as a nature reserve car park
22 HAYLING BILLY COASTAL PATH. www.gps-routes.co.uk
23 HAYLING ISLAND: Goods shed now the Station Theatre. www.hayling-dramatics.hampshire.co.uk
24 2ft gauge HAYLING SEASIDE RAILWAY. www.haylingseasiderailway.com
25 CENTURION WAY. www.gps-routes.co.uk
26 SELSEY: Site cleared as a children's play area
27 MILL HILL: Mill Hill Tunnel now used as a shooting range
28 YARMOUTH: Station building now a café
29 FRESHWATER CAUSEWAY
30 WHITWELL: Holiday accommodation available in station building. www.whitwellstation.co.uk
31 MERSTONE: Site cleared as a car park
32 Parts of the SANDOWN – NEWPORT CYCLE PATH. www.wightlink.co.uk
33 BRADING: Station also home to an exhibition and visitor centre
34 Part of the YAR RIVER TRAIL. www.ldwa.org.uk
35 ISLE OF WIGHT STEAM RAILWAY. www.iwsteamrailway.co.uk
36 SMALLBROOK JUNCTION*: Network station only open when the ISLE OF WIGHT STEAM RAILWAY is operating

LEGEND FOR MAP 5A

1 EBURY WAY. www.gps-routes.co.uk
2 12in gauge RUISLIP LIDO RAILWAY. www.ruisliplidorailway.org
3 WEST CROYDON: Original station building now a shop
4 LONDON TRAMLINK. www.tfl.gov.uk
5 Part of the WEY SOUTH PATH. www.gps-routes.co.uk
6 WORTH WAY. www.ldwa.org.uk
7 FOREST WAY. www.eastsussex.gov.uk
8 SPA VALLEY RAILWAY. www.spavalleyrailway.co.uk
9 GROOMBRIDGE: Station building shared with Withyham Parish Council
10 TUNBRIDGE WELLS WEST: Original station building now the Smith & Western hotel and restaurant. www.smith-western.com
11 PETWORTH: Now a guest house, complete with four restored Pullman carriages. www.old-station.co.uk
12 AMBERLEY MUSEUM & HERITAGE CENTRE: Extensive narrow gauge network. www.amberleymuseum.co.uk
13 Part of the DOWNS LINK. www.westsussex.gov.uk
14 Brighton Seafront: 2ft 8½in gauge VOLKS ELECTRIC RAILWAY (formerly BRIGHTON ELECTRIC RAILWAY). www.volkselectricrailway.co.uk
15 BLUEBELL RAILWAY. www.bluebell-railway.co.uk
16 LAVENDER LINE. www.lavender-line.co.uk
17 GLYNDE: Station building now a paragliding school
18 HEATHFIELD: Booking office now a shop
19 CUCKOO TRAIL. www.eastsussex.gov.uk
20 POLEGATE: Station building (closed 1986) now the Old Polegate Station bar and restaurant. oldpolegatestation.co.uk

LEGEND FOR MAP 8A

1 MONMOUTH TROY: Station building re-erected at WINCHCOMBE on the GLOUCESTERSHIRE WARWICKSHIRE RAILWAY
2 COLEFORD (closed to passengers 1917): Home to the COLEFORD GREAT WESTERN RAILWAY MUSEUM. www.colefordgwr.150.com
3 Part of the FAMILY CYCLE TRAIL. www.forestry.gov.uk
4 DEAN FOREST RAILWAY. www.deanforestrailway.co.uk
5 TINTERN: Now a visitor centre with a tearoom, refurbished carriages, a signal box exhibition gallery and a 5in gauge railway. www.tintern.org.uk
6 Part of the WYE VALLEY WALK. www.wyevalleywalk.org
7 WARMLEY: Down platform shelter now a food kiosk
8 BRISTOL & BATH RAILWAY PATH. www.bristolbathrailwaypath.org.uk
9 AVON VALLEY RAILWAY. www.avonvalleyrailway.org
10 BATH (later BATH GREEN PARK): Station building now a market/offices/events space
11 TWO TUNNELS GREENWAY. www.twotunnels.org.uk
12 MIDFORD: Being rebuilt by the NEW SOMERSET & DORSET RAILWAY. newsomersetanddorsetrailway.org
13 YATTON: Home to the Strawberry Line community café. www.strawberrylinecafe.co.uk
14 WESTON-SUPER-MARE: First station site (closed 1866) now a commemorative garden
15 SANDFORD: Now part of a retirement village
16 STRAWBERRY LINE. www.thestrawberryline.co.uk
17 WINSCOMBE: Site cleared as the Old Station Millennium Green open community space
18 AXBRIDGE: Station building now a youth centre
19 MIDSOMER NORTON (later MIDSOMER NORTON SOUTH): Operating base of the SOMERSET & DORSET RAILWAY HERITAGE TRUST. www.sdjr.co.uk
20 Part of Chilcompton Tunnel now a shooting range
21 EAST SOMERSET RAILWAY. www.eastsomersetrailway.com
22 GLASTONBURY: Former island platform canopy re-erected as the market car park shelter
23 2ft gauge GARTELL LIGHT RAILWAY. newglr.weebly.com
24 YEOVIL JUNCTION: Former GWR transfer shed home to the YEOVIL RAILWAY CENTRE with visitor centre and art gallery. www.yeovilrailway.freeservers.com
25 Part of the STOP LINE WAY
26 WEST SOMERSET RAILWAY. www.westsomersetrailway.v.ticket.co.uk
27 Trackbed of former WEST SOMERSET MINERAL RAILWAY. www.westsomersetmineralrailway.org.uk
28 SOMERSET & DORSET RAILWAY TRUST MUSEUM. www.sdrt.org
29 BLUE ANCHOR: Station building home to the BLUE ANCHOR RAILWAY MUSEUM

LEGEND FOR MAP 9A

1 SEVERN VALLEY RAILWAY. www.svr.co.uk
2 KIDDERMINSTER RAILWAY MUSEUM. www.krm.org.uk
3 HARTLEBURY: Former station building now the Tap House pub. www.thetaphousehartlebury.co.uk
4 FENCOTE: Station restored as private residence but open to the public on special occasions - see railway press for announcements
5 ROWDEN MILL: Station restored as private residence but open to the public on special occasions - see railway press for announcements
6 1ft 3in gauge EVESHAM VALE LIGHT RAILWAY. www.evlr.co.uk
7 Part of the MONARCH'S WAY. www.ldwa.org.uk
8 GLOUCESTERSHIRE WARWICKSHIRE RAILWAY. www.gwsr.com
9 WINCHCOMBE RAILWAY MUSEUM & GARDENS. www.winchcomberailwaymuseum.co.uk
10 Part of the LEDBURY TOWN TRAIL. www.walkjogrun.net
11 Part of the FAMILY CYCLE TRAIL. www.forestry.gov.uk
12 MONMOUTH TROY: Station building re-erected at WINCHCOMBE on the GLOUCESTERSHIRE WARWICKSHIRE RAILWAY
13 COLEFORD (closed to passengers 1917): Home to the COLEFORD GREAT WESTERN RAILWAY MUSEUM. www.colefordgwr.150.com
14 DEAN FOREST RAILWAY. www.deanforestrailway.co.uk
15 Part of the WYE VALLEY WALK. www.wyevalleywalk.org
16 TINTERN: Now a visitor centre with a tearoom, refurbished carriages, a signal box exhibition gallery and a 5in gauge railway. www.tintern.org.uk
17 NOTGROVE: Now a Caravan Club site. www.caravanclub.co.uk
18 TETBURY: Site largely cleared as a car park and picnic area
19 MALMESBURY: Station building re-erected at BLUNSDON on the SWINDON & CRICKLADE RAILWAY
20 SWINDON & CRICKLADE RAILWAY. www.swindon-cricklade-railway.org
21 Swindon Works: Now home to STEAM (MUSEUM OF THE GREAT WESTERN RAILWAY). www.steam-museum.org.uk
22 Part of the CHISELDON TIMBERLAND TRAIL. www.gps-routes.co.uk
23 CHISELDON & MARLBOROUGH RAILWAY PATH. www.gps-routes.co.uk
24 SUMMERTON WAY
25 Western end of the STRATFORD & MORETON TRAMROAD trackbed

The end of the line! Looking north at Rhymney station on 23 June 2013. Until BR truncated it it carried on to Rhymney Bridge where, in a similar fashion to many of the valley lines, it made a connection with the former London & North Western Railway's Abergavenny – Dowlais route: the "Heads of the Valleys" line. *Paul Smith*

LEGEND FOR MAP 14A

1 PENMAENPOOL: Site now a car park with the main station building part of the George III Hotel and the signal box an RSPB information centre and observation point
2 MAWDDACH TRAIL. www.mawddachtrail.co.uk
3 DINAS MAWDDWY: Engine shed now a mill shop and café. www.merionmill.co.uk
4 2ft 3in gauge CORRIS RAILWAY. www.corris.co.uk
5 TALERDDIG: Station house now the Station Guest House
6 2ft 6in gauge WELSHPOOL & LLANFAIR LIGHT RAILWAY. www.wllr.org.uk
7 WELSHPOOL: Former station building now a visitor centre, shop and café
8 LLANSANTFFRAID: Now the Station Restaurant
9 LEATON: Now a B&B. www.theoldstationshropshire.co.uk
10 BISHOP'S CASTLE RAILWAY & TRANSPORT MUSEUM. www.bcrailway.co.uk
11 1ft 11¾in gauge VALE OF RHEIDOL LIGHT RAILWAY. www.rheidolrailway.co.uk
12 Part of the WYE VALLEY WALK. www.wyevalleywalk.org
13 RHAYADER: Site now used by Powys County Council's Highways Department
14 Part of the former ELAN VALLEY RAILWAY system now a walkway. www.elanvalley.org.uk
15 LLANDRINDOD: One signal box relocated to the southbound platform and converted into a museum. visitmidwales.com
16 KNIGHTON: Former station building now a veterinary centre
17 BUILTH ROAD: Low level station building now the Cambrian Arms pub
18 NEW RADNOR: Now holiday accommodation and caravan park. www.oldstationcaravanpark.co.uk
19 STANNER: Now used by Herefordshire County Council's Highways Department
20 EARDISLEY: Station building re-erected at RAVEN SQUARE on the WELSHPOOL & LLANFAIR LIGHT RAILWAY
21 MOORHAMPTON: Now a Caravan Club site. www.caravanclub.co.uk
22 ERWOOD: Now an arts and crafts centre. www.erwood-station.co.uk
23 TRAM INN: Now part of a garage
24 PONTRILAS: Now holiday accommodation. www.railwayholidays.co.uk
25 ABERBRAN: Now a Caravan Club site. www.caravanclub.co.uk
26 TALYBONT-ON-USK: Now the Talybont Outdoor Education Centre
27 Part of the TAFF TRAIL. www.tafftrail.org.uk

LEGEND FOR MAP 15A

1 MIDDLEWOOD WAY. www.cheshireeast.gov.uk
2 SETT VALLEY TRAIL. www.derbyshire.gov.uk
3 MONSAL TRAIL. www.peakdistrict.gov.uk
4 HASSOP: Now a café, bookshop and cycle-hire business. www.hassopstation.co.uk
5 Part of the HIGH PEAK TRAIL. www.peakdistrictcycleways.com
6 WHITEGATE: Now a visitor centre and car park for the WHITEGATE WAY
7 WHITEGATE WAY. www.cheshirewestandchester.gov.uk
8 BROXTON: Site cleared as a car park
9 CREWE HERITAGE CENTRE. www.creweheritagecentre.co.uk
10 WHEELOCK RAIL TRAIL. www.cheshireeast.gov.uk
11 SALT LINE. www.cheshireeast.gov.uk
12 BIDDULPH VALLEY WAY. www.cheshireeast.gov.uk
13 10¼ in gauge RUDYARD LAKE STEAM RAILWAY. www.rlsr.org
14 Part of the STAFFORDSHIRE WAY. www.staffordshire.gov.uk
15 HARTINGTON: Site now a picnic area with the restored signal box a visitor centre
16 HULME END: Station building now a visitor centre and rebuilt engine shed a tearoom. www.teajunctionhulmeend.co.uk
17 TISSINGTON: Site now cleared as car park and picnic area for the TISSINGTON TRAIL. www.peakdistrictcycleways.com
18 MANIFOLD WAY. www.peakdistrictcycleways.com
19 WATERHOUSES: Site largely cleared as a car park with a cycle-hire business in the narrow gauge goods shed
20 CHURNET VALLEY RAILWAY. www.churnet-valley-railway.co.uk
21 ALTON: Now holiday accommodation. www.landmarktrust.org.uk
22 FOXFIELD RAILWAY. www.foxfieldrailway.co.uk
23 APEDALE VALLEY LIGHT RAILWAY: Museum collection of narrow gauge industrial equipment with a 2ft gauge operational line in the Apedale Heritage Centre. www.avlr.org.uk
24 SILVERDALE: Station building re-erected at the APEDALE VALLEY LIGHT RAILWAY
25 CHARTLEY: Waiting room re-erected at the AMERTON RAILWAY
26 2ft gauge AMERTON RAILWAY. amertonrailway.co.uk
27 Part of the (Staffordshire) MILLENNIUM WAY. www.ldwa.org.uk
28 WOLVERHAMPTON HIGH LEVEL: Former gateway building now the gateway to the 'bus station
29 WOLVERHAMPTON LOW LEVEL: Station building now an events venue. www.grandstation.co.uk
30 MIDLAND METRO. nxbus.co.uk
31 CHASEWATER RAILWAY. www.chasewaterrailway.co.uk
32 SHREWSBURY ABBEY: Site largely cleared as a car park with building restored by the SHREWSBURY RAILWAY HERITAGE TRUST. shrewsburyrht.org.uk
33 BERRINGTON: Now a cattery
34 TELFORD STEAM RAILWAY. telfordsteamrailway.co.uk
35 Part of the SILKIN WAY. www.ldwa.org.uk
36 IRON BRIDGE & BROSELEY: Site cleared as a car park
37 Part of the SEVERN WAY. www.ldwa.org.uk
38 COALPORT ([GWR] later COALPORT WEST): Holiday accommodation available in two converted carriages. www.coalportstation.com
39 PRESTHOPE: Now a Caravan Club site. www.caravanclub.co.uk
40 Part of the JACK MYTTON WAY. www.ldwa.org.uk
41 SEVERN VALLEY RAILWAY. www.svr.co.uk
42 CODSALL: Former station building now the Station pub
43 WOMBOURN: Station building now a café. therailwaycafe.vpweb.co.uk
44 HIMLEY: Site cleared as a car park and picnic area for the SOUTH STAFFORDSHIRE RAILWAY WALK. www.sstaffs.gov.uk
45 TYSELEY LOCOMOTIVE WORKS. www.tyseleylocoworks.co.uk

LEGEND FOR MAP 19A

1 Part of the NORTH WALES PATH. www.ldwa.org.uk
2 1ft 3in gauge RHYL MINIATURE RAILWAY. www.rhylminiaturerailway.co.uk
3 Line slewed by new section of the A55
4 LLANERCHYMEDD: Base of the ANGLESEY CENTRAL RAILWAY preservation company. www.leinamwlch.co.uk
5 Britannia Bridge now also carries the A55
6 PENRHYN CASTLE RAILWAY MUSEUM. www.nationaltrust.org.uk
7 Operating base of the DALGARROG RAILWAY SOCIETY on former industrial railway trackbed. http://dolgarrograilway.wix.com/dolgarrog-railway
8 2ft gauge PENRHYN QUARRY RAILWAY. penrhynquarries.webs.com
9 Walkway to Port Penrhyn being created using parts of the trackbeds of the BETHESDA branch and the parallel 1ft 10¾in gauge industrial PENRHYN QUARRY RAILWAY
10 LON LAS MENAI CYCLEWAY. www.cyclingnorthwales.co.uk
11 Carnarvon Tunnel under town centre now a roadway
12 1ft 11½in gauge WELSH HIGHLAND RAILWAY. www.festrail.co.uk
13 Trackbed of BRYNGWYN BRANCH now a footpath
14 1ft 11½in gauge LLANBERIS LAKE RAILWAY mainly on trackbed of 4ft gauge industrial PADARN RAILWAY. www.lake-railway.co.uk
15 LLANBERIS: Branch line station now a shop and café; trackbed northwards now sections of the A4086 and LLANBERRIS LAKE WALK. www.walesdirectory.co.uk
16 800mm gauge SNOWDON MOUNTAIN RAILWAY. www.snowdonrailway.co.uk
17 LON EIFION CYCLEWAY. www.cyclingnorthwales.co.uk
18 PORTHMADOG: Station building now the Station Inn; Former Beddgelert Sidings now occupied by the 1ft 11½in gauge WELSH HIGHLAND HERITAGE RAILWAY. www.whr.co.uk
19 1ft 11½in gauge FESTINIOG RAILWAY. www.festrail.co.uk
20 BETWS-Y-COED: Former goods yard now home to the CONWY VALLEY RAILWAY MUSEUM with operational miniature railway and tramway lines. www.conwyrailwaymuseum.co.uk
21 LLANGOLLEN RAILWAY. www.llangollen-railway.co.uk
22 CORWEN: Now a sales centre
23 CYNWYD: Now a sales centre
24 1ft 11⅝in gauge BALA LAKE RAILWAY. www.bala-lake-railway.co.uk

LEGEND FOR MAP 20A

1 WIRRAL WAY. www.gps-routes.co.uk
2 BROUGHTON & BRETTON: Now a veterinary centre
3 WHITEGATE WAY. www.cheshirewestandchester.gov.uk
4 WHITEGATE: Now a visitor centre and car park for the WHITEGATE WAY
5 BROXTON: Site cleared as a car park
6 CREWE HERITAGE CENTRE. www.creweheritagecentre.co.uk
7 WHEELOCK RAIL TRAIL. www.cheshireeast.gov.uk
8 SALT LINE. www.cheshireeast.gov.uk
9 BIDDULPH VALLEY WAY. www.cheshireeast.gov.uk
10 APEDALE VALLEY LIGHT RAILWAY: Museum collection of narrow gauge industrial equipment with a 2ft gauge operational line in the Apedale Heritage Centre. www.avlr.org.uk
11 SILVERDALE: Station building re-erected at the APEDALE VALLEY LIGHT RAILWAY
12 Part of the (Staffordshire) MILLENNIUM WAY. www.ldwa.org.uk2
13 GLYNDYFRDWY: Station building now holiday accommodation. www.stationholiday.co.uk
14 LLANGOLLEN RAILWAY. www.llangollen-railway.co.uk
15 GLYNCEIRIOG: Base for the NEW GLYN VALLEY TRAMWAY & INDUSTRIAL HERITAGE TRUST. www.glynvalleytramway.co.uk
16 DOLYWERN: Building preserved
17 PONTFADOG: Building preserved as a display museum
18 CHIRK [GVT]: Site subject to restoration by the GLYN VALLEY TRAMWAY TRUST
19 OSWESTRY: Operating base of the CAMBRIAN HERITAGE RAILWAYS. www.cambrianrailways.com
20 Rides over the former Nantmawr goods branch operated by the TANAT VALLEY LIGHT RAILWAY. www.nantmawrvisitorcentre.co.uk
21 LLYNCLYS SOUTH: Short rides operated by the CAMBRIAN HERITAGE RAILWAYS. www.cambrianrailways.com

LEGEND FOR MAP 21A

1 AYSGARTH: Holiday accommodation available in station building. www.wensleydalerailway.com
2 WENSLEYDALE RAILWAY. www.wensleydalerailway.com
3 MASHAM: Station yard now a camp site and former goods shed a café. www.oldstation-masham.co.uk
4 Part of the NIDDERDALE WAY. www.ldwa.org.uk
5 PATELEY BRIDGE: Station house now a B&B. www.stationhouse-pateleybridge.co.uk
6 BELL BUSK: Station building now the Tudor House B&B. www.malhamhotels.co.uk
7 EMBSAY & BOLTON ABBEY STEAM RAILWAY. www.embsayboltonabbeyrailway.org.uk
8 ILKLEY: Former station building and platforms now retail premises
9 INGROW WEST: MUSEUM OF RAIL TRAVEL (www.vintagecarriagetrust.org) and the INGROW LOCO MUSEUM & WORKSHOP (ingrowlocomuseum.com) both adjacent to the station
10 KEIGHLEY & WORTH VALLEY RAILWAY. kwvr.co.uk
11 SOWERBY BRIDGE: Surviving portion of the former station building now the Jubilee Refreshment Rooms bar. www.jubileerefreshmentrooms.co.uk
12 MARSDEN: Former goods shed now home to a local history exhibition.
13 MANCHESTER METROLINK. www.metrolink.co.uk
14 LONGDENDALE TRAIL. www.gps-routes.co.uk
15 GLOSSOP: Part of the former station buildings and platforms now part of a supermarket
16 SETT VALLEY TRAIL. www.derbyshire.gov.uk
17 MIDDLEWOOD WAY. www.cheshireeast.gov.uk
18 PANNAL: Station building now a convenience store
19 WETHERBY YORK ROAD (closed to passengers 1902): Now the Engine Shed dance venue. www.engineshedwetherby.co.uk
20 HARLAND WAY. www.hedgehogcycling.co.uk
21 BENINGBROUGH: Station building now a restaurant with holiday accommodation available in five converted Pullman carriages. www.thesidingshotel.com
22 Former 1ft 6in gauge SAND HUTTON LIGHT RAILWAY
23 YORK: Former engine shed and other buildings now home to the NATIONAL RAILWAY MUSEUM. www.nrm.org.uk
24 DERWENT VALLEY LIGHT RAILWAY. www.dvlr.org.uk
25 NABURN: Station building now holiday accommodation and a café. www.naburnstation.co.uk
26 Part of the TRANS PENNINE TRAIL. www.transpenninetrail.org.uk
27 WHELDRAKE: Station building re-erected at MURTON PARK on the DERWENT VALLEY LIGHT RAILWAY
28 SKIPWITH & NORTH DUFFIELD: Holiday accommodation available in three converted carriages and former loading bay. www.skipwithstation.com

Ex-GWR 4200 Class 2-8-0T No.4270 at Toddington station on 23 July 2014 on the preserved Gloucestershire Warwickshire Railway.
Paul Jordan

An LMS platform ticket issued by BR on 31 March 1956! It was not uncommon for stations to hold stocks of pre-printed tickets for less-frequented destinations, or access to platforms for many years before they were exhausted. This station exists today as a tram stop on the Manchester Metrolink line to Stalybridge
(See note on Edmondson railway tickets on Page xxv)

Passengers waiting at Penhelig station on 18 February 2015, looking east. This station was opened as Penhelig Halt by the GWR on 8 May 1933 and is unusually located on a short length of track between two tunnels

Paul Jordan

GAZETTEER 1 - 1923 Maps

Map references of stations open as of 1 January 1923, indexed alphabetically letter by letter. Adjacent stations sharing a common name are accorded the one entry.

ABBEYDORE 14 F5
ABBEY FOR WEST DEREHAM 11 A5, 17 F5
ABBEYHILL 30 Inset F4
ABBEY TOWN 26 C4
ABBEY WOOD 40 D5
ABBOTSBURY 3 F2
ABBOTSFORD FERRY 30 E5
ABBOTS RIPTON 11 B2
ABELOUR 36 D5
ABER 19 D3
ABERAMAN 43 D2
ABERANGELL 14 A2
ABERAVON SEASIDE 43 F3
ABERAYRON 13 D4
ABERBEEG 43 B2
ABERBRAN 14 F2
ABERCAIRNY 33 F4
ABERCANAID & PENTREBACH 43 C2
ABERCARN 43 B3
ABERCHALDER 32 A5, 35 G4
ABERCRAVE 43 E1
ABERCWMBOI HALT 43 C2
ABERCYNON 43 C3
ABERDARE 43 D2
ABERDEEN JOINT 37 G4
ABERDOUR 30 A3
ABERDOVEY 13 B5
ABERDYLAIS 43 F2
ABEREDW 14 E3
ABERERCH 19 F1
ABERFAN 43 C2
ABERFELDY 33 D3
ABERFFRWD 14 C1
ABERFOYLE 29 A4, 33 G1
ABERGAVENNY 43 A1
ABERGAVENNY BRECON ROAD 43 A1
ABERGAVENNY JUNCTION 43 A1
ABERGELE & PENSARN 19 D5
ABERGWILI 13 G4
ABERGWYNFI 43 E3
ABERGYNOLWYN 13 B5
ABERLADY 30 B5
ABERLLEFENI 14 A1
ABERLOUR 36 E5
ABERMULE 14 B4
ABERNANT 43 D2
ABERNETHY 33 F5
ABERSYCHAN & TALYWAIN 43 A2
ABERSYCHAN LOW LEVEL 43 A2
ABERTHAW 43 C5
ABERTILLERY 43 B2
ABERTRIDWR 43 C3
ABERTYSSWG 43 C2
ABERYSTWYTH 13 C5
ABINGDON 10 F2
ABINGTON 30 E2
ABOYNE 34 A3, 37 G1
ABY 17 A3
ACCRINGTON 24 D5
ACHANALT 35 D4
ACH-NA-CLOICH 32 E3
ACHNASHEEN 35 D3
ACHNASHELLACH 35 D2
ACHTERNEED 35 D5
ACKLINGTON 31 G5
ACKWORTH 42 C5
ACLE 18 E4
ACOCK'S GREEN & SOUTH YARDLEY 15 G5
ACREFAIR 20 F2
ACTON 39 C3
ACTON BRIDGE 45 D5
ACTON TOWN 39 D3
ADDERBURY 10 C2
ADDERLEY 15 C2, 20 F4
ADDERLEY PARK 13 Inset C4
ADDIEWELL 30 C2
ADDINGHAM 21 C2
ADDLESTONE 5 C2
ADISHAM 6 C4
ADLESTROP 9 D5
ADLINGTON (Cheshire) 45 A5
ADLINGTON (Lancs) 45 D1
ADMASTON 15 E2
ADVIE 36 E4
AFON WEN 19 F1
AINDERBY 21 A3, 28 G1
AINSDALE 45 F1
AINSDALE BEACH 45 F1
AINSWORTH ROAD HALT 45 B2
AINTREE 45 F3
AINTREE RACECOURSE 45 F3
AIRDRIE 44 B2
AIRDRIE SOUTH 44 B2
AIRMYN 21 E5
AIRTH 30 A1
AKELD 31 E3
AKEMAN STREET 10 E3
ALBERTA PLACE PLATFORM 43 B5
ALBERT ROAD HALT 1 Inset A1
ALBION 13 Inset B2
ALBRIGHTON 15 F3
ALCESTER 9 B4
ALDEBURGH 12 C4

ALDEBY 12 A5, 18 F5
ALDERLEY EDGE 45 A5
ALDERMASTON 4 A3
ALDERSGATE STREET 40 C1
ALDERSHOT NORTH CAMP & SOUTH
FARNBOROUGH 4 B5, 5 C1
ALDERSHOT TOWN 4 B5
ALDGATE 40 C2
ALDGATE EAST 40 C2
ALDIN GRANGE FOR BEARPARK 27 D5
ALDRIDGE 15 F4
ALEXANDRA DOCK 45 F3, Inset G3
ALEXANDRA PALACE 40 A1
ALEXANDRA PARK (Glasgow) 44 D2
ALEXANDRA PARK (Lancs) 45 A3
ALEXANDRIA 29 B3
ALFORD (Aberdeen) 37 F2
ALFORD (Lincs) 17 A3
ALFORD HALT 3 C2, 8 F5
ALFRETON & SOUTH NORMANTON 41 E3
ALGARKIRK & SUTTERTON 17 D2
ALLANFEARN 36 D1
ALLANGRANGE 36 D1
ALLENDALE 27 C3
ALLERTON (Lancs) 45 E4
ALLERTON (Yorks) 21 C4
ALLOA 30 A2
ALLOWAY 29 F3
ALMELEY 14 E5
ALMONDBANK 33 E5
ALNE 21 B4
ALNESS 36 C1
ALNMOUTH 31 F5
ALNWICK 31 F5
ALPERTON FOR PERIVALE 39 B2
ALRESFORD (Essex) 12 E2
ALRESFORD (Hants) 4 C3
ALREWAS 15 E5
ALSAGER 15 C3, 20 E5
ALSAGER ROAD 15 C3, 20 E5
ALSOP-EN-LE-DALE 15 C5
ALSTON 27 D2
ALTCAR & HILLHOUSE 45 F2
ALTHORNE 6 A2, 12 G1
ALTHORPE 22 F1
ALTHORP PARK 10 B3
ALTNABREAC 38 D2
ALTOFTS & WHITWOOD 42 B5
ALTON (Hants) 4 C4
ALTON (Staffs) 15 C4
ALTRINCHAM & BOWDON 45 B4
ALVA 30 A1, 33 G4
ALVECHURCH 9 A4
ALVERSTONE 4 F3
ALVERTHORPE 42 C3
ALVES 36 C4
ALVESCOT 10 E1
ALYTH 34 D1
ALYTH JUNCTION 34 D1
AMBERGATE 41 E2
AMBERLEY 5 F1
AMBLE 31 F5
AMERSHAM 10 F5
AMESBURY 4 C1
AMISFIELD 26 A3
AMLWCH 19 C1, 23 G2
AMMANFORD 43 G1
AMMANFORD COLLIERY HALT 43 G1
AMOTHERBY 22 B1
AMPLEFORTH 21 B5
AMPTHILL 10 C5, 11 D1
ANCASTER 16 C5, 17 C1
ANDERSTON CROSS 44 Inset F4
ANDOVER JUNCTION 4 C2
ANDOVERSFORD 9 D4
ANDOVERSFORD & DOWDESWELL 9 D4
ANDOVER TOWN 4 C2
ANERLEY 40 F2
ANGEL ROAD 5 A3
ANGERTON 27 A4
ANGLING CLUB COTTAGE
PLATFORM 30 E5
ANGMERING 5 F25
ANNAN 26 B4
ANNBANK 29 E4
ANNESLEY 41 E4
ANNFIELD PLAIN 27 C5
ANNITSFORD 27 B
ANN STREET HALT 45 D4
ANSDELL & FAIRHAVEN 24 E2
ANSTON 41 A4
ANSTRUTHER 34 G3
APPERLEY BRIDGE & RAWDON 42 A2
APPIN 32 D4
APPLEBY (Lincs) 22 F2
APPLEBY (Westmorland) 27 E2
APPLEDORE 6 E2
APPLETON 45 D4
APPLEY BRIDGE 45 D2
ARBIRLOT 34 D3
ARBROATH 34 D3
ARDDLEEN 14 A4
ARDINGLY 5 E3

ARDLEIGH 12 E2
ARDLER 34 D1
ARDLEY 10 D2
ARDLUI 32 F5
ARDROSSAN 29 D3
ARDROSSAN PIER 29 D3
ARDROSSAN SOUTH BEACH 29 D3
ARDROSSAN TOWN 29 D3
ARDSLEY 42 B3
ARDWICK 45 A3
ARENIG 19 F4
ARGOED 43 B2
ARISAIG 32 B5
ARKHOLME 24 B4
ARKSEY 21 F5
ARKWRIGHT TOWN 41 C3
ARLECDON 26 E3
ARLESEY & SHEFFORD ROAD 11 D2
ARLEY 9 A2
ARLEY & FILLONGLEY 16 G1
ARMADALE 30 C2
ARMATHWAITE 27 D1
ARMITAGE 15 E5
ARMLEY 42 A3
ARMLEY & WORTLEY 42 A3
ARNAGE 37 E4
ARNSIDE 24 A3
ARRAM 22 D2
ARROCHAR & TARBET 32 G5
ARTHINGTON 21 D3
ARTHOG 13 A5
ARUNDEL 5 F1
ASCOT & SUNNINGHILL 4 A5, 5 B1
ASCOTT-UNDER-WYCHWOOD 10 D1
ASFORDBY 16 E3
ASH 4 B5, 5 C1
ASHBOURNE 15 C5
ASHBURTON 2 C2
ASHBURY 1 B5
ASHBURY'S FOR BELLE VUE 45 A3
ASHBY 16 E1
ASHBY MAGNA 16 G2
ASHCHURCH 9 D3
ASHCOTT 3 C2, 8 E4
ASHDON HALT 11 D4
ASHEY 4 F3
ASHFORD (Kent) 6 D2
ASHFORD (Middlesex) 5 B2
ASH GREEN 4 B5, 5 C1
ASHINGTON 27 A5
ASHLEY 45 B4
ASHLEY & WESTON 16 F2
ASHLEY HILL 3 Inset F1
ASHPERTON 9 C2
ASHTEAD 5 C2
ASHTON 2 C3
ASHTON (CHARLESTOWN) 21 Inset A2
ASHTON HALL 24 C3
ASHTON-IN-MAKERFIELD 45 D3
ASHTON OLDHAM ROAD 21 Inset A2
ASHTON PARK PARADE 21 Inset A2
ASHTON-UNDER-HILL 9 C4
ASHTOWN 6 C4
ASHURST 5 D4
ASHWATER 1 B5
ASHWELL 16 E4
ASHWELL & MORDEN 11 D2
ASHWELLTHORPE 12 A3, 18 F3
ASKAM 24 A1
ASKERN 21 E5
ASKRIGG 21 A1, 27 G3
ASLOCKTON 16 C4
ASPALL & THORNDON 12 C3
ASPATRIA 26 D3
ASPLEY GUISE HALT 10 C5
ASTLEY 45 C3
ASTON 13 Inset B4
ASTON BOTTERELL SIDING 15 G2
ASTON-BY-STONE 15 D3, 20 F5
ASTON CANTLOW HALT 9 B5
ASTON ROWANT 10 F3
ASWARBY & SCREDINGTON 17 D1
ATHELNEY 3 D1, 8 F3
ATHERSTONE 16 F1
ATHERTON 45 C2
ATHERTON CENTRAL 45 C2
ATTADALE 35 E2
ATTENBOROUGH 41 G4
ATTERCLIFFE 42 G4
ATTERCLIFFE ROAD 42 G4
ATTLEBOROUGH 12 A2, 18 F2
ATTLEBRIDGE 18 E3
AUCHENDINNY 30 C4
AUCHENGRAY 30 D2
AUCHENHEATH 30 D1
AUCHENMADE 29 D3
AUCHINCRUIVE 29 F3
AUCHINDACHY 37 D1
AUCHINLECK 29 F5
AUCHLOCHAN HALT 30 E1
AUCHMACOY 37 E4
AUCHNAGATT 37 D4
AUCHTERARDER 33 F4

AUCHTERHOUSE 34 E1
AUCHTERLESS 37 D3
AUCHTERMUCHTY 34 F1
AUDLEM 15 C2, 20 F4
AUDLEY 15 C3, 20 E5
AUDLEY END 11 E4
AUGHTON PARK HALT 45 E2
AULDBAR ROAD 34 D3
AULDEARN 36 D3
AULDGIRTH 26 A2
AUTHORPE 17 A3
AVIEMORE 36 F2
AVOCH 36 D1
AVONBRIDGE 30 B2
AVONCLIFF HALT 3 B4
AVON LODGE 4 E1
AVONMOUTH DOCK JOINT
3 A2, 8 C4, 9 G1
AVONWICK 2 D2
AWRE FOR BLAKENEY 8 A5, 9 E2
AWSWORTH 41 F3
AXBRIDGE 3 B1, 8 E3
AXMINSTER 2 B5
AYCLIFFE 28 E1
AYLESBURY 10 E4
AYLESFORD 6 C1
AYLSHAM 18 D3
AYNHO 10 D2
AYNHO PARK PLATFORM 10 D2
AYOT 11 F2
AYR 29 F3
AYSGARTH 21 A1, 27 G4
AYTON 31 C3

BACKWORTH 28 B1
BACTON 14 F5
BACUP 20 A5
BADMINTON 9 G3
BAGGROW 26 D4
BAGILLT 20 D1
BAGSHOT 4 B5, 5 C1
BAGULEY 45 B4
BAGWORTH & ELLISTOWN 16 E2
BAILDON 42 A2
BAILEY GATE 3 E4
BAILLIESTON 44 C3
BAINTON 22 C2
BAKER STREET 39 C5
BAKEWELL 15 B5
BALA 19 F4
BALADO 30 A3, 33 G5
BALA JUNCTION 19 F4
BALCOMBE 5 E3
BALDERSBY 21 A3
BALDERTON 20 E5
BALDOCK 11 E2
BALDOVAN 34 E2
BALDRAGON 34 E2
BALDWIN'S HALT 43 F3
BALERNO 30 C3
BALFRON 29 A4
BALGOWAN 33 F4
BALHAM & UPPER TOOTING 39 E5
BALLABEG 23 C2
BALLACHULISH FERRY 32 D3
BALLACHULISH (GLENCOE) 32 D3
BALLASALLA 23 C2
BALLATER 34 A1
BALLAUGH 23 A2, 25 G4
BALLINDALLOCH 36 E4
BALLINGHAM 9 D1
BALLINLUIG 33 D4
BALLOCH 29 B3
BALLOCH PIER B3
BALMORE 44 E1
BALNACOUL 36 C5
BALNE 21 E5
BALQUHIDDER 33 F2
BALSHAW LANE & EUXTON 45 D1
BAMBER BRIDGE 24 Inset C2
BAMFORD 15 A5
BAMFURLONG 45 D2
BAMPTON (DEVON) 7 G5
BAMPTON (OXON) 10 E1
BANAVIE 32 C3
BANAVIE PIER 32 C3
BANBURY BRIDGE STREET 10 C2
BANBURY MERTON STREET 10 C2
BANCHORY 34 A4
BANFF 37 C2
BANFF BRIDGE 37 C2
BANGOR 19 D2
BANGOR-ON-DEE 20 F2
BANKFOOT 33 E5
BANK HALL 45 F3
BANKHEAD (Aberdeen) 37 F4
BANKHEAD (Lanark) 30 D2
BANKNOCK 30 B1
BANKS 24 E2
BANNISTER GREEN HALT 11 E5
BANNOCKBURN 30 A1
BANSTEAD & BURGH HEATH 5 C3
BARASSIE 29 E3

TULLIBARDINE 33 F4
TULLOCH 32 B5
TULSE HILL 40 E1
TUMBLE 7 A3
TUMBY WOODSIDE 17 C2
TUNBRIDGE WELLS 5 D5
TUNSTALL 15 C3, 20 E5
TURNBERRY 29 G2
TURNCHAPEL 1 Inset A2
TURNHAM GREEN 39 D3
TURNHOUSE 30 B3
TURRIFF 37 D3
TURTON & EDGWORTH 45 B1
TURVEY 10 B5
TUTBURY 15 D5
TUXFORD 16 B4
TWEEDMOUTH 31 C3
TWENTY 17 E2
TWICKENHAM 39 E2
TWIZELL 31 D3
TWYFORD 4 A5, 10 G4
TWYWELL 10 A5
TY CROES 19 D1
TYDD 17 E3
TYLDESLEY 45 C2
TYLERS ARMS PLATFORM 43 B2
TYLORSTOWN 43 D2
TYLWCH 14 C2
TYNDRUM 32 E5
TYNE DOCK 28 B1
TYNEHEAD 30 C5
TYNEMOUTH 28 B1
TYSELEY 15 G5
TYTHERINGTON 8 B5, 9 F2

UCKFIELD 5 E4
UDDINGSTON 44 C3
UDDINGSTON WEST 44 C3
UDNY 37 E4
UFFCULME 2 A4, 8 G1
UFFINGTON 10 F1
UFFINGTON & BARNACK 17 F1
UFFORD BRIDGE 17 F1
ULBSTER 38 E4
ULCEBY 22 E3
ULLESKELF 21 D4
ULLESTHORPE & LUTTERWORTH 16 G2
ULLOCK 26 E3
ULVERSTON 24 A2
UMBERLEIGH 7 F3
UNION BANK FARM HALT 45 D4
UNION MILLS 23 B2
UNSTONE 41 B2
UP EXE 2 A3
UPHALL 30 C3
UPHOLLAND 45 D2
UPLAWMOOR 44 G4
UPMINSTER 5 A5
UPPER BANK 43 G3
UPPER BATLEY 42 B3
UPPER BIRSTALL 42 B2
UPPER BOAT HALT 43 C3
UPPER BROUGHTON 16 D3
UPPER GREENOCK 29 B3
UPPER HOLLOWAY 40 B1
UPPER LYDBROOK 8 A4, 9 E1
UPPER PONTNEWYDD 43 A3
UPPER SOUDLEY HALT 8 A5, 9 E2
UPPER SYDENHAM 40 F2
UPPERTHORPE & KILLAMARSH 41 B3
UPPER WARLINGHAM 5 C3
UPPINGHAM 16 F4
UPTON 45 F4
UPTON & BLEWBURY 10 F2
UPTON & NORTH ELMSALL 42 D5
UPTON MAGNA 15 E1
UPTON-ON-SEVERN 9 C3
UPTON PARK 40 B4
UPWELL 17 F4
UPWEY 3 F3
UPWEY JUNCTION 3 G3
UPWEY WISHING WELL HALT 3 F3
URALITE HALT 6 B1
URMSTON 45 B3
URQUHART 36 C5
USHAW MOOR 27 D5
USK 8 B3
USWORTH 28 C1
UTTERBY HALT 22 G4
UTTOXETER 15 D5
UXBRIDGE 5 A2, 10 G5
UXBRIDGE HIGH STREET 5 A2, 10 G5
UXBRIDGE ROAD 39 D4
UXBRIDGE VINE STREET 5 A2, 10 G5

VALLEY 19 Inset B2
VARTEG 43 A2
VAUXHALL 40 D1
VAUXHALL & DUDDESTON 13 Inset C4
VELVET HALL 31 D3
VENN CROSS 8 F1
VENTNOR 4 G3
VENTNOR TOWN 4 G3
VERNEY JUNCTION 10 D3
VERWOOD 3 E5
VICARAGE CROSSING HALT 20 E1
VICTORIA (London) 39 D5
VICTORIA (Mon) 43 B2
VICTORIA PARK 40 B3
VICTORIA PARK, WHITEINCH 44 F2

VIRGINIA WATER 5 B1
VOWCHURCH 14 F5
VULCAN HALT 45 D3

WADBOROUGH 9 C3
WADDESDON 10 E4
WADDESDON ROAD 10 E3
WADDINGTON 16 B5, 17 B1
WADDON 5 C3
WADEBRIDGE 1 C2
WADHURST 5 E5
WADSLEY BRIDGE 42 G4
WAEN AVON 43 B1
WAENFAWR 19 E2
WAINFLEET 17 C4
WAKEFIELD KIRKGATE 42 C4
WAKEFIELD WESTGATE 42 C4
WAKERLEY & BARROWDEN 16 F5
WALBERSWICK 12 B5
WALCOT 15 E1
WALDRON & HOREHAM ROAD 5 F5
WALESWOOD 41 A3
WALHAM GREEN 39 D4
WALKDEN B2
WALKER 28 B1
WALKERBURN 30 E5
WALKER GATE 28 C1
WALKERINGHAM 22 G1
WALL 27 B3
WALLASEY 45 F3
WALLASEY VILLAGE 45 G3
WALL GRANGE 15 C4
WALLINGFORD 10 F3
WALLINGTON 5 C3
WALLSEND 28 B1
WALMER 6 C5
WALPOLE 17 E4
WALSALL 13 Inset A2
WALSALL WOOD 15 F4
WALSDEN 21 E1
WALSINGHAM 18 D1
WALTHAM 22 F4
WALTHAM CROSS & ABBEY 11 G3
WALTHAMSTOW 40 A3
WALTON 17 F2
WALTON & ANFIELD 45 F3
WALTON FOR HERSHAM 5 C2
WALTON-IN-GORDANO 3 A1, 8 C3
WALTON JUNCTION 45 F3
WALTON-ON-THE-NAZE 12 E3
WALTON PARK 3 A1, 8 C3
WAMPHRAY 26 A3, 30 G3
WANBOROUGH 5 C1
WANDSWORTH COMMON 39 E5
WANDSWORTH ROAD 40 E1
WANDSWORTH TOWN 39 E5
WANLOCKHEAD 30 F2
WANSFORD 11 A1, 17 F1
WANSFORD ROAD 11 A1, 17 F1
WANSTEAD PARK 40 B4
WANSTROW 3 C3, 8 E5
WANTAGE 10 F1
WANTAGE ROAD 10 F1
WAPPENHAM 10 C3
WAPPING 40 C2
WAPPING DOCK 45 Inset G5
WARBLINGTON HALT 4 E4
WARBOYS 11 B2
WARCOP 27 F2
WARDHOUSE 37 E2
WARDLEWORTH 45 A1
WARE 11 F3
WAREHAM 3 F4
WARGRAVE 4 A5, 10 G4
WARK 27 B3
WARKWORTH 31 F5
WARLINGHAM 5 C3
WARMINSTER 3 C4
WARMLEY 3 A3, 8 C5
WARNHAM 5 D2
WARRINGTON ARPLEY 45 C4
WARRINGTON BANK QUAY HIGH LEVEL
                                     45 D4
WARRINGTON BANK QUAY LOW LEVEL
                                     45 D4
WARRINGTON CENTRAL 45 D4
WARSOP 41 C4
WARTHILL 21 C5
WARTLE 37 E3
WARWICK 10 B1
WARWICK (MILVERTON) 10 B1
WASHFORD 8 E1
WASHINGBOROUGH 16 B5, 17 B1
WASHINGTON 28 C1
WASSAND 22 D3
WATCHET 8 E1
WATCHINGWELL 4 F2
WATERBEACH 11 C4
WATERFALL 23 B2
WATERFOOT 24 E5
WATERHOUSES (Derbys) 15 C5
WATERHOUSES (Durham) 27 D5
WATERINGBURY 6 C1
WATERLOO (Lancs) 45 F3
WATERLOO (London) 40 D1
WATERLOO HALT 43 B3
WATERLOO JUNCTION 40 D1
WATERLOO ROAD (Lancs) 24 D2
WATERLOO ROAD (Staffs) 15 C3, 20 E5
WATER ORTON 15 F5

WATERSIDE 29 F4
WATFORD HIGH STREET 5 A2, 11 G1
WATFORD JUNCTION 5 A2, 11 G1
WATFORD WEST 5 A2, 11 G1
WATH 42 E5
WATH-IN-NIDDERDALE 21 B2
WATH-ON-DEARNE 42 E5
WATLINGTON 10 F3
WATNALL 41 F4
WATSON'S CROSSING HALT 21 E1
WATTEN 38 D4
WATTON 18 F1
WAVERTON 15 B1, 20 E3
WAVERTREE 45 F4
WEARHEAD 27 D3
WEAR VALLEY JUNCTION 27 E5
WEASTE 45 B3
WEAVERTHORPE 22 A2
WEDNESBURY 13 Inset A2
WEDNESFIELD 15 Inset E3
WEEDON 10 B3
WEELEY 12 E3
WEELSBY ROAD HALT 22 F4
WEETON 21 C3
WELBURY 28 F1
WELDON & CORBY 16 G4
WELFORD & KILWORTH 10 A3, 16 G3
WELFORD PARK 4 A2
WELLFIELD 28 D1
WELL HALL FOR NORTH ELTHAM 40 E5
WELLING 40 E5
WELLINGBOROUGH 10 B5
WELLINGTON (Salop) 15 E2
WELLINGTON (Somerset) 8 G2
WELLINGTON COLLEGE 4 A5
WELLOW 3 B3, 8 D5
WELLS 18 C1
WELLS PRIORY ROAD 3 C2, 8 E4
WELLS TUCKER STREET 3 C2, 8 E4
WELNETHAM 12 C1
WELSHAMPTON 20 F2
WELSHPOOL 14 B4
WELSH ROAD HALT 20 D2
WELTON 10 A3
WELWYN 11 F2
WELWYN GARDEN CITY HALT 11 F2
WEM 15 D1, 20 G3
WEMBLEY HILL 39 B3
WEMBLEY PARK 39 B3
WEMYSS BAY 29 C2
WEMYSS CASTLE 30 A4, 34 G1
WENDLEBURY HALT 10 D2
WENDLING 18 E1
WENDOVER 10 E4
WENHASTON 12 B5
WENNINGTON 24 B4
WENSLEY 21 A2, 27 G4
WENTWORTH & HOYLAND COMMON 42 F4
WENVOE 43 C5
WERN LAS 14 A5, 20 G2
WEST AUCKLAND 27 E5
WESTBOURNE PARK 39 C5
WEST BROMPTON 39 D5
WEST BROMWICH 13 Inset B2
WESTBROOK 14 F4
WESTBURY (Salop) 14 A5
WESTBURY (Wilts) 3 B4
WEST CALDER 30 C2
WESTCLIFF-ON-SEA 6 A2
WESTCOMBE PARK 40 D4
WEST CORNFORTH 28 D1
WESTCOTT 10 E3
WESTCRAIGS 30 C2
WEST CROSS 43 G3
WEST CROYDON 5 C3
WEST CULTS 37 G4
WEST DERBY 45 F3
WEST DRAYTON & YIEWSLEY 5 B2, 10 G5
WEST EALING 39 C2
WEST END LANE 39 B5
WESTENHANGER 6 D3
WESTERFIELD 12 D3
WESTERHAM 5 C4
WESTERTON 44 E2
WEST FERRY 34 Inset E5
WESTFIELD 30 B2
WESTGATE-IN-WEARDALE 27 D3
WESTGATE-ON-SEA 6 B4
WEST GOSFORTH 27 B5
WEST GREEN 40 A2
WEST GRINSTEAD 5 E2
WEST HALLAM 41 F3
WEST HALTON 22 E2
WEST HAM 40 C4
WESTHAM HALT 3 G3
WEST HAMPSTEAD 39 B5
WEST HARROW HALT 39 A1
WEST HARTLEPOOL 28 D2
WESTHEAD HALT 45 E2
WEST HOATHLY 5 E3
WESTHOUGHTON 45 C2
WESTHOUSES & BLACKWELL 41 D3
WEST INDIA DOCKS 40 C3
WEST JESMOND 27 Inset
WEST KENSINGTON 39 D4
WEST KILBRIDE 29 D2
WEST KIRBY 20 C1, 24 G1
WEST LEIGH 45 C3
WEST LEIGH & BEDFORD 45 C3
WEST MEON 4 D4

WEST MILL 11 E3
WESTMINSTER 40 D1
WESTMOOR 14 E5
WEST MOORS 3 E5
WEST NEWPORT 34 Inset F4
WEST NORWOOD 40 F1
WESTOE LANE 28 B1
WESTON (Lincs) 17 E2
WESTON (Somerset) 3 A3, 8 D5
WESTON & INGESTRE 15 D4
WESTON-ON-TRENT 16 D1
WESTON-SUB-EDGE 9 C5
WESTON-SUPER-MARE 3 B1, 8 D3
WESTON-SUPER-MARE EXCURSION
                          PLATFORM 3 B1, 8 D3
WEST PENNARD 3 C2, 8 E4
WEST ROUNTON GATES 28 F1
WEST RUNTON 18 C3
WEST ST LEONARDS 6 F1
WEST TIMPERLEY 45 B4
WEST TINSLEY 42 G4
WEST VALE 42 C1
WEST WEMYSS 30 A4, 34 G1
WEST WICKHAM 40 G3
WESTWOOD 42 F4
WEST WORTHING 5 F2
WEST WYCOMBE 10 F4
WETHERAL 27 C1
WETHERBY 21 C4
WETTON MILL 15 B4
WETWANG 22 C2
WEYBOURNE 18 C2
WEYBRIDGE 5 C2
WEYHILL 4 B2
WEYMOUTH QUAY 3 G3
WEYMOUTH TOWN 3 G3
WHALEY BRIDGE 15 A4
WHALLEY 24 D4
WHAPLODE 17 E3
WHARRAM 22 B1
WHATSTANDWELL 41 E2
WHAUPHILL 25 C4
WHEATHAMPSTEAD 11 F2
WHEATLEY 10 E3
WHEELOCK 15 B2, 20 E4
WHELDRAKE 21 C5
WHERWELL 4 C2
WHETSTONE 16 F2
WHIFFLET 44 B3
WHIFFLET HIGH LEVEL 44 B3
WHIFFLET LOW LEVEL 44 B3
WHIMPLE 2 B4
WHIMSEY HALT 8 A5, 9 E2
WHIPPINGHAM 4 F3
WHISSENDINE 16 E4
WHISTLEFIELD 29 A3
WHITACRE 15 F5
WHITBURN 30 C2
WHITBURN COLLIERY 28 B1
WHITBY TOWN 28 F4
WHITBY WEST CLIFF 28 F4
WHITCHURCH (Glam) 43 B4
WHITCHURCH (Hants) 4 B3
WHITCHURCH (Salop) 15 C1, 20 F3
WHITCHURCH DOWN PLATFORM 1 C5
WHITE BEAR 45 D2
WHITEBOROUGH 41 D3
WHITECHAPEL 40 C2
WHITE COLNE 12 E1
WHITECRAIGS 44 E4
WHITECROFT 8 A5, 9 E2
WHITEDALE 22 D3
WHITEFIELD 45 B2
WHITEGATE 15 B2, 20 D4
WHITE HART LANE 5 A3
WHITEHAVEN BRANSTY 26 E2
WHITEHAVEN CORKICKLE 26 E2
WHITEHOUSE 37 F2
WHITEHURST HALT 20 F2
WHITEINCH 44 F2
WHITE MOSS LEVEL CROSSING HALT 45 E2
WHITE NOTLEY 11 F5
WHITERIGG 44 A2
WHITHORN 25 D4
WHITLAND 7 A1, 13 G3
WHITLEY BAY 28 B1
WHITLEY BRIDGE 21 E5
WHITLINGHAM 18 F3
WHITMORE 15 C3, 20 F5
WHITNEY-ON-THE-WYE 14 E4
WHITRIGG 26 C4
WHITSTABLE HARBOUR 6 B3
WHITSTABLE TOWN & TANKERTON 6 B3
WHITSTONE & BRIDGERULE 1 A4
WHITTINGHAM 31 F4
WHITTINGTON (Derby) 41 B2
WHITTINGTON (Salop) 20 G2
WHITTLESEA 11 A2, 17 G2
WHITTLESFORD 11 D3
WHITTON 22 E2
WHITWELL (Derby) 41 B4
WHITWELL (Isle of Wight) 4 G3
WHITWELL & REEPHAM 18 E2
WHITWICK 16 E2
WHITWORTH 45 A1
WHYTELEAFE 5 C3
WICK 38 D4
WICKENBY 17 A1
WICKFORD 6 A1
WICKHAM 4 E3

EDMONDSON RAILWAY TICKETS

In the very early days of railway travel tickets were hand written in a similar fashion to those issued for stagecoach passengers. However, this method inevitably created long hold-ups when dealing with the much larger number of rail travellers. Allied to this was the inherent poor record-keeping, which could lead to pilfering of revenue by staff.

Thomas Edmondson, a Station Master on the Newcastle & Carlisle Railway, invented a system of issuing pre-numbered and printed card tickets and this was first introduced on the Manchester & Leeds Railway in the early 1840s. It rapidly became adopted nationally and was the standard for the Railway Clearing House when that was established in 1842.

The system was used in Britain until totally superseded by computer-issued tickets on BR in February 1990. Happily, many heritage railways continue to use them and three such examples are shown here:

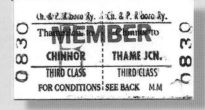

GAZETTEER II - 2015 Maps

Map references of stations opened or renamed since 1 January 1923 and open or closed as of 1 January 2015. Entries in *italics* are for stations under construction but not open as of 1 January 2015 [with projected opening date].

Replacement stations of the same name are not included (unless relocated to another line), nor are heritage railway stations sharing a common name.

Whilst every effort has been made to ensure that the station names in this Railway Atlas are correct, it should be remembered that in some cases a choice has had to be made from a number of contenders:

- the name generally used by the owning company
- the name that appeared in (non-company) timetables
- the name used by other railway companies for through-ticketing purposes
- and even the name on the station's signs

For example, establishing just how 'official' the suffix 'FOR SUCH-AND-SUCH A PLACE' was has been fraught with difficulty – and can sometimes still be, as the above photos show! Or, when was a halt not a 'HALT' – or even a 'PLATFORM'? Wherever possible, names of stations currently open are those given by the appropriate national and heritage railway official websites.

For historical and commercial reasons, in the pre-Grouping era a town served by two companies might well have had two stations of exactly the same name; post-Grouping, some degree of differentiation came in, especially if the two stations now belonged to one owner. Other name changes, in more recent years, have included the widespread dropping of HIGH LEVEL and LOW LEVEL where one station has been closed (as at WOLVERHAMPTON) or the two have been integrated (as at LICHFIELD TRENT VALLEY), and the general loss of apostrophes (as at KINGS NORTON).

In the interests of historical accuracy, any verifiable corrections to the station names used – or indeed to any other aspect of this Railway Atlas – will be welcomed by the compilers.

WITH THANKS TO ...

Margaret Donnison
Paul Jordan
Members of the Engine Shed Society for updating us with information regarding the current status of steam sheds and diesel/electric depots (www.engineshedsociety.co.uk)
And finally, to everyone who took the time and trouble to offer their comments on the first edition of this atlas

Further information regarding many of the closed stations may be found on the excellent Disused Stations website: www.disused-stations.org.uk/